NORTHWEST TREES

Part of the pleasure of reading *Northwest Trees* stems from its curious tidbits...Reading *Northwest Trees* provides an opportunity for readers to branch out and learn more about familiar and foreign trees.

—*Klamath Falls Herald and News*

Stephen Arno's 1977 classic is a book of true beauty [and] the new 30th anniversary edition should be even more exquisite...This book is so rich in detailed, gorgeous illustrations that it should appeal to all book lovers, no matter what their degree of tree-huggability.

—*Portland Mercury*

A masterpiece

—*The Stranger,* **Seattle**

Ramona Hammerly's illustrations are worth the price of admission to *Trees,* although Stephen Arno's text, updated for the 30th anniversary edition of this classic, is just as important. Far more than an identification book, *Trees* provides a sense of place and the character of specific trees as well as the scientific facts.

—*The Olympian*

Northwest Trees is just the right size to fill a hiker's holiday stocking. This 30th anniversary edition of a Northwest classic can be enjoyed any time of the year, so treat someone else or even give yourself a copy to take on the next hike...[and] Hammerly's detailed black-and-white drawings of needles, cones, leaves, twigs, and fruits make tree identification not only easier but a pleasure.

—*Seattle Post-Intelligencer*

A beautiful and meticulously illustrated book... This sounds like a typical botany guide, but *Northwest Trees* goes a step further and explains the whys.

—*Inside Bozeman* (MT) *Magazine*

ANNIVERSARY EDITION

NORTHWEST TREES

Identifying and Understanding
the Region's Native Trees

STEPHEN F. ARNO & RAMONA P. HAMMERLY

THE MOUNTAINEERS BOOKS

THE GREATER NORTHWEST

Legend:
- Greater Northwest
- - - - - Continental Divide

SASKATCHEWAN

ALBERTA

BRITISH COLUMBIA

BOREAL FOREST

BOREAL FOREST & ASPEN WOODLANDS

FOOTHILL FOREST &

SUBALPINE ROCKY MTN FOREST

INTERMOUNTAIN

INTERMOUNTAIN DRY

INTERMOUNTAIN DRY FOREST

COAST RANGE

WET COASTAL MOUNTAIN FOREST

DRY INTERIOR COASTAL FOREST

WET COASTAL FOREST

Athabasca River

Columbia River

Fraser River

Bow River

Edmonton

Calgary

Jasper NP

Banff NP

Glacier NP

Yoho NP

Kootenay NP

Kamloops

Kelowna

Manning PP

N. Cascades NP

Prince George

Williams Lake

Vancouver

Tweedsmuir PP

Garibaldi PP

Vancouver Island

Strathcona PP

Victoria

Olympic NP

GREAT PLAINS

MONTANA

WYOMING

MIDDLE ROCKY MOUNTAINS

Billings

Yellowstone River

Yellowstone NP

Missouri River

Great Falls

Lethbridge

SHORTGRASS PRAIRIE & RIVERSIDE TREES

DRY FOOTHILLS FOREST

Helena

SUBALPINE ROCKY MTN FOREST

Craters of the Moon NM

Idaho Falls

UTAH

ASPEN GROVES

Waterton Lakes NP

Glacier NP

Clark Fork River

Missoula

BITTERROOT MTNS

MOIST FOREST

Lewiston

Salmon River

IDAHO

SAGEBRUSH-GRASS & RIVERSIDE TREES

Sawtooth NRA

Boise

Snake River

FOREST

Spokane

WASHINGTON

INTERMOUNTAIN DRY FOREST

BLUE MTNS

OREGON

SAGEBRUSH GRASS

Mt Rainier NP

Columbia River

Deschutes River

SAGEBRUSH & JUNIPER GRASS

Bend

Crater Lake NP

Seattle

Tacoma

FOREST

FOREST COASTAL MOUNTAIN FOREST

WET COASTAL MOUNTAIN DRY FOREST

CASCADE

Mt St Helens NM

Portland

Willamette River

COAST RANGE COASTAL DRY INTERIOR

WET COASTAL

SISKIYOU MTNS

Medford

Oregon Caves NM

NEVADA

CALIFORNIA

N

PACIFIC OCEAN

0   100   200
miles

THE MOUNTAINEERS BOOKS
*is the nonprofit publishing arm of The Mountaineers, an
organization founded in 1906 and dedicated to the exploration,
preservation and enjoyment of outdoor and wilderness areas.*

1001 SW Klickitat Way, Suite 201, Seattle, WA 98134

Editor: Kris Fulsaas
Cover, Book Design, and Layout: Mayumi Thompson
Cartographer: Moore Creative Designs

Cover illustration: Ramona P. Hammerly
Frontispiece: *Whitebark pine at timberline*

Library of Congress Cataloging-in-Publication Data
Arno, Stephen F.
  Northwestern trees : identifying and understanding our native trees /
Stephen F. Arno ; illustrated by Ramona Hammerly. — Rev. ed.
     p. cm.
  Includes bibliographical references and index.
  ISBN 978-1-59485-041-7 (paperack)
  1. Trees—Northwest, Pacific. I. Hammerly, Ramona P. II. Title.
QK484.N95A75 2007
582.1609795—dc22

                    2007020267

ISBN (paperback): 978-1-59485-041-7
ISBN (ebook): 978-1-59485-316-6

CONTENTS

ACKNOWLEDGMENTS

My son, Matthew Arno, a restoration forestry contractor, urged me to develop this new edition and to include new ecological knowledge of our trees along with what it implies for forest stewardship. The following reviewers provided helpful suggestions that improved the book: Peter Achuff, national botanist, Parks Canada, Waterton Lakes National Park, Alberta; James Habeck, retired professor, University of Montana, Missoula; Frank Lang, retired professor, Southern Oregon University, Ashland; Ronald Mastrogiuseppe, Crater Lake Institute, Crater Lake National Park, Oregon; Robert Van Pelt, forest ecologist and author of *Forest Giants of the Pacific Coast* (University of Washington Press, 2001); and John Worrall, retired professor, University of British Columbia, Vancouver.

Both Ramona Hammerly and I would like to thank Deb Easter, new editions editor at The Mountaineers Books, for her continual encouragement and help at all stages of the book's development.

Some of the miniature sketches used in the identification guide (key), as well as some showing foliage of naturalized trees, are from Sudworth, *Forest Trees of the Pacific Slope* (U.S. Forest Service, 1908), and some are from Hitchcock and others, *Vascular Plants of the Pacific Northwest* (1955–69), with permission from the University of Washington Press.

—*Stephen F. Arno*

INTRODUCTION:
THE WHY AND WHAT OF THIS BOOK

Nearly three decades after it first appeared, *Northwest Trees* continues to be in demand despite the advent of many new books focusing on tree identification. Evidently people value a book that delves deeper, capturing the character of native trees in beautiful, meticulously accurate drawings and conveying the qualities of each species in an engaging account. New knowledge of native trees spurred us to develop this updated edition, which we also expanded to encompass the "Greater Northwest." Our 1977 book covered southern British Columbia, Washington, and northern parts of Oregon and Idaho. We now include southern Oregon with its rich assortment of interesting trees, and we extend eastward through the Rockies to include trees of southwestern Alberta, most of Idaho and Montana, and the Yellowstone Park area of northwestern Wyoming (see map).

This book profiles more than sixty native species that commonly attain treelike stature, defined as 20 feet (6 m) or taller. Drawings and narrative portray each tree's general characteristics, where it lives, its appearance, how it fits into the environment, how it responds to natural and man-made disturbances, and how people have used and valued it through the ages.

For example, western redcedar was "the tree of life" to coastal Native peoples, who used it for clothing, shelter, and transportation and to procure and preserve food. We note how Natives of the interior Northwest peeled bark from ponderosa pines to obtain the sugary inner bark and that some bark-peeling scars made a few hundred years ago can still be seen on living trees. Douglas-fir is well-known, but how many people realize that this exceptional species adapts to habitats ranging from coastal rain forest to high mountain sites and arid plains east of the

Rockies? Readers meet our region's two species of deciduous conifers called larch—one a towering tree that survives great fires, the other a short, sturdy dweller of alpine peaks so hardy it leafs out in June while still standing in snow. Its companion, whitebark pine, bears nutlike seeds that birds and squirrels compete to harvest—the birds ultimately "planting" new seedlings, while the squirrels' seed caches provide essential food for grizzly bears. The little Pacific yew supplied bows for Northwest Natives, but in the 1990s it became famous, and threatened with overexploitation, as the prime source for a cancer cure. In parts of Idaho, this low-growing tree can outcompete and ultimately replace the spruce and fir that soar high above it.

The Northwest's broadleaf trees are also intriguing. They include the broad-crowned bigleaf maples in coastal rain forests that are laden with thick drapes of hanging moss, which in turn support a crop of ferns—a photographer's delight. In contrast, hunched-over netleaf hackberry trees provide welcomed shade in the barren bottom of torrid Hells Canyon. Hackberry is one of the many fruit- and nut-bearing broad-leaved trees we profile.

The identification guide, or "key," uses the simplest, most-reliable characteristics and nontechnical language to help distinguish each species. However, keys are artificial constructs aimed at helping people sort out the messy, often intergrading divisions in nature that we call "species." For our key, we have used the best information available from various sources and translated it from technical features and terminology, but we cannot make it *perfect*, nor can we construct it so that people can apply it without reading and study of a tree's most accessible features. However, we believe this is a superior key to Northwest trees for general audiences.

THE GREATER NORTHWEST: HOME OF REMARKABLE TREES

This book covers trees of the Greater Northwest, a region nearly twice the size of Texas. Our region's abundance of trees developed under the influence of a climate spawned in the North Pacific Ocean. Oceanic air masses dry out as they push inland through rugged mountains, mixing with air masses from the center of the continent that are hotter in summer and colder in winter. Still, our region is the only place in North America where Pacific coast tree species spread inland to the crest of the Rocky Mountains. Highly variable geology and soils also contribute to the diversity of the Northwest's trees. Although our region has about equal numbers of conifer and broad-leaved species, conifers dominate the forests and are among the largest and oldest of their kind in the world. In contrast, most other temperate-zone forests worldwide are made up mostly of deciduous broad-leaved trees such as oaks and maples.

Ecologists explain why this is so (Waring and Franklin 1979): Conifers are better adapted to the Northwestern climate, which has ample moisture in the cool part of the year followed by drought in summer. Most other temperate regions have higher rainfall and humidity during summer. Our conifers are leafed out and ready to begin growth processes in the cool, wet seasons that abut winter—whenever temperatures stay mostly above freezing. Coastal conifers become active during mild periods in winter, while inland conifers activate in spring well before broad-leaved trees dare leaf out and expose tender shoots and new leaves to a sharp frost or snow. On the other hand, during hot, dry periods in summer, conifers can go dormant to conserve moisture while broad-leaved trees have their succulent foliage exposed to the drought.

The gigantic proportions attained by many Northwest conifers provide a buffer against environmental stress including drought and limited supplies of nutrients (Waring and Franklin 1979). Large, fire-resistant trees can survive low-intensity fires, which were common until the early 1900s in some of our inland forests. Many of our tree species are adapted to age-old patterns of fires, be they stand-replacing fires at intervals of a century or more; frequent, low-intensity fires perhaps once a decade; or mixed-severity fires occurring at irregular intervals. Other tree species take over in the absence of fire and other disturbances.

Several species of trees and associated undergrowth plants are essentially confined to the Greater Northwest: western larch, alpine larch, Pacific silver fir, noble fir, and grand fir. Others are restricted to our region except that they also extend southward into the mountains of California: western white pine, whitebark pine, coastal Douglas-fir, Pacific yew, bigleaf and vine maples, Pacific dogwood, Pacific madrone, and cascara. North of our region, boreal forests dominate, including white spruce and black spruce. South of our region, forest types associated with California (such as redwood, gray pine, and Jeffrey pine), the Great Basin (for example, pinyon and bristlecone pines), and the central Rocky Mountains (for instance, blue spruce and Rocky Mountain white fir) appear.

Some Northwestern species are confined to the coastal environment west of the Cascades (for example, Sitka spruce, Pacific silver fir, bigleaf maple, and several other broad-leaved trees). Others are coastal but also occupy the wet "inland maritime" area centered on northern Idaho (western hemlock, western redcedar, red alder, and cascara). Some are inland species (western larch, western juniper, water birch, and netleaf hackberry). Others are widespread geographically (Douglas-fir, subalpine fir, and black cottonwood). However, nearly all species are confined to one or two of the three elevational zones: low, middle, and high altitudes.

We—the author, artist, and publisher—hope this book will stimulate readers to investigate the broader subjects of forest ecology and stewardship. Many publications provide additional information. See References at the back of this book.

HOW TO USE THE KEYS

Nontechnical keys (like the ones in this book) rely on simple, accessible characteristics to help people identify what botanists have designated as individual species, based on technical characteristics. There is considerable variation within a species, and similar species often intergrade. Thus, keys are not infallible, but the ones presented here, used carefully, should correctly identify the vast majority of native trees most of the time.

1. The first key that follows is for conifers (having leaves that are needle- or scalelike), and the second key is for broad-leaved trees. Start at the top of the appropriate key for the specimen you wish to identify. Read the first set of paired, alternative statements and choose the one that fits best.

2. Then read the paired statements below that alternative (or branch) in the key. Again, choose the statement that fits the tree you are trying to identify.

3. Continue to follow the best alternatives downward through the key (noting that the keys' pages are numbered separately from the rest of this book's pages) until you arrive at a species name and page number.

4. Turn to that page in the main text and read the species description to see if it matches the tree in question.

5. If it doesn't match, go back to the beginning of the key and try again. If the key doesn't lead to a species whose description fits, perhaps the tree is an introduced species. A local horticulturist or extension forester may be able to identify the species.

GUIDE TO IDENTIFYING NORTHWEST TREES

CONIFERS (leaves needlelike or scalelike)

Note: > means "greater than"
< means "less than"

leaves needlelike; = or > ½ in. (12 mm) long

leaves scalelike; < ½ in. (12 mm) long: **cypress family, key p. 2**

needles not clustered

twigs smooth where old needles have fallen off

buds not large and sharp-pointed; cones without three-prong bracts

twigs of current year turn brown; needles not sharp-pointed: **true firs, key p. 5**

large trees; bark thick, red-brown, fibrous; small woody cone: **redwood, p. 146**

buds large, sharp-pointed; cones have three-prong bracts: **Douglas-fir, p. 71**

twigs warty where old needles have fallen off

needles sharp; bark has loose scales: **spruces, key p. 4**

twigs of current year remain green; needles pointed, 2-ranked on twigs

small tree; bark thin, purplish, and scaly; fruit red, berrylike: **Pacific yew, p. 143**

needles blunt; bark without loose scales (hemlocks)

needles plump, spread from all around twig; cones > 1¼ in. (3 cm) long: **mountain hemlock, p. 85**

needles flat and spread horizontally; cones < 1 in. (2.5 cm) long: **western hemlock, p. 79**

needles clustered

clusters of 2–5 hard evergreen needles: **pines, key p. 3**

clusters of > 10 soft deciduous needles (larches)

current-year twigs not woolly; low or mid elevations: **western larch, p. 43**

current-year twigs woolly; grows at high elevations: **alpine larch, p. 49**

Continuation from key page 1, top right: leaves scalelike, < ½ in. (12 mm) long

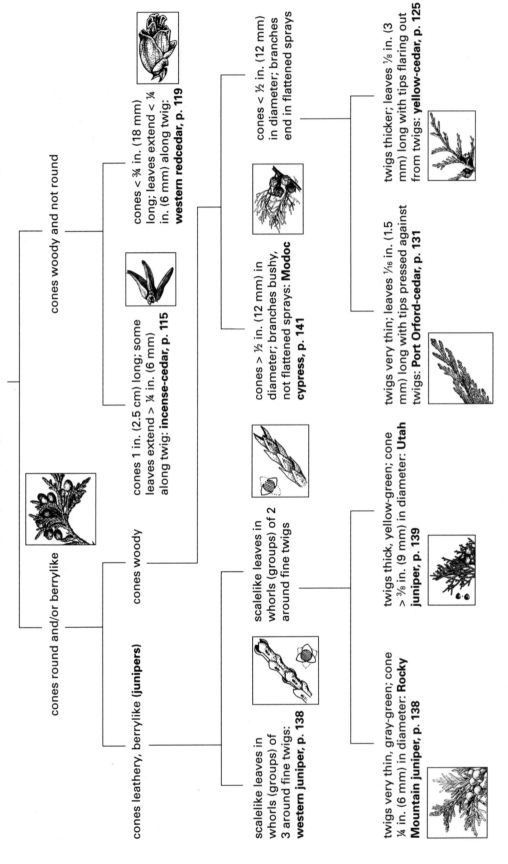

cones round and/or berrylike

cones woody and not round

cones leathery, berrylike (**junipers**)

cones woody

cones 1 in. (2.5 cm) long; some leaves extend > ¼ in. (6 mm) along twig: **incense-cedar, p. 115**

cones < ¾ in. (18 mm) long; leaves extend < ¼ in. (6 mm) along twig: **western redcedar, p. 119**

cones < ½ in. (12 mm) in diameter; branches end in flattened sprays

cones > ½ in. (12 mm) in diameter; branches bushy, not flattened sprays: **Modoc cypress, p. 141**

twigs thicker; leaves ⅛ in. (3 mm) long with tips flaring out from twigs: **yellow-cedar, p. 125**

twigs very thin; leaves ¹⁄₁₆ in. (1.5 mm) long with tips pressed against twigs: **Port Orford-cedar, p. 131**

scalelike leaves in whorls (groups) of 3 around fine twigs: **western juniper, p. 138**

scalelike leaves in whorls (groups) of 2 around fine twigs

twigs thick, yellow-green; cone > ⅜ in. (9 mm) in diameter: **Utah juniper, p. 139**

twigs very thin, gray-green; cone ¼ in. (6 mm) in diameter: **Rocky Mountain juniper, p. 138**

Continuation from key page 1: pines

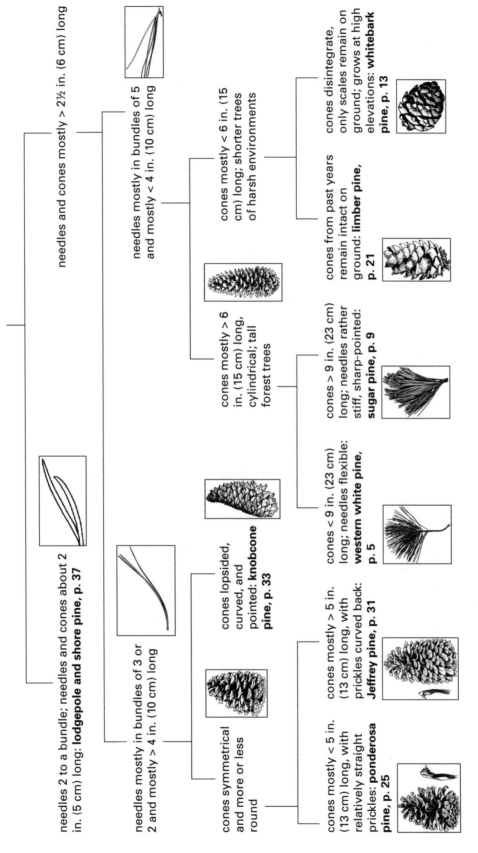

needles and cones mostly > 2½ in. (6 cm) long

needles 2 to a bundle; needles and cones about 2 in. (5 cm) long: **lodgepole and shore pine, p. 37**

needles mostly in bundles of 5 and mostly < 4 in. (10 cm) long

needles mostly in bundles of 3 or 2 and mostly > 4 in. (10 cm) long

cones mostly < 6 in. (15 cm) long; shorter trees of harsh environments

cones disintegrate, only scales remain on ground; grows at high elevations: **whitebark pine, p. 13**

cones from past years remain intact on ground: **limber pine, p. 21**

cones mostly > 6 in. (15 cm) long, cylindrical; tall forest trees

cones > 9 in. (23 cm) long; needles rather stiff, sharp-pointed: **sugar pine, p. 9**

cones < 9 in. (23 cm) long; needles flexible: **western white pine, p. 5**

cones symmetrical and more or less round

cones lopsided, curved, and pointed: **knobcone pine, p. 33**

cones mostly > 5 in. (13 cm) long, with prickles curved back: **Jeffrey pine, p. 31**

cones mostly < 5 in. (13 cm) long, with relatively straight prickles: **ponderosa pine, p. 25**

Continuation from key page 1: spruces

trees of higher elevations, > 2000 ft. (600 m), or E of Cascade Crest; needles stout, not flattened

trees atop and E of Cascades and B.C. Coast Range; cones < 3 in. (8 cm) long

cone scales broadest near tip; firm, smooth-textured, rounded, have smooth edges: **hybrid white spruce, p. 67**

low-elevation coastal tree; needles flattened, whitish on one side: **Sitka spruce, p. 55**

trees of SW Oregon, NW Calif.; crown has long, drooping branchlets; cones > 3 in. (8 cm) long: **Brewer spruce, p. 66**

cone scales broadest near base; thin, papery, crinkled, not rounded, have jagged edges: **Engelmann spruce, p. 63**

Continuation from *key page 1*: true firs

lower branches have many needles > 1½ in. (4 cm) long; needles flat and spread more or less horizontally from twigs (intermediate forms may be hybrids)

needles shiny dark green on top, whitish beneath; spreading horizontally in 2 comblike rows, producing flat branchlets: **grand fir, p. 95**

needles have whitish bloom on both surfaces, thus appearing pale grayish green; many upturned so twigs are not flat: **white fir, p. 95**

needles < 1½ in. (4 cm) long; if needles are flat, many point forward on top of twigs

needles shiny dark green on top, whitish beneath; some spread horizontally forward, covering twig: **Pacific silver fir, p. 91**

needles not markedly 2-toned; not spreading horizontally forward covering twig

needles stiff and turning up in brushlike pattern; young twigs brownish; mature trees not spire-shaped (intermediate forms may be hybrids)

twigs imperfectly brushlike; young twigs greenish; mature trees have narrow spire shape: **subalpine fir, p. 101**

needles have tiny ridge on upper surface; top of twig visible between needles; bark has vertical and horizontal breaks creating plates; cones < ½ covered with papery bracts: **Shasta red fir, p. 109**

needles have tiny groove on upper surface; top of twig nearly hidden by dense needles; bark has prominent vertical ridges; cones (in tree top) > ½ covered with papery bracts: **noble fir, p. 109**

BROAD-LEAVED TREES

Note: > means "greater than"
< means "less than"

leaves compound—several leaflets attached to a leaf stem with a bud on the twig at leaf base, but not at the leaflets: **continued on key p. 12**

leaves attached alternately; twigs and buds in alternate pattern: **continued on key p. 7**

leaves simple—one blade and a leaf stem

leaves attached opposite each other in pairs; twigs and buds opposite each other

leaves oval, not lobed; large white blossoms; fruit wingless: **Pacific dogwood, p. 217**

leaves lobed, maplelike; fruit with 2 large wings **(maples)**

many leaves > 7 in. (18 cm) across: **bigleaf maple, p. 201**

leaves < 7 in. (18 cm) across

most leaves > 5 in. (13 cm) across, deeply lobed, silvery on undersides: **silver maple, p. 223**

leaves < 5 in. (13 cm) across, not silvery on undersides

leaves with 7–9 lobes with triangular points, making them somewhat star-shaped: **vine maple, p. 209**

leaves with 3 lobes

leaf edges have few teeth (large and rounded); native to SE Idaho and southward: **bigtooth maple, p. 210**

leaf edges have many small pointed or slightly rounded teeth: **Rocky Mountain maple, p. 207**

Continuation from key page 6, upper left: leaves simple, attached alternately

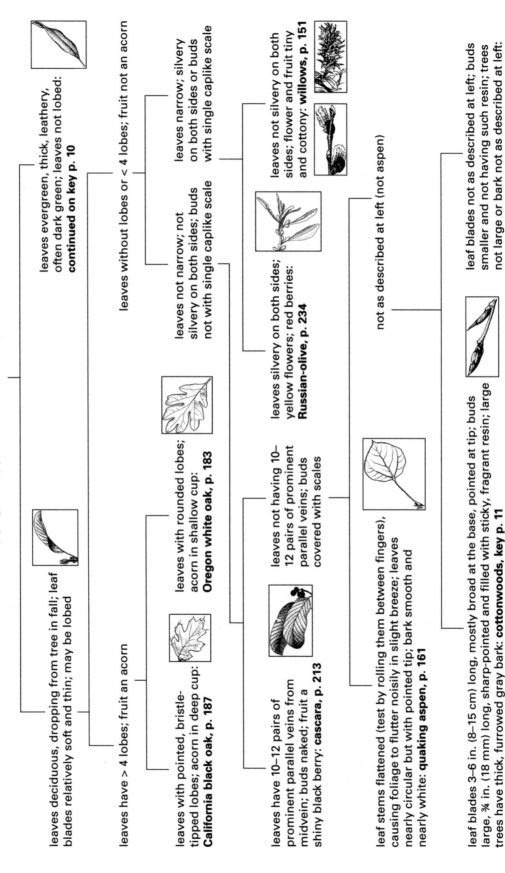

leaves deciduous, dropping from tree in fall; leaf blades relatively soft and thin; may be lobed

leaves evergreen, thick, leathery, often dark green; leaves not lobed: **continued on key p. 10**

leaves have > 4 lobes; fruit an acorn

leaves without lobes or < 4 lobes; fruit not an acorn

leaves with pointed, bristle-tipped lobes; acorn in deep cup: **California black oak, p. 187**

leaves with rounded lobes; acorn in shallow cup: **Oregon white oak, p. 183**

leaves not narrow; not silvery on both sides; buds not with single caplike scale

leaves narrow; silvery on both sides or buds with single caplike scale

leaves have 10–12 pairs of prominent parallel veins from midvein; buds naked; fruit a shiny black berry: **cascara, p. 213**

leaves not having 10–12 pairs of prominent parallel veins; buds covered with scales

leaves silvery on both sides; yellow flowers; red berries: **Russian-olive, p. 234**

leaves not silvery on both sides; flower and fruit tiny and cottony: **willows, p. 151**

leaf stems flattened (test by rolling them between fingers), causing foliage to flutter noisily in slight breeze; leaves nearly circular but with pointed tip; bark smooth and nearly white: **quaking aspen, p. 161**

not as described at left (not aspen)

leaf blades 3–6 in. (8–15 cm) long, mostly broad at the base, pointed at tip; buds large, ¾ in. (18 mm) long, sharp-pointed and filled with sticky, fragrant resin; large trees have thick, furrowed gray bark: **cottonwoods, key p. 11**

leaf blades not as described at left; buds smaller and not having such resin; trees not large or bark not as described at left: **continued on key p. 8**

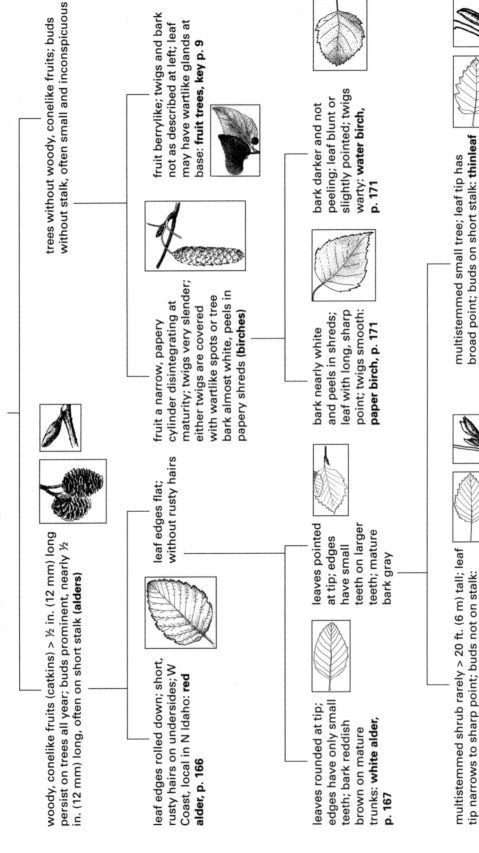

Continuation from key page 7, bottom right: simple deciduous leaves, not lobed, leaf stems often not flattened, etc.

woody, conelike fruits (catkins) > ½ in. (12 mm) long persist on trees all year; buds prominent, nearly ½ in. (12 mm) long, often on short stalk **(alders)**

trees without woody, conelike fruits; buds without stalk, often small and inconspicuous

fruit berrylike; twigs and bark not as described at left; leaf may have wartlike glands at base: **fruit trees, key p. 9**

fruit a narrow, papery cylinder disintegrating at maturity; twigs very slender; either twigs are covered with wartlike spots or tree bark almost white, peels in papery shreds **(birches)**

bark darker and not peeling; leaf blunt or slightly pointed; twigs warty: **water birch, p. 171**

bark nearly white and peels in shreds; leaf with long, sharp point; twigs smooth: **paper birch, p. 171**

multistemmed small tree; leaf tip has broad point; buds on short stalk: **thinleaf alder, p. 167**

leaf edges rolled down; short, rusty hairs on undersides; W Coast, local in N Idaho: **red alder, p. 166**

leaf edges flat; without rusty hairs

leaves pointed at tip; edges have small teeth on larger teeth; mature bark gray

leaves rounded at tip; edges have only small teeth; bark reddish brown on mature trunks: **white alder, p. 167**

multistemmed shrub rarely > 20 ft. (6 m) tall; leaf tip narrows to sharp point; buds not on stalk: **Sitka alder, p. 167**

Continuation from key page 8, upper right: native and naturalized fruit trees

leaves not deeply lobed in different patterns; fruit not raspberrylike

leaves very rough to the touch; leaf blades with 3 prominent veins spreading from base of leaf stem: **netleaf hackberry, p. 199**

flowers and fruit mostly in clusters

some leaves deeply toothed or even lobed; fruit like small apple or rosehip

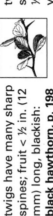

twigs with few or no spines; fruit often > ½ in. (12 mm) long, yellow to red: **Pacific crab apple, p. 197**

leaves not deeply toothed; fruit cherrylike

twigs have many sharp spines; fruit < ½ in. (12 mm) long, blackish: **black hawthorn, p. 198**

leaf tips pointed

leaves < 2 in. (5 cm) long; fruit a tiny, very bitter cherry, about ¼ in. (6 mm) across and black: **Mahaleb cherry, p. 231**

some leaves with deep lobes in different patterns; small raspberrylike fruit: **white mulberry, p. 232**

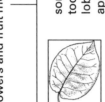

leaves not especially rough; blades not having 3 prominent veins spreading from base of leaf stem

flowers and fruit borne singly

fruit a plum about 1 in. (2.5 cm) long: **Klamath plum (Oregon), p. 195**; **cherry plum (Idaho), p. 232**; **American plum (Montana), p. 195**

fruit an apricot, about 1½ in. (4 cm) long: **apricot, p. 232**

flowers and fruit borne in small clusters

flowers and fruit borne in cylindrical clusters > 4 in. (10 cm) long: **chokecherry, p. 193**

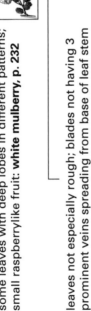

leaf tips rounded: **bitter cherry, p. 193**

leaves > 3 in. (8 cm) long; fruit a sweet cherry, pale yellow or dark red, but smaller than domestic cherries: **Mazzard cherry, p. 231**

Continuation from key page 7, top right: leaves evergreen, thick, leathery, not lobed

leaf underside not golden; fruit not a spiny bur

leaves green above, golden yellow on underside; fruit a large, spiny bur: **golden chinkapin, p. 175**

leaves have strong camphor smell when crushed, like medicated jellies or cough drops: **California-laurel, p. 225**

leaves without exceptional smell when crushed

bark orange-brown and flaking off in papery strips, revealing chartreuse inner bark; leaves shiny dark green above, pale silvery green below: **Pacific madrone, p. 221**

bark and leaves not as described at left

leaves mostly < 3 in. (8 cm) long; some have prickly edges like holly; fruit an acorn whose cup is not covered with bristles: **canyon live oak, p. 191**

leaves mostly > 3 in. (8 cm) long, not prickly, have prominent parallel veins often ending in tooth on the edge; fruit an acorn in bristle-covered cup: **tanoak, p. 179**

Continuation from key page 7, bottom left: cottonwoods
(Note: intermediate forms may be hybrids, not covered in this key)

leaves narrow, mostly > 2½ times longer than broad: **narrowleaf cottonwood, p. 158**

leaves relatively broad, mostly < 2 times longer than broad

most leaves shaped like broad triangles, flat across base; same green color on both surfaces; leaf stem markedly flattened (roll between fingers)

leaves have large, curved teeth; glands tiny or absent at junction of leaf stem and blade; S Idaho: **Frémont cottonwood, p. 233**

leaves with smaller teeth; conspicuous glands at leaf base; S Idaho, central Montana: **plains cottonwood, p. 158**

many leaves have rounded bases or are more oval than triangular; brown-streaked and paler green on lower surface; leaf stem round or oval

mature leaves about as wide as long, generally triangular; capsules that hold cottony seeds split in 3 segments; widespread in NW: **black cottonwood, p. 155**

mature leaves longer than wide, broadly oval; capsules that hold cottony seeds split in 2 segments; Canadian Rockies: **balsam poplar, p. 158**

Continuation from key page 6, top left: leaves compound

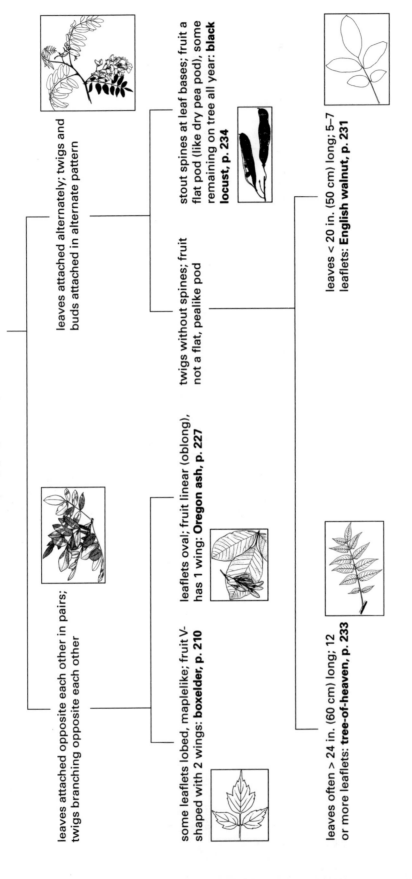

leaves attached opposite each other in pairs; twigs branching opposite each other

some leaflets lobed, maplelike; fruit V-shaped with 2 wings: **boxelder, p. 210**

leaflets oval; fruit linear (oblong), has 1 wing: **Oregon ash, p. 227**

leaves attached alternately; twigs and buds attached in alternate pattern

stout spines at leaf bases; fruit a flat pod (like dry pea pod), some remaining on tree all year: **black locust, p. 234**

twigs without spines; fruit not a flat, pealike pod

leaves often > 24 in. (60 cm) long; 12 or more leaflets: **tree-of-heaven, p. 233**

leaves < 20 in. (50 cm) long; 5–7 leaflets: **English walnut, p. 231**

Ramona
Hammerly '75

PART I CONIFERS

WESTERN WHITE PINE

Pinus monticola, Pine family—Pinaceae

Across most of its natural distribution, from central British Columbia to California's Sierra Nevada, western white pine grows scattered among forests dominated by firs and hemlocks. The pine stands out as a handsome tree with checkered bark and a slender, open crown adorned with long, dangling cones that contrasts with its thick-canopied associates.

Western white pine once dominated the forest over large areas of northern Idaho. Its great columnar trunks stood close together and soared upward, supporting a canopy 200 feet (60 m) high. These were the preeminent lumber-producing timberlands of the Rocky Mountains. Over much of the last century, heavy logging, devastating wildfires, a crippling fungal disease, and an epidemic of bark beetles laid waste to Idaho's magnificent white-pine forest. Now, though, with the help of geneticists and foresters, this beleaguered species is making a comeback in and beyond northern Idaho.

Where It Grows

Western white pine grows between sea level and about 5000 feet (about 1500 m) elevation in southwestern British Columbia and western Washington. It also inhabits moist areas of the Blue Mountains in eastern Washington and Oregon. In Oregon, the species' affinity for moist sites generally confines it to between 2000 and 6000 feet (600 and 1800 m) in the Cascades and coastal ranges. Near its southern limits, in the Sierra Nevada, it finds suitably cool and moist conditions between about 7000 and 10,500 feet (2100 and 3200 m) elevation. Western white pine also occupies the moist, inland-maritime forests of southeastern British Columbia, northeastern Washington, northern Idaho, and northwestern Montana as far east as Glacier National Park.

Appearance

Young western white pines have narrow, open crowns made up of very regularly spaced whorls (distinct layers) of branches arising from the same level on the main stem. One can estimate the age of a young tree by counting the annually produced branch whorls.

Even relatively young western white pines commonly bear some of the long, slender cones. The cones, often used in wreaths and other decorations, are 6 to 11 inches (15 to 28 cm) long, slightly curved, and covered with thin,

1"

western white pine

pitchy scales. The cones, which remain intact on the forest floor for a few years, are useful for identification of tall trees whose foliage is out of reach.

All "white pines"—including sugar, whitebark, and limber pine—bear their needlelike leaves in bundles (fascicles) of five. Western white pine needles are noticeably more slender, flexible, and whitish blue-green than those of whitebark pine, which sometimes grows nearby at high elevations. Western white pine needles are lined with minute teeth—detected by feeling them—while needles on whitebark pine are smooth. Sugar pine, an associated species in Oregon, has needles that are stiffer, somewhat plumper, and darker in color (bluish green).

Mature western white pine trees have bark that appears checkered or cut into small, regular units, unlike any other Northwestern tree. Still another notable feature of old trees, especially those in the Northern Rockies, is the way uppermost boughs often stretch out and upward.

Ecological Role

Western white pine grows in relatively humid regions or in moist sites in the mountains. Although it is intermediate in shade tolerance— the ability to compete with other species in a dense forest—its principal associates include highly shade-tolerant true firs and hemlocks. Thus, in order to compete for growing space, western white pine requires occasional disturbances, notably fire. Historically, white pine benefited from its ability to survive understory fires that burned along the ground at low intensity and killed many of the fire-sensitive firs and hemlocks. Stand-replacement fires killed most trees but often favored western white pine because it regenerates well in burned areas—sometimes from seeds surviving in green cones in tall trees. Western white pine commonly outgrows its competitors in the aftermath of fire, logging, or other disturbances.

This species also succeeds by being exceptionally well adapted to poor soils. On gravelly soils compacted by the massive continental glacier that inundated the Puget Sound area, white pines outgrow even the ubiquitous coastal Douglas-fir, attaining diameters of 36 inches (90 cm) by the time Douglas-fir of the same age are half that thick. Western white pine also thrives at the margins of bogs on the Olympic Peninsula. On high, stony ridges in the southern Cascades and Sierra Nevada, western white pine often develops into a stout, rugged sentinel rising out of the boulders.

Human History

Ethnobotanists who have studied tribal uses of plants throughout the Greater Northwest report that western white pine's resinous gum was chewed to relieve or treat coughing (Moerman 1998). Native peoples coated whaling and fishing equipment and fastened arrowheads on shafts with the tree's pitch. This species was apparently utilized less than other pines that bear large seeds or grow in dry regions where the extensively useful western redcedar wasn't available. However, aboriginal peoples weren't mass-producing lumber.

Pioneer lumbermen considered western white pine and its close relative eastern white pine (*Pinus strobus*), native to eastern North America, among the world's finest softwoods. Eastern white pine produced the prime lumber used in early Colonial houses as well as square timbers and thousands of huge masts for sailing ships. The English monarchy even blazed certain prime specimens with a broad arrow to reserve them for the Royal Navy.

The wood of both eastern and western white pines is light in color and weight but comparatively strong. Its grain is often so straight and even that the wood can be sliced across the grain with ease. The wood takes nails without splitting, works well, is not very resinous, and takes finishes nicely. It has historically been prized for window and door frames and moldings. It is an outstanding wood for carving. A favorite whittler's project is to take a block of white pine and fashion it into a chain composed of many interlocking links—an operation hard for the novice even to visualize.

Western white pine has an epochal relationship to the development of forestry in western North America. By 1880, unregulated harvest had removed much of the original eastern white pine forest, and lumbermen's attention shifted to the even larger western white pine timber found in the Coeur d'Alene and Saint Joe river drainages of northern Idaho (Strong 1970). This was before the forest reserves (later called national forests) were established, at a time when government policy favored disposal of western lands to aid settlement and development. Two transcontinental railroads that passed through northern Idaho, with their branch lines, totaled 4000 miles (6400 kilometers) of track and required 10 million ties, many of which were milled from western white pine. By the early 1900s, sawmills in the Coeur d'Alene River drainage alone were annually producing up to half a billion board feet of largely white pine lumber, enough to build 50,000 small houses. One big mill operated by the Ohio Match Company sawed white pine into planks that were cut up into wooden match sticks!

Uncontrolled logging might have cleared off all the primeval western white pine forests, as had happened with eastern white pine. Fortunately, the era of conservation intervened—aided by President Theodore Roosevelt and Chief Forester Gifford Pinchot. Millions of acres were placed into federal forest reserves, but the problem of what to do about wildfires plagued efforts to protect the forests. A crisis arose in August 1910, when a violent windstorm fanned multiple fires into a conflagration that engulfed 3 million acres (1.2 million ha), including part of the town of Wallace, Idaho, and a few backwoods settlements. This holocaust centered in Idaho's white pine region became the impetus for the federal forestry campaign to eliminate fire. Two generations later, in the late 1970s, forest agencies recognized that attempts to exclude fire from forests were ultimately counterproductive, and they adopted new policies promoting comprehensive management of fire and fuels—a policy that is practiced in some areas but not in others (Arno and Allison-Bunnell 2002).

Another monumental event in 1910 directly impacted western white pine. A Eurasian disease, white pine blister rust (*Cronartium ribicola*), was accidentally imported to Vancouver, British Columbia, on eastern white pine seedlings that had been grown in France (McDonald and Hoff 2001). By the 1920s, blister rust had spread eastward, via windblown spores, to the white pines of northern Idaho. The rust fatally damages white pine trees (including whitebark, limber, and sugar pines). In the 1930s, federal forestry agencies responded to this worsening plague by launching a multimillion-dollar program to save white pines. For three decades, thousands of people were employed to grub out and chemically poison currant and gooseberry bushes (genus *Ribes*) from British Columbia and California and eastward to Glacier and Yellowstone national parks. By thus destroying this alternate host necessary for completion of the blister rust's life cycle, foresters hoped to save white pines.

However, rust spores can be carried many miles downwind in moist air masses. The *Ribes* eradication program proved futile, as did a direct chemical attack on blister rust. In 2005, Forest Service pathologists in Moscow, Idaho, discovered that two species of native forest herbs—a lousewort (*Pedicularis*) and a paintbrush (*Castilleja*)—can also serve as alternate hosts for blister rust. Since the 1960s, efforts have concentrated on breeding the small percentage of white pines that exhibit natural resistance to blister rust. Since 1970, millions of naturally resistant western white pine seedlings have been planted

Reopening a trail in northern Idaho's white pine forest after the 1910 fire. (U.S. Forest Service, Region 1 photo)

and have generally grown well on logged sites in northern Idaho and adjacent areas. Also, natural rust resistance seems increasingly evident in wild young white pines growing on logged, burned, or other disturbed sites, even in areas where the species is less abundant. Periodic disturbance by logging or fire that opens up the forest provides western white pine an opportunity to regenerate in large numbers. This allows rust-resistant individuals to get established and eventually pass on some of their genetic resistance to subsequent generations. Western white pine is probably at greatest risk in natural areas west of the Cascade crest, where fire is still effectively excluded and logging, to create new habitat for white pine, is not allowed.

SUGAR PINE

Pinus lambertiana, Pine family—Pinaceae

Sugar pine is often described in poetic terms as the most regal of the world's 100 or so species of pine. It is the largest of all the pines, with old trees commonly attaining 4 to 8 feet (1.2 to 2.4 m) in diameter and over 200 feet (60 m) in height, and it bears huge, pendant cones at the tips of great, spreading limbs. The upper-crown branches on old trees commonly reach out 25 feet (8 m) or more, as if to demonstrate dominion over the other forest species. The legendary aura associated with sugar pine (see Human History) began with explorer David Douglas's heroic and perilous discovery of this forest giant in the remote mountains of southwestern Oregon. In addition to its inspirational image, sugar pine has long served humans as a source of sustenance and high-quality lumber.

Where It Grows

Sugar pine grows on relatively moist sites at middle elevations in the mountains of Oregon and California, where it is part of a diverse mixed-conifer forest. On the western slope of the Cascades east of Eugene, Oregon, it is usually found between elevations of 1700 and 3700 feet (500 and 1100 m), but in Oregon's eastern and southern Cascades and in the Siskiyous, it ascends to 5000 feet (1500 m) or higher. Small populations of sugar pine are scattered northward along the Cascades a few miles past Mount Jefferson. The species is more abundant farther south, in forests west of Crater Lake and in the Siskiyous. Small populations also occupy isolated higher mountains east of the Cascades, south of Bend, Oregon. Sugar pine becomes more abundant along the western slope of the Sierra Nevada in California.

Appearance

Young sugar pines have broad, conical canopies extending down near the ground, with distinctive bluish-green foliage made up of 3- to 4-inch-long (8- to 10-cm-long) needles borne in clusters of five. Young trees grow more slowly than associated ponderosa pine, but growth accelerates when they reach pole size, and then they sustain higher grow rates than their associates. Thus, sugar pine typically becomes the largest tree in the mountains of southern Oregon and California, except for the scattered groves of giant sequoia in the Sierra Nevada.

As sugar pines grow and mature, lower branches are shaded out, die, and eventually fall away, leaving a long, clear trunk supporting a canopy high overhead. Development of clear boles was no doubt aided by the scorching and pruning effect of frequent, moderate-intensity surface fires that occurred in many stands prior to about 1900. Bark on mature trees is reddish brown to purple, irregularly fissured, and 2 to 4 inches (5 to 10 cm) thick.

Sugar pines often live 300 to 400 years or more. As they mature, some of the upper-crown branches commonly extend great distances horizontally, imparting a distinctive shape to mature sugar pines that a keen observer can identify from a mile or farther away. A few of the upper-crown branches in an old tree may reach out so far that they create an eccentric or even a bizarre shape.

Sugar pine cones are mostly 10 to 14 inches (25 to 35 cm) long, and some are longer yet. Before ripening, they are narrow, green, and heavy—2 to 4 pounds (1 to 2 kg). Thus, they fall like a missile when cut off by squirrels high overhead! Cones that mature on the tree dry out and turn brown, and their scales flex open. This releases the large,

sugar pine

in crowded forests, unlike shade-tolerant species.) Over the past century, the shade-tolerant competitors have proliferated in many of these forests due to the elimination of understory fires and to logging that removed sugar pines while leaving many of the competitors. The shade-tolerant species commonly form dense understories that increase stress on sugar pines and heighten their vulnerability to bark beetle attack. Historically, fires favored sugar pine because of its thicker bark and high, open canopy, which make it more fire-resistant than some of its competitors, and the fact that fires create openings suitable for regeneration.

Like western white pine, sugar pine is vulnerable to white pine blister rust. The rust's impact on sugar pine has so far been less severe than on western white and whitebark pines growing in more northerly latitudes where a damp climate seems more favorable to the disease. In sugar pine, rust-caused mortality is often most noticeable on saplings—the potential giant trees of the future. Loss of young sugar pines is exacerbated on much of the landscape by a diminished amount of disturbance that favors sugar pine regeneration.

Many of the older western white and sugar pines have now been killed by a native bark beetle—the mountain pine beetle (*Dendroctonus ponderosae*). The larvae live in and tunnel through the soft inner bark layer (cambium), girdling the tree. Beetle outbreaks are enhanced by drought and overcrowded forest conditions that weaken the pines and make them more vulnerable. Employing silvicultural cutting treatments and prescribed fire to thin out competing trees and as a substitute for the historical role of fire might help restore sugar pine as monarch of the forest.

winged seeds that average about 2100 per pound (4600 per kg)—nearly as big as pinyon pine nuts. Later, the open cones fall to the ground, where they remain intact for a few years unless gathered up by humans as decorations.

Ecological Role

Sugar pine usually grows scattered in mixed stands with other species ranging from shade-intolerant ponderosa pine to mid-tolerant coastal Douglas-fir and western white pine to shade-tolerant incense-cedar and true firs. (Shade-intolerant trees do not compete well

Human History

Sugar pine provided two types of food eagerly sought by Native peoples (Moerman 1998). Several tribes harvested sugar pine seeds, which were eaten raw, roasted (and sometimes stored for winter use), boiled, pounded and mixed with cold water, dried, powdered, made into small cakes, eaten in a mush, or pulverized and made into a spread comparable to peanut butter. The sweet inner bark was gathered and eaten directly or mixed with other foods or dried into a "powdered sugar." The pitch, also sweet at certain times, was chewed as gum. It oozes out of wounds on the trunk, becomes white, and tastes sweet, thus giving the tree its common name; however, on account of its laxative properties, it was eaten only in limited quantities. The taste is attributed to a sugar-alcohol called pinitol.

Sugar pine was first described in 1826 by botanical explorer David Douglas, a young Scot who was hosted by John McLoughlin, the Hudson's Bay Company's Chief Factor at Fort Vancouver, near present-day Vancouver, Washington. After seeing the large pine seeds and a gigantic cone brought in by Indians and trappers, Douglas became eager to locate the intriguing new species of pine that grew somewhere in the headwaters of the Willamette River (a detailed account is in Davies 1980). After five weeks of arduous travel southward through western Oregon in stormy fall weather, Douglas encountered an alarmed Indian. After establishing peaceful intentions, Douglas drew a sketch of the cone from the pine he was seeking out. The Indian pointed to the hills off to the south. Several hours later, Douglas reached the great pines, the largest of which had blown down. Douglas reported its circumference as equivalent to 18.4 feet (5.6 m) in diameter near the ground and 5.5 feet (1.7 m) in diameter at 134 feet (41 m). The tree's total length was 215 feet (65 m). Today the largest known sugar pine is 11.7 feet (3.6 m) in diameter—at 4.5 feet (1.4 m) above the ground. It may be that the basal circumference figure attributed to Douglas is in error, but there is little doubt that the tree was gargantuan.

Douglas described the giant pines as having smooth trunks with branches only high above the ground, and these having cones hanging from their tips "like small sugar-loaves in a grocer's shop" (Davies 1980). The cones were so high up that Douglas had to clip them from the branches using his gun. The noise soon attracted eight Indians who were painted with red earth, well armed, and anything but friendly. Douglas tried to explain to them that he only wanted some cones, but they showed every inclination toward doing him harm. Finally he faced off against the entire group, cocking his gun and pulling a pistol from his belt. After several minutes of anxious confrontation, the Indian leader made a sign for tobacco, which Douglas indicated they would get only if they fetched him some cones. As soon as they left his sight, Douglas grabbed his three cones and some twigs and hastily retreated across the many miles to his camp. That evening he recorded his discomfort while lying in the grass, gun at his side and writing by the flicker of a piece of burning pitch-wood, in constant expectation of being attacked.

Because of the remoteness of most sugar pines in Oregon and a slow rate of settlement in their vicinity, nineteenth-century exploitation of the species was limited. Frank Lang, a forest ecologist and resident of Ashland, Oregon, has found numerous places where a large sugar pine had been felled long ago and milled into lumber right where it lay.

In contrast, the 1849 California Gold Rush brought throngs of European Americans to the doorstep of that state's sugar pine country. Here, huge sugar pines were plundered on tens of thousands of acres of unprotected government land long before national forests and national parks were established. The magnificent trees with their prodigious volume of clear wood, similar to but larger than eastern white and western white pines, made choice lumber; but they were often used wastefully. Today, much less sugar pine is harvested, and it is carefully processed into high-value lumber products, similarly to western white pine.

WHITEBARK PINE

Pinus albicaulis, Pine family—Pinaceae

Whitebark pine is a sturdy and picturesque tree that accentuates the beauty and ecological diversity of high mountain habitats. This slow-growing pine of the remote ridges and peaks was little known to most foresters and ecologists until the 1980s. By then, studies revealed that whitebark pine functions as a keystone species in the high mountain ecosystem. Its pea-sized, nutlike seeds serve as a critical food source for wildlife, including grizzly bears. It also helps stabilize the snowpack and erodible soils on steep mountain slopes, thereby protecting the high quality of water emanating from alpine watersheds in places where few if any other trees can grow.

Unfortunately, in much of its range, whitebark is now heavily damaged by epidemics of white pine blister rust and bark beetles and, due to suppression of fires, it has little opportunity to regenerate. Recognizing the implications of this catastrophic decline, biologists and land managers are trying out strategies to restore whitebark pine communities (Tomback and others 2001).

Where It Grows

Whitebark pine grows in the highest-elevation forest and at timberline along the entire Rocky Mountain chain from central British Columbia and Alberta southward through western Wyoming. In the coastal mountain ranges and the Cascades, whitebark pine is more narrowly confined to the timberline zone, where trees occur only in patches. Here, it extends from west-central British Columbia southward to the high Cascades and California's Sierra Nevada. It also inhabits most of the high mountain ranges between the Cascades and the Rockies, including Oregon's Blue Mountains. White-

bark pine does not grow among the high peaks on Vancouver Island, but small populations inhabit a few ridges in the dry, rain-shadow zone of the northeastern Olympic Mountains. This tree becomes more abundant eastward across the Northwest toward the Rocky Mountains. In relatively dry mountains of southwestern Montana and east-central Idaho, whitebark pine becomes a major component of the subalpine forest.

Appearance

Whitebark pine saplings often have a narrow, pyramidal crown, but they are slow-growing and seldom develop the distinct annual whorls of branches that characterize faster-growing trees. Young trees have smooth, light gray bark, which gave rise to both the common and scientific names for this species. As they gradually mature, whitebark pines often develop a broad, irregular crown made up of multiple-branch trunks. Trees growing on good sites in moist subalpine forests often develop a straight trunk 80 feet (25 m) or taller resembling associated lodgepole pines. However, whitebark pines have five needles per cluster (versus two in lodgepole pines), and even their dead snags can often be distinguished by the large, upward-ascending branches at the top.

At higher elevations, where the forest begins to break up into groves of trees and meadows, whitebark gains more living space and develops a stout, shorter trunk and a large, spreading crown. These trees provide plump blue grouse a place to roost and eat buds while protected from winter's onslaughts and marauding goshawks. "Ghost forests" of great, spreading whitebark pines that died in a massive bark beetle epidemic in the 1930s still stand in many

whitebark pine snag

areas, a testimony to the durability of their resin-impregnated wood.

On extremely windy, cold, and snowbound sites, whitebark pine takes on a variety of stunted growth forms. These include short, stout, multi-stemmed trees with broad, rounded crowns. In harsher sites, whitebark forms thickets of shrublike trees with wind-battered stems—a form known as *krummholz,* which is German for "crooked wood." Finally, above tree line, white-bark forms "alpine scrub," or cushion *krummholz,* consisting of dense, wind-pruned shrubs barely knee-high, often arising in the lee of a boulder.

Whitebark pine needles are about 3 inches (8 cm) long and borne in clusters of five. They are coarse and yellow-green, in contrast with the fine, silvery green needles of the western white pine saplings that sometimes grow among the whitebark pine at its the lower elevational limits.

Whitebark pine cones are quite unusual and have long been a source of conjecture and confusion. As they mature, held upright at the tip of the tree's upper branches, the cones are

whitebark pine krummholz

whitebark pine

dark purple, egg-shaped, and 2 to 3½ inches (5 to 9 cm) long. Cones on the tree are generally reduced to remnants after Clark's nutcrackers break them open. Whole cones are found intact on the ground only for a few hours while squirrels are harvesting them. Thus, unlike other pines, whitebark is identified by an absence of cones beneath it. The broken cone-scales are found in abundance on the ground, however, and are useful for identification.

Whitebark's cones are destined to be harvested by animals, and the pine depends entirely on the jaylike Clark's nutcracker to disperse its seed in a manner that allows it to regenerate (Lanner 1996; Tomback 2001). Because of this animal-dependent relationship, whitebark pine seeds have no ordinary mechanism for dispersal. When, rarely, some cones are left unharvested in the tree, they do not open sufficiently for the nutlike seeds to drop out. Even if they did, the trees are short and the heavy seeds have no wing, so they would fall beneath the parent tree rather than into a suitable opening for regeneration. Chipmunks, other small animals, and birds quickly devour any seeds that happen to fall to the ground.

Ecological Role

Most relatively shade-intolerant (sun-loving) trees, such as whitebark pine, are able to persist in mixed forests by regenerating and growing more rapidly in burned and other disturbed sites than their shade-tolerant competitors. In contrast, whitebark is slow to establish and in its growth thereafter. Despite this disadvantage, whitebark has historically been able to prosper in two different ecological situations:

First, whitebark is part of self-perpetuating or climax communities at timberline, where climatic and site conditions are so austere that there are always open spaces for trees to colonize. Examples include the communities of stunted whitebark pine near Timberline Lodge on Oregon's Mount Hood and at Sunrise Park on Mount Rainier in Washington.

The second situation occurs when whitebark pine is perpetuated as a result of disturbances that open up the high-elevation forest. This happens especially where fires are frequent enough to allow whitebark to compete with other trees because of its special means of seed dispersal and its superior hardiness on severely exposed, burned sites. Historically, these disturbance-dependent whitebark pine communities are estimated to have covered perhaps 3 million acres (1.2 million ha) in the Rocky Mountains south of Canada—far more area than climax whitebark pine communities.

Clark's nutcrackers. The pea-sized whitebark seeds average about 2600 per pound (5700 per kg) but, unlike seeds of most pines, do not have a papery wing attached to aid wind transport. This makes it easy for Clark's nutcrackers to rapidly extract seeds from a cone and swallow them into their throat pouch. These raucous black, white, and gray birds issue harsh *kr-a-a-a*s as they pound away on the purple cones to claim the seeds.

Ecologist Ronald Lanner (1996) and ornithologist Diana Tomback (2001) explain the nutcracker's mutually beneficial (symbiotic) relationship with whitebark pine. A nutcracker may gather 100 or more seeds in its pouch before flying off to cache them, often miles away. When flying with a bulging throat pouch, the nutcracker looks like a miniature pelican. Nutcrackers cache small groups of seeds about an inch below the soil surface, leaving no telltale signs of their activity; thus the seeds are safe from predation by rodents or other birds. Each nutcracker can precisely relocate thousands of cache sites and retrieve the seeds during the following year or so to use as food for itself and its young.

However, nutcrackers also leave many caches unretrieved, and the seeds germinate and grow into whitebark pine seedlings. Nutcrackers prefer relatively open sites for caching, such as burned areas, and this is advantageous for regeneration of the relatively shade-intolerant pine. Essentially all natural regeneration of whitebark pine arises from seed caches made by nutcrackers, and because of this origin, multiple pine saplings commonly grow up in tight clusters. This form of seed distribution allows whitebark to colonize large burned areas more efficiently than its competitors that rely on wind transport of their seed.

Squirrels and bears. Tree squirrels compete with nutcrackers for the whitebark pine seed crop (Mattson and others 2001). Squirrels harvest whole cones and store most of them

whitebark pine **krummholz**

Clark's nutcracker harvesting pine nuts

red squirrel feeding on pine nuts

in middens in their underground burrows, rotten logs, or tree cavities. These storehouses allow squirrels to feed on pine seeds for a year or longer after harvesting a cone crop. The storehouses also make large quantities of seeds available to black and grizzly bears, who raid the middens, as well as to ground-dwelling rodents. Squirrels are workaholics that harvest enough cones to feed themselves as well as the marauding bears.

Bears roll and crush the cones under their paws and are able to separate the seeds well enough that they consume few of the coarse cone scales—attested to by the content of bear scat, which consists largely of seed shells. Whitebark pine seeds are so sought-after, nutritious, and nonperishable that bears will subsist largely on them for the entire year following a good cone crop. Upon emerging from hibernation in spring, bears dig down through a few feet of snowpack to reach cone middens. In the greater Yellowstone Park area, grizzly bears depend heavily on whitebark pine seeds, and in years following poor cone crops, bear-human conflicts are more frequent as bears range more widely in search of food.

Human History

Many Native peoples harvested whitebark pine seeds for food, often roasting them, cooking them as porridge, or mixing them with dried berries. Bud Cheff (1993), who grew up among traditional Salish people in western Montana, recounts long camping trips in the high mountains during the 1920s when they gathered packhorse loads of whitebark pine cones for later extraction and use of the seeds as food.

Ironically, at about the same time that biologists recognized whitebark pine as a critical component of its high mountain ecosystem, they also discovered serious threats to this tree and that its bountiful cone crops were already becoming a thing of the past in some regions. By the 1990s, blister rust disease, compounded by bark beetle attacks, had killed or severely damaged most mature whitebark pines in northwestern Montana, northern Idaho, and parts of Washington, and this dual plague was spreading both southward and to the north. Blister rust commonly kills the uppermost, cone-bearing branches first. Thus, many areas, such as Montana's Whitefish Range, that once produced copious whitebark pine cone crops heavily used by bears no longer provide this resource.

Whitebark pine is besieged by epidemics of mountain pine beetle, a native tree-killer whose outbreaks have increased dramatically in response to a pattern of warmer-than-average summers and winters, unusually favorable for sustaining high beetle populations. Whitebark pines weakened by blister rust are especially vulnerable, but also a high proportion of whitebark pine stands are old and are crowded with competing subalpine fir and other shade-tolerant trees as a result of seventy years of fire suppression. Despite their remote location, fires in whitebark pine communities tend to grow slowly due to cool and humid conditions and are easily suppressed using aerial access. Historically, many fires that swept through whitebark pine habitats started at lower elevations where today fires are quickly controlled.

Like western white pine, whitebark pine is highly susceptible to the imported blister rust disease. Both pine species also have a small proportion of their populations—less than 5 percent—that exhibit some form of genetically based resistance to rust damage. Since about 1970, naturally rust-resistant western white pine seedlings have been propagated in nurseries and planted in substantial numbers in logged areas of northern Idaho and vicinity. The knowledge and technology behind this successful breeding program could be used similarly to help embattled whitebark pine populations. However, whitebark pine represents a more difficult restoration problem for several reasons. Western white pine is a fast-growing, valuable tree in forests that are actively managed for lumber production; thus it is propagated in the process of forest management. Whitebark pine has essentially no commercial value and is slow-growing and difficult—thus expensive—to propagate in its remote habitats.

Overall, the best management alternatives for restoring whitebark pine are to allow lightning fires to burn in whitebark habitat and to use prescribed fire in strategic places. Also, in areas where rust damage is severe, rust-resistant seedlings can be planted in burns and other relatively open sites. The Whitebark Pine Ecosystem Foundation (*www.whitebarkfound.org*) is working to counteract the decline of whitebark pine through educational initiatives, focused research, and technical assistance and grants for restoration projects.

LIMBER PINE

Pinus flexilis, Pine family—Pinaceae

Limber pine is best known as a stalwart little tree clinging to stony wind-scoured ridges. Artists and photographers love the gnarled limber pines perched on rock outcrops at Saint Mary Lake beneath the towering peaks of Glacier National Park, Montana, and the battered pines at tree line on Trail Ridge Road in Rocky Mountain National Park, Colorado. Limber pine tends to occupy fringes of the forest, not the forest itself. It takes on many forms adapting to a hostile environment. Wherever it grows, limber pine provides habitat for wildlife. Although it is often confused with whitebark pine, there are distinct differences, and the two species are not closely related. Like other five-needle pines, in many areas limber pine has been badly damaged by blister rust and bark beetles.

Where It Grows

Limber pine inhabits scattered locations from Banff National Park, Alberta, to the 10,000-foot-high (3050-m-high) mountains rising east of Los Angeles. In the Greater Northwest, it is mostly confined to semi-arid sites from Alberta and eastern Idaho to northwestern Wyoming. Often mixed with inland Douglas-fir, limber pine forms an elfin woodland of bushy trees about 20 feet (6 m) tall at the edge of the Great Plains, immediately east of the Continental Divide. This pygmy forest of the high plains could be compared to the pinyon-juniper woodland that covers lower slopes of desert mountain ranges farther south.

Limber pine also colonizes dry, windy ridges at middle elevations, especially on coarse limestone soils and other infertile substrates. From the arid mountains near Sun Valley in east-central Idaho southward through the Great Basin and Southern Rockies, limber pine commonly forms the alpine timberline on

severely exposed sites. It is the only companion of ancient bristlecone pines (*Pinus longaeva*) at elevations of 11,000 to 12,000 feet (3350 to 3650 m) on peaks rising out of the Great Basin. Some isolated patches of limber pine occur far west of its usual distribution on droughty limestone or other largely barren rock types, notably on steep faces at only about 3000 feet (900 m) elevation along the Kicking Horse River near Golden, British Columbia, and at high elevation sites in Oregon's Wallowa and Strawberry mountains.

Appearance

Limber pine exhibits a myriad of shapes as influenced by its wide range of habitats. In the elfin woodland on the high plains, the short, compact trees have irregular, rounded crowns. Trees in middle-elevation sites tend to grow erect, often about 40 feet (12 m) tall, but still with irregular shapes and usually not a single straight stem like ponderosa or lodgepole pines have. Generally, the limber pine's main stem is crooked or divides into multiple ascending trunks in the upper crown. Limbs tend to be very long and often have upswept tips. At the alpine tree line, limber pines grow as stout, craggy trees; wind-shaped *krummholz* with tattered, flaglike leaders reaching up into the hostile elements; trees with a single prostrate trunk appressed against the stony ground; and wind-pruned cushion shrubs. These fascinating timberline forms can be seen by hikers who climb to the 9500-foot (2900-m) level on the west slope of Mount Borah south of Challis, Idaho.

Limber pine bears needles in clusters of five, about 3 inches (7.5 cm) long, similar to those of whitebark pine. The two species occasionally grow together on rocky,

limber pine krummholz

wind-scoured sites at moderately high elevations—for example, at about 7000 feet (2100 m) on the ridge southeast of Red Mountain near Lincoln, Montana. Few people can distinguish the two species as seedlings or saplings. However, once the trees are about 8 inches (20 cm) in diameter and seventy years of age, they will have produced cones, and differences become obvious.

Limber pine's new cones (which are two years old) are bright green in early summer. They turn light brown as they mature. In contrast, whitebark pine's new cones are dark purple in summer before turning brown in September—although they seldom remain intact on the trees that long, due to animal predation. Limber pine cones are larger—4 to 6 inches (10 to 15 cm) long—than whitebark cones and do not disintegrate. Like cones of most other pines, they dry out, the scales

spread open, and seeds are released while cones are still on the tree. Then the empty cones fall to the ground, where they remain intact for several years. They look generally

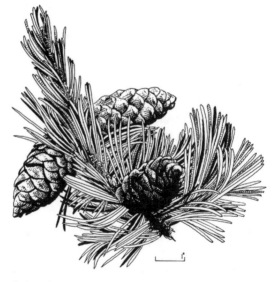

limber pine

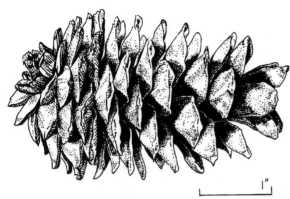

limber pine cone

Ecological Role

Limber pine is shade-intolerant and unable to sustain itself on sites where other conifers form moderately dense woodlands or forests. Thus, by default it inhabits infertile substrates and droughty sites exposed to a particularly hostile climate—such as lower and alpine timberlines and wind-battered ridges. Scattered inland Douglas-fir coexist with limber pine in all but the driest and coldest habitats, where Rocky Mountain juniper and Engelmann spruce, respectively, are likely associates instead.

like western white pine cones, except they are shorter and have thicker scales. These durable cones on the ground distinguish limber pine from whitebark. Pollen cones may also aid identification; they are generally reported to be yellow in limber pine and bright reddish in whitebark.

Limber pine seeds are sought out by animals, and, as with whitebark pine, seed caches abandoned by the Clark's nutcracker are the major source of successful regeneration. Limber pine seeds weigh about half as much as those of whitebark pine, averaging about 4900 per pound (10,800 per kg). Some are wingless, and others have an ineffective, rudimentary wing, suggesting that limber pine evolved from ancestors that bore winged seeds.

Ron Lanner's book *Made for each other: A symbiosis of birds and pines* (1996) describes probable origins of bird-dependent pines and concludes that limber and whitebark pines are *not* closely related. Instead, limber pine has co-evolved with birds to be like whitebark and its other stone pine relatives (group *Cembrae*) that include the Swiss and Siberian stone pines. Limber pine itself is genetically part of the white pines (group *Strobus*) together with eastern white, western white, and sugar pine. These other members of the *Strobus* group bear seeds with wings that can be transported by the wind.

Historically, fire seems to have had little effect on limber pine communities at middle and high elevations, because surface fuel is inherently sparse. Some of the very slow-growing trees in these habitats in the Greater Northwest are 500 or occasionally even 1000 years old and have scars from occasional low-intensity fires. However, at lower elevations, comparison of historic landscape photos and modern retakes show that some limber pine woodlands expanded dramatically into former grasslands during the twentieth century, probably as a result of livestock grazing and fire suppression that disrupted the historical pattern of frequent grass fires (Gruell 1983).

Limber pine's highly discontinuous distribution is intriguing. Perhaps Clark's nutcracker seed caching is responsible for some of the small limber pine populations far to the west of their normal range on special rock types. Where limber pine is accessible to black or grizzly bears, its seeds, also available in squirrel caches, become an important food source for them. This is notable along the Rocky Mountain Front in northern Montana and southern Alberta, where limber pine woodlands occur at the junction of mountains and high plains.

Since the 1990s, some limber pine communities have been badly damaged or largely destroyed by blister rust and by bark beetle epidemics, especially at low elevations where the trees were likely weakened by drought. Some of these stands had expanded greatly during the twentieth century. The Whitebark Pine Ecosystem Foundation (*www.whitebarkfound .org*) is concerned about limber pine communities and is involved in efforts to survey, evaluate, and restore them.

Human History

A compilation of early botanical exploration in Montana reports that limber pine seeds were an important food source for some Native peoples (Blankinship 1905). Limber pine is seldom mentioned in connection with European-American settlement and development of the West, probably because of its remoteness from habitable areas and its lack of economic value. Today, picturesque limber pines are a prominent feature of one major natural area: Craters of the Moon National Monument in south-central Idaho. Here scattered, enduring limber pines colonize the stark black lava. A much-photographed limber pine—the Burmis pine, now a dead snag—is a landmark along Highway 3, about 6 miles (11 km) east of the Frank Slide in southern Alberta.

PONDEROSA PINE

Pinus ponderosa, Pine family—Pinaceae

Ponderosa pine is a quintessential symbol of the expansive, semi-arid landscape of the American West. Typically it is the first forest tree to greet travelers emerging from a tiresome journey across steppes covered with nothing taller than sagebrush or bushy junipers. Its stout trunk is clad in handsome orange-brown bark, and its big, sturdy branches support a luxuriant canopy of long-needled foliage. Ponderosa borders the desert because it is superior to other forest trees in adapting to drought. It also is finely attuned to a dry environment historically shaped by frequent fires. Ponderosas commonly lived 500 years or more in part because of fires burning beneath them every decade or so.

In the early 1900s, ponderosa pine was still found in sunny, parklike forests dominated by large trees, but today many of these places are radically changed. Crowded with small trees (often firs) and deadfall, they are prone to severe wildfires and epidemics of insects and disease. These forests now contain millions of homes and other developments. At long last, some private landowners and managers of public lands are carrying out treatments designed to restore a semblance of the historic grandeur to ponderosa pine forests.

Where It Grows

Ponderosa pine is characteristic of relatively warm, dry forests throughout the West, from southern British Columbia to southern California, New Mexico, and South Dakota. Ponderosa is absent from some regions that have short, cool summers punctuated by frequent frost, such as southern Alberta, the greater Yellowstone Park area, and much of the Great Basin. It also grows poorly in damp coastal environments, and thus it is absent from most of western Washington and southwestern British Columbia. Isolated populations occur in a few areas west of the Cascades, notably at the head of Ross Lake in southernmost British Columbia, the Fort Lewis prairies near Tacoma, Washington, and the Willamette Valley in Oregon. In southwestern Oregon and northwestern California, the maritime climate is confined to a narrow band along the coast, and east of this the ponderosa becomes common.

Ponderosa is well adapted to the warm, dry mountain country between the Cascade crest and the Continental Divide. For example, in central Idaho it descends to 1000 feet (300 m) elevation in deep canyons, but it also prospers as high up as 6500 feet (2000 m) on south-facing ridges.

Appearance

Healthy young ponderosa pines have broad crowns made up of regular whorls of long limbs. The canopy is rather open, with branches well separated. Their foliage consists of 5- to 8-inch-long (13- to 20-cm-long) needles mostly borne in groups of three. (Ponderosa pines east of the Continental Divide often bear needles in clusters of two.) Also, the large buds at the tips of branches are protected by a tuft of long needles. These characteristics help ensure that some of the small trees survive low-intensity fires. Young trees have rough, dark-brown bark, but as they age, the bark gradually becomes bright orange-brown and is divided into plates by a network of dark fissures—a favorite subject of artists and photographers.

As young trees grow tall, their lower branches normally die. Historically, they were pruned by repeated fires, resulting in mature trees having a branch-free trunk extending high

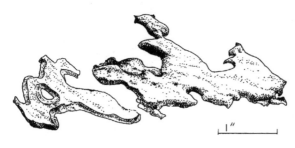

flakes of ponderosa pine bark

above the ground. Botanical explorer David Douglas named these trees "ponderosa" (related to "ponderous") because of their great size. On good sites, the largest old trees commonly attain diameters of 4 feet (1.2 m) and heights of 130 feet (40 m) or more. The biggest individual ponderosas in Washington, Oregon, California, and Idaho are 7 feet (2 m) or more in diameter and about 200 feet (60 m) tall. Trees greater than 500 years old can often be distinguished by especially smooth and pale orange bark and a flat-topped canopy composed of great gnarled branches and thin, ropy branchlets.

Ponderosa pine cones are often abundant on and underneath the trees. They are mostly 3 to 5 inches (8 to 13 cm) long, egg-shaped, and purple when the squirrels fell them but becoming brown and almost spherical when they dry and the scales flex open. The back of each scale is armed with a sharp prickle that sticks out and soon teaches people to be careful when handling these cones.

Ecological Role

Ponderosa pine is shade intolerant, so if more shade-tolerant trees are present, they tend to replace ponderosa in forests that are protected from fire and other major disturbances. Such associates include inland Douglas-fir, grand fir, white fir, and incense-cedar. How is it, then, that a shade-intolerant species became one of the most widespread trees in the American West? Its success is due to two traits: superior drought tolerance and adaptation to frequent fires.

In large parts of its distribution, ponderosa pine forests develop in sites too dry for

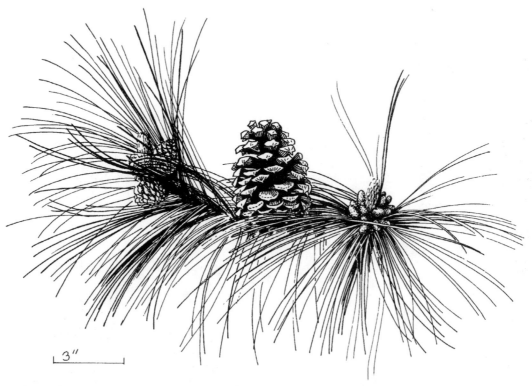

ponderosa pine

Douglas-fir and other less drought-tolerant trees. These pure ponderosa forests border the Columbia Basin desert, for example, along Interstate 90 west of Spokane, Washington. They also occupy droughty pumice soils around Bend, Oregon, and extensive areas in eastern Montana. Physiologists learned that ponderosa pines are superior in accessing and conserving moisture. In one historic study (Bates 1924), year-old seedlings attained a height of only 3 inches (8 cm) but developed taproots nearly 24 inches (60 cm) long. Because of these deep roots, gardeners find it difficult to successfully transplant ponderosa saplings.

Other studies (Smith 1985; U.S. Forest Service 1990) disclosed that during summer drought, the ponderosa is able to close its leaf pores to prevent water loss better than other conifers, and its seedlings are able to withstand exceedingly high temperatures—162 degrees F (72 C)—at the ground surface. These attributes allow ponderosas to colonize rocky or sandy soils that dry out to lethal levels in the upper 24 to 36 inches (60 to 90 cm) but remain moist farther down. Central Oregon's Lost Forest, northeast of Christmas Valley, is a dramatic example. Here a pure stand of ponderosa pine thrives amid a vast desert where less than 10 inches (25 cm) of precipitation falls in the average year, evidently as a result of water available deep under the sandy surface.

In much of its historic distribution in the Greater Northwest, ponderosa pine prospered despite competition from more shade-tolerant firs, due to its ability to survive frequent low-intensity fires, protected by thick bark and other fire-resistant features (Arno and Allison-Bunnell 2002). When organized fire suppression and logging of large pines disrupted this historic ecosystem, young firs were able to take over. Many dense fir forests east of the Cascades still have remnants of huge ponderosa pines that were logged long ago. Old ponderosa stumps can be identified by a core of sound pine pitch-wood—light colored and smelling of fresh pitch when carved with a knife.

Pitch-filled stumps often preserve a sequence of scars from ancient fires. One stump from a tree felled in 1906 near Hamilton, Montana, had scars from thirty-one fires between about 1545 and 1883 (Gruell and others 1982). Other nearby stumps and live trees had scars from twelve additional fires during that period. Also, a thick layer of ponderosa's distinctive orange bark, complete with puzzle-shaped bark flakes, is often found by scraping away litter at the base of old stumps.

Ponderosa historically prospered on south- and west-facing slopes and other sites where tree litter and grass were dry and combustible for long periods during most years. Ponderosa virtually ensured frequent burning by providing its own light fuel in prodigious quantities. Any homeowner in a ponderosa forest can attest to this after gathering 1 to 2 tons per acre (2 to 4 tonnes per ha) of shed needles and cones from around the house and outbuildings each year. This material is the ideal fuel that fire scientists use for experimental burning in combustion chambers!

Frequent burning triggered pitch flows into the base of ponderosa pine trees, which in turn produced durable trunks. Thus, snags of old-growth ponderosa pines commonly remain standing for 50 to 150 years and provide excellent habitat for woodpeckers and a variety of cavity-nesting birds and small mammals. Conversely, large second-growth ponderosas have seldom experienced fires; thus they rot and fall within a few years of dying.

Black bears like large old ponderosas for

Opposite: Giant old ponderosa pine in a pasture near Arlee, north of Missoula, Montana, in 1933. (U.S. Forest Service, Region 1 photo)

glacier lilies with ponderosa pine needles

climbing "exercises," their claw tracks often extending a dozen feet or higher up the smooth, pillarlike trunk and numerous scratch marks etched into the tree's charred, hardened fire scar.

Human History

There are at least 200 published references to specific Native American uses of ponderosa pine (Moerman 1998). Native peoples used ponderosa stems and limbs as a building material and for firewood; they used the gum as a salve or ointment; needles were boiled to make a solution used for cough and fever; seeds were eaten; dried pitch was chewed as gum; needles and fine roots were employed in making baskets; trunks were fashioned into dugout canoes; pitch was used as a glue and a waterproofing agent; and twigs served as twirling sticks in making fire.

Direct evidence of one widespread use of ponderosa pine by aboriginal peoples can still be seen today: bark-peeling scars on old-growth trees. Women would harvest the tree's sugar-rich inner bark, or sap layer, in late spring by removing the outer bark with axes and sharpened poles. As a result, a large oval peeling scar extended several feet up one side of the trunk, from the starting point at 12 to 24 inches (30 to 60 cm) above the ground. The inner bark layer (appearing like wet felt) could be eaten directly or used to sweeten and help preserve foods being dried or cooked. Trees were not girdled or killed by bark-peeling, and the cameo-shaped scars—which are now smaller than their original size due to healing—can be seen at the Swan Valley Ecosystem Center at Condon and Indian Trees Campground at Sula in western Montana and along major tributaries of the Salmon River in Idaho. More than

JEFFREY PINE *(Pinus jeffreyi)*

Jeffrey pine is an intriguing cousin of ponderosa pine that mainly inhabits the mountains of California but also extends north throughout much of the Siskiyou Mountains in southwestern Oregon, where it is abundant along US 199 south from Cave Junction. In the northern part of its range—the Klamath and Siskiyou mountains—Jeffrey pine is largely confined to infertile soils derived from rock rich in heavy metals (serpentine, etc.) that impede the growth of most conifers. In most of its range in California, Jeffrey pine tends to grow at higher elevations or on frostier sites than ponderosa tolerates.

Jeffrey pine's appearance is very similar to ponderosa's. The cones provide one obvious distinction. Cones of Jeffrey pine are 5 to 10 inches (13 to 25 cm) long, which is larger than ponderosa cones, and are not prickly when handled since the prickles curve inward instead of pointing outward.

One subtle difference is that the bark of old Jeffrey pines tends to be reddish-brown, in contrast to the orange- or yellow-brown bark of ponderosas. Jeffrey pine bark often has a vanilla- or pineapplelike fragrance in warm weather. The two pine species can hybridize but normally do not, because Jeffrey pine releases pollen significantly later than does ponderosa.

Left: Jeffrey pine cone; right: ponderosa pine cone

100 individual bark-peeling scars examined on ponderosa pines in the Bob Marshall Wilderness, Montana, dated from 1665 to the early 1900s (Östlund and others 2005).

Northwestern ponderosa pines were the first forest trees encountered by pioneers on the Oregon Trail who had struggled for months to cross sagebrush deserts in what is now Wyoming and southern Idaho. When these beleaguered pilgrims finally reached eastern Oregon's Blue Mountains, their diaries chronicle the beauty and promise embodied in the first sentinels of western forest (Evans 1990). The big, tall, full-crowned ponderosas they beheld were associated with necessities that had been scarce or nonexistent during most of their journey: clear streams, green meadows for pasture, shade and shelter, firewood, and a source of lumber for building homesteads.

Throughout much of the inland West, old-growth ponderosa pine became the major source of lumber for building settlements and even for railroad ties in the nineteenth and early twentieth centuries, because of its widespread accessibility and good quality. By the mid-twentieth century, much of the historic old-growth ponderosa—termed "yellow pine" in the lumber trade—had been replaced by dense stands of young ponderosa and fir that had grown up in the absence of thinning fires. Paradoxically, the dark-barked young ponderosas, termed "bull pine," are of low value for lumber, because boards sawn from them readily warp and split.

Some foresters and landowners with ponderosa pine forests have become interested in mimicking historic conditions (Arno and Fiedler 2005). This involves thinning and using selective harvests to create open stands of vigorous trees of many ages, including large ponderosas. Where possible, prescribed fire is employed to reduce ingrowth of small trees (especially firs) and accumulations of fuel. Burning also recycles nutrients beneficial for biological diversity and wildlife forage. A modest but sustainable quantity of high-value yellow pine logs can be produced using this kind of "restoration forestry," which simulates the primeval ponderosa pine ecosystem.

KNOBCONE PINE

Pinus attenuata, Pine family—Pinaceae

A tree fancier who encounters knobcone pine in its natural habitat immediately recognizes it as an eccentric among the Northwestern conifers. In a region known for stately or at least straight and slender pines, knobcone, which grows at moderate elevations, is a curious exception. Under crowded conditions on rocky sites, knobcone pine develops a scrawny, misshapen form, while in open stands on gentle topography it becomes a bushy tree with long branches extending nearly to ground level. In appearance and considering its typical hot, dry habitat, knobcone pine is more comparable to the gray or foothills pine (*Pinus sabiniana*) and Coulter pine (*P. coulteri*) native to California than to other Northwestern trees.

Its large, odd-shaped cones are another peculiar feature. Clusters of cones hang on indefinitely, accumulating on the tree. While fire readily kills knobcone pines, it also releases seeds stored in the closed (serotinous) cones, thereby allowing this species to produce new seedlings and to repopulate the burned site.

Where It Grows

Knobcone pine inhabits hot, dry sites on rocky slopes and poor, coarse soils in southwestern Oregon, between 1000 and 2500 feet (300 and 750 m) elevation. It is also widely scattered through northern California, mostly in rugged terrain. In Oregon it extends northward in isolated patches to the foothills west and east of Cottage Grove. It is reportedly common in the North Umpqua drainage near Toketee Reservoir east of Roseburg, Oregon. Knobcone pine achieves perhaps its greatest abundance starting a few miles inland from the ocean in Curry County and extending into the western part of Josephine County, Oregon. Here, it is seen at several points along US

199 in the vicinity of Cave Junction and southward in the Smith River Canyon just across the border in California.

Appearance

Knobcone pine is a small tree, usually 30 to 60 feet (9 to 18 m) tall. In dense stands, it is easily distinguished by its spindly, ill-proportioned form. Under open conditions on less severe sites, it has a full canopy of whitish-green foliage and abundant, odd-looking cones clinging to its trunk and principal branches. The needles are in bundles of three and are mostly 3½ to 5 inches (9 to 13 cm) long. The bark is thin—smooth and gray on young stems and turning darker and scaly on older trunks.

The cones are 3½ to 6 inches (9 to 15 cm) long and almost conical but curved inward toward the stem to which they are attached. They encircle the main stem and principal branches in tightly clinging clusters, pointing toward the base of the stem. Cones are borne in abundance even on saplings only about 6 feet (2 m) high. Most cones remain closed for an indefinitely long period, but some cones have scales that flex open, giving a ragged appearance. The outer side of each closed cone is swollen and covered with the knoblike projections that give the tree its common name.

Ecological Role

Knobcone pine occupies sites that are too droughty, hot, or infertile for most other Northwestern trees. It is especially abundant on the iron- and magnesium-rich rocks (serpentine, etc.) of the Siskiyous, other volcanic rocks, and coarse, droughty soils derived from them. Knobcone pine is short-lived, commonly surviving only 100 years or so, and it appears to

be shade intolerant, intolerant of competition, in comparison to other trees.

However, it has historically avoided being replaced by more shade-tolerant species, such as Douglas-fir or tanoak, by adapting to exceptionally harsh sites and being able to regenerate rapidly after fire. The hot, dry sites it occupies are highly susceptible to fire. Fires merely scorch and fail to consume many of the tree's dense, closed cones, so the seeds inside survive. The fire's heat melts the resin that seals cones shut. Thus, soon after the fire, the scales flex open, allowing knobcone pine seeds to be among the first to fall into the nutrient-rich ash seedbed and to establish the first seedlings on the burned site.

Human History

Knobcone pine has been of little interest to humans, since its seeds are small and its trunk is of poor form and made up of weak, exceptionally knotty wood. In cultivation, knobcone pine can become a luxuriant, bushy tree that is well adapted to drought.

knobcone pine

LODGEPOLE PINE AND SHORE PINE

Pinus contorta, Pine family—Pinaceae

Lodgepole pine and shore pine are different subspecies within the same species, *Pinus contorta*, which is widespread and well known but much more diverse and complex than most people realize. In the Greater Northwest, we have an inland, mountain form called lodgepole pine (primarily *P. contorta* subspecies *latifolia*) and a coastal lowland form called shore pine (*P. contorta* ssp. *contorta*).

Lodgepole pine is best known as the small, straight, slender tree that dominates millions of acres among the inland mountain ranges, often growing in dog-hair stands—where the trees are crowded "as dense as the hair on a dog's back."

Lodgepole is generally short-lived and depends on occasional fires to regenerate and maintain its abundance. Without disturbances, other tree species that are longer-lived, larger, and more effective competitors (shade-tolerant) tend to take over.

Shore pine has a different specialty. It colonizes infertile sites near sea level along the Pacific coast where other trees grow poorly, if at all. Shore pine contrasts from its inland cousin by being heavily limbed and crooked—hence fitting the scientific name *contorta* that acknowledges explorer David Douglas's original description of this coastal tree. Although shore pine along the coast clearly contrasts with

Opposite: lodgepole pine; above: shore pine

inland lodgepole pine, from the Puget Sound area northward the two subspecies meet and intergrade confusingly along the western slope of the Cascades and British Columbia coastal ranges.

A third form of this species, Sierra lodgepole pine (*P. contorta* ssp. *murrayana*), occupies the high mountains of California and evidently intergrades northward with lodgepole pine (ssp. *latifolia*) in Oregon. Sierra lodgepole can maintain its diameter growth for hundreds of years, thus achieving impressive girth, and it is not necessarily dependent on fires for its perpetuation (U.S. Forest Service 1990).

Comparative Appearance

Lodgepole pine and shore pine are the only native Northwestern pines with short needles—about 2 inches (5 cm) long—in bundles of two. Vigorous seedlings and small saplings have needles 3 to 5 inches (8 to 13 cm) long. The two subspecies bear similar needles and cones, except that foliage tends to be yellow-green in lodgepole pine and dark green in shore pine.

Lodgepole and shore pines also have distinctive little cones 1½ to 2 inches (4 to 5 cm) long with a prickle on the back of each cone scale. Often, closed and open cones remain on the trees for many years. In trees whose canopies are high overhead, the cones stand out like little burrs, aiding identification. Both shore

shore pine cone

pine and lodgepole are precocious and prolific cone bearers, usually yielding some viable seeds by about ten years of age—perhaps an adaptation to frequent fire.

Mature lodgepole pines usually have thin, scaly, gray-brown bark, which is easily peeled off with a pocket knife. In contrast, mature shore pines have moderately thick, corky, dark brown bark divided by deep fissures in a checkered pattern. Interestingly, low-elevation lodgepole pines near Priest Lake in northern Idaho have the thick, dark bark and other features of shore pine (Johnson 1995).

LODGEPOLE PINE

Where It Grows

Lodgepole pine is abundant across a broad range of elevations in the inland mountains of the Greater Northwest, including the eastern slope of the Cascades. It is ubiquitous throughout interior British Columbia and the Rocky Mountains of Alberta, save for extremely dry sites and the highest alpine areas. It also extends northward to the Yukon Territory. South of the Greater Northwest, lodgepole is confined to increasingly high elevations, commonly reaching 11,000 feet (3350 m) in southern Colorado.

Appearance

Lodgepole pines in the Greater Northwest are usually small trees with a straight, slender trunk. On dry, rocky sites, mature trees may be only 8 inches (20 cm) in diameter and about 40

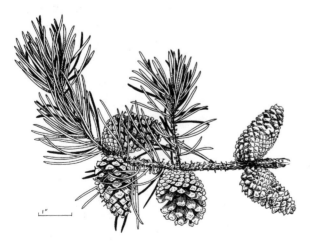

lodgepole pine

feet (12 m) tall, while on deep soils in sheltered valleys, they commonly surpass 16 inches (40 cm) in diameter and 90 feet (27 m) in height.

After fire or logging, lodgepole pine seedlings often become established more abundantly and grow more rapidly than other species; thus, lodgepole saplings on relatively open sites have narrow, pyramidal canopies. By the time young trees reach 15 feet (4.5 m) in height, their lower branches die. By about 70 years of age, lodgepole pines typically have a narrow, thin canopy that starts high above the ground, and their diameter and height growth has slowed dramatically. In stands more than 100 years old, lodgepole pines have usually been surpassed in height and diameter by associated western larch, Engelmann spruce, and Douglas-fir.

For other characteristics, see Comparative Appearance, above.

Ecological Role

Lodgepole pine can tolerate a very broad range of growing conditions, and it forms pure stands in habitats too adverse for other species, such as on the high-elevation volcanic substrates of central Oregon. At Crater Lake National Park, pure, even-aged stands of lodgepole pine grow on droughty pumice flats where ground-surface temperatures reach 140 degrees F (40 C) on sunny summer days but can plummet to freezing before dawn (U.S. Forest Service 1990).

On the eastern slope of the Cascades, lodgepole also occupies a thin layer of soil resting atop hardened clay. This band of soil is soggy for long periods because water cannot drain through the clay pan. Lodgepole develops a shallow rooting system and forms pure stands. Ponderosa pine occupies adjacent well-drained and thus droughty soils but gives way to lodgepole in low-lying frost-pocket sites. New lodgepole pine seedlings can withstand growing-season temperatures as low as 15 degrees F (−9 C) without injury (Cochran and Berntsen 1973).

Nevertheless, in most situations lodgepole pine must compete with other, more shade-tolerant trees. In these habitats, lodgepole depends upon fires to help it compete, and it can benefit from fires of contrasting intensities (Arno 2000). Historically, in some cold, dry mountain forests, creeping fires of low intensity killed lodgepole's principal competitor, the highly fire-sensitive subalpine fir. Lodgepole pine has a low level of fire resistance, vastly superior to that of the fir, and thus it often survived creeping fires.

Old lodgepole pines frequently bear scars from one or more historic fires. These appear as a narrow, upside-down V (or multiple, nested Vs) of bare, dead wood often extending several feet up from the ground. Fire scars are accompanied by charcoal on burned twigs, old bark, or other nearby wood, which helps differentiate them from the irregularly shaped scars caused by bark beetle attacks. Porcupines also leave telltale scars when they feed on the inner bark of lodgepole pines. In winter, these slow-moving creatures spend much of their time in tree canopies, chewing off bark in irregularly shaped patches scattered all along the tree trunk.

Often in the mountain forests, fires of variable intensities killed patches of trees, creating openings that allowed fast-developing lodgepole saplings to regain dominance despite an abundance of more competitive (shade-tolerant) trees. Lodgepole pine is commonly the most abundant seed source in a mixed forest because it produces and retains large numbers of both open and closed cones. The open cones rain thousands of small, winged seeds almost every year. The closed (serotinous) cones remain shut, storing and protecting viable seeds. Then, when a fire burns the trees, these cones open slowly in response to the heat, and seeds fall into the cooled, ashy seedbed.

On relatively productive sites, lodgepole pine tends to be short-lived and is largely replaced by other conifers within about 80 years. Cold, moist habitats such as high-elevation spruce-fir forests often have no lodgepole because these habitats burned so infrequently. In cold, dry habitats, such as the 7500-foot (2300-m) Yellowstone Park plateau of northwestern Wyoming, lodgepole persists far longer—some trees surviving more than 300 years. Thus, lodgepole might continue to dominate even where intervals between fires averaged three centuries.

In addition to coping with competing tree species and fires, lodgepole pine is subject to two major plagues: the parasitic plant dwarf mistletoe (*Arceuthobium*) and mountain pine beetles. Both these agents were historically kept in check when fires were relatively frequent. Dwarf mistletoe is comparable to the Christmas mistletoe except that it has tiny, scalelike leaves. After the sticky dwarf mistletoe seed lands on a branch, it germinates and sends a rootlike growth into the branch, removing nutrients and causing the branch to swell and often to produce the bushy growth called a "witch's broom." The small, yellow dwarf mistletoe plant can be seen growing out of the limbs, especially in summer when its fruiting bodies form. These are little capsules that explode at maturity, hurling the seed several feet and thus allowing the infection to spread slowly. The sticky seeds can attach themselves to a bird's foot and thereby occasionally get transported a long distance to another tree.

Mountain pine beetles kill trees by tunneling into the inner bark and then raising their brood (larvae) there. A vigorous lodgepole pine will "pitch out" attacking beetles, in effect drowning them in sticky pitch. However, beetles can gang up on a tree, using pheromones (chemical signals) to attract other beetles. Such attacks can overpower a tree's defenses when it is already weakened by drought or excessive competition. Beetles require larger trees— greater than 8 inches (20 cm) in diameter— for brood development and are particularly favored by extensive forests of old lodgepole pines where most trees have poor vigor. Thus,

periodic fires that recycle lodgepole pine forests tend to keep beetle epidemics in check. In contrast, prolonged periods without fire allow forests to become old and vulnerable to attack. Unusually cold weather in summer or winter can also help control beetle populations.

Human History

The straight, slender stems of lodgepole pines have traditionally been a favorite material for housing (Hart 1976). Lodgepole was the prime source of tepee poles used by Native Americans in the Rocky Mountains and nearby high plains. Native peoples often traveled long distances to get the slender, strong, lightweight stems of small lodgepole pine trees that, when covered with animal skins, served as their mobile lodges. Women cut and peeled twenty-five to thirty poles about 25 feet (8 m) long for each tepee, then dried them in the sun. As the poles were dragged for many miles from one camp area to another, they wore out and thus had to be replaced annually.

Native peoples used the thin inner bark of lodgepole pine as an emergency food for themselves and especially for horses. At a meadow near Lolo Pass on the Idaho-Montana divide, large quantities of lodgepole pines, now dead, have bark-peeling scars dating from the 1877 Nez Perce escape from U.S. Army subjugation. These trees are artifacts from when Chief Joseph led his people along with perhaps 3000 ponies on their unsuccessful march toward Canada and freedom (Beal 1963).

The first European-American settlers also preferred the smooth, straight, easy-to-peel trunks of lodgepole pine for their log cabins. Today, builders of expensive log homes pay dearly to acquire large dead lodgepole pines with uniformly round stems and minimal taper. Rural residents favor lodgepole for posts and rail fences. Lodgepole pine is also sawn into lumber and is popular for firewood.

Recently, lodgepole pine became the focus

of a forest management conundrum. Suppression of fires for more than seventy years has allowed lodgepole pine forests to age across large landscapes and become highly susceptible to mountain pine beetle epidemics. Beetles killed most lodgepole pines on about 15 million acres (6 million ha) in British Columbia alone during the first few years of the twenty-first century. This glut of dead timber contributes to the hazard of large, severe wildfires—which would presumably trigger development of young forests of lodgepole pine.

Canadians have stepped up the harvest of beetle-killed lodgepole pine. Also, starting in 1983, managers in Banff National Park, Alberta, and neighboring national parks began conducting stand-replacement burns in selected areas as a substitute for historical fires, to help re-create a landscape mosaic that includes young forests and thereby restores biodiversity and reduces hazard of beetle epidemics and gigantic wildfires (Arno and Fiedler 2005). Prescribed fires are conducted after the snow melts off in spring, at a time when wildfire hazard is relatively low and seasonal tourism is in a lull.

There is a precedent for using human-ignited fires in these national parks. At several locations in the lodgepole pine forest in and near Banff National Park, remains of earth-sheltered pit houses and other artifacts indicate that humans have been part of this ecosystem for a few thousand years. Anthropological evidence indicates that human-caused fires have been important for hundreds of years or longer in Alberta's mountain valleys, which are within traditional hunting grounds of the Blackfeet and other Native peoples (Kay and others 1999; Stewart 2002). This burning evidently attracted plains bison up into mountain valleys, where they could be hunted (White and others 2001). Also, on the west slope of the Rockies in the Kootenay River valley, explorer David Thompson noted that tribal people frequently set surface fires to clear brush and attract game to the subsequent new growth (Nisbet 1994).

In U.S. national forests, environmental concerns and litigation have largely prevented timber harvesting in aging or dead lodgepole pine. However, managers of wilderness areas and national parks in Idaho and Montana have allowed lightning-ignited fires that do not threaten developed areas to burn and restore historic natural patterns in lodgepole pine forests.

SHORE PINE
Where It Grows
Shore pine occupies sand dunes, swamp, muskeg, bedrock, and other extremely infertile sites in the coastal lowlands from northern California northward through the Alaska Panhandle. Shore pine also colonizes logged, burned, or otherwise disturbed habitats on poor-quality mineral soils, such as compacted glacial gravels or hardpan.

Appearance
In hostile substrates, shore pine grows stunted, contorted, and bushy but seldom has to compete with other trees. On less-severe sites, shore pines grow straight but are squatty and with relatively large limbs often extending nearly to the ground. For additional characteristics, see Comparative Appearance, above.

Ecological Role
In some places in the Puget Sound basin, fires were frequent enough in centuries past to perpetuate shore pine, Oregon white oak, and other shade-intolerant species that without disturbance are replaced by Douglas-fir or other more competitive trees.

Human History
Shore pine was historically sought out for pitch (as a fastener and sealant) and resinous gum (for chewing and medicinal use) by coastal tribes, evidently in much the same manner as was western white pine (Moerman 1998).

WESTERN LARCH

Larix occidentalis, Pine family—Pinaceae

People who see western larch for the first time are immediately impressed by its tall, ramrod-straight form and narrow, pyramidal crown made up of fine, bright-green needles that contrast with the somber dark green of most conifers. In autumn, larch foliage transforms to a stunning golden yellow that seems to light up whole mountainsides. Then a few weeks later the needles fall, making newcomers think these barren conifers are dead.

Western larch grows faster and larger than most of its associates, and it can survive many of the fires that kill other trees. Also, after fire or logging opens up a forest, the shade-intolerant (sun-loving) larch are among the first trees to seed in and regenerate. Larch needs these advantages because it faces stiff competition from a host of more shade-tolerant species.

On good sites, the imposing orange- or purplish-brown trunks of old western larch trees often attain 4 feet (120 cm) in diameter and 180 feet (55 m) in height, making them the largest of the world's eleven or so species of larch. Monarch western larch 500 to 1000 years old often have heart rot that allows woodpeckers to create cavities, which provide nesting sites for a variety of birds and small mammals.

"Is it larch or tamarack?" People familiar with forests of the northeastern United States and Canada often identify western larch at first sight as "tamarack," because of its obvious similarity to the tamarack or eastern larch (*Larix laricina*). Tamarack is a smaller tree that usually grows on boggy ground and can be found growing naturally in the boreal forest east of Jasper, Alberta, and in northern British Columbia. The name "tamarack" is often applied colloquially to any species of larch and in the Sierra Nevada to lodgepole pine.

Where It Grows

Western larch is essentially restricted to the Columbia River drainage east of the Cascade crest from about the latitude of Bend in central Oregon and Weiser in west-central Idaho (44 degrees N) northward to the vicinity of Kamloops in interior British Columbia (51 degrees N). Within its limited geographic distribution, western larch is locally abundant on moist mountain slopes at lower and middle elevations, up to about 6000 feet (1800 m) on average.

Larch is sparse in the Cascades, but it can be found here and there along the eastern slope from central Washington to northern Oregon. It becomes more abundant in the Blue Mountains and other ranges farther east. It is plentiful west of the Continental Divide in Montana and southeastern British Columbia, but only scattered individual trees are found in the drier climatic region immediately east of the divide.

Appearance

Western larch forms a slender sapling whose pointed crown projects above its competitors. It grows rapidly, developing a high, open canopy that filters but does not block sunlight. At maturity, it is usually the tallest tree in the forest. Finally, the oldest larches become grizzled patriarchs with a storm-battered top and a cinnamon-colored, pillarlike trunk incised by blackened fire scars.

Western larch needles are about 1½ inches (4 cm) long, bright yellow-green, and soft, unlike the hardened needles of firs and other evergreen conifers. Most of the larch foliage grows in tufts on the end of small, woody spur shoots. Tips of growing shoots bear needles singly from all around the twig, as with Douglas-fir. In winter, the leafless larch branches are readily

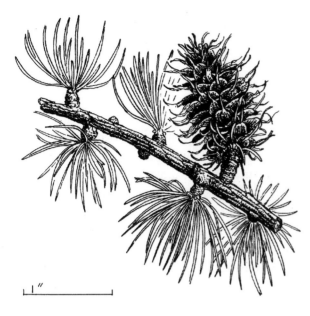

western larch

or perhaps just the green cones in some tree tops survive fires, and they can shower light-weight seeds onto the burned site.

Larch and lodgepole pine produce the fastest-growing saplings in much of the inland forest, which helps them get established ahead of more shade-tolerant competitors, including Douglas-fir and grand fir. While lodgepole pine matures and ceases height growth at an early age, western larch keeps growing much longer and may eventually become twice as tall. Larch can also persist several centuries between fires, while competition from shade-tolerant trees becomes increasingly intense.

The history and development of the exceptional "big larch forest" at Seeley Lake in western Montana illustrates how this species benefits from fire. The Lolo National Forest recreation

identified by their lumpy appearance. The cones are only 1 to 1½ inches (2.5 to 4 cm) long and have a long, pointed bract sticking out far beyond the end of each cone scale.

The bark becomes very thick and flaky on mature trees. It is deeply furrowed into large, orange-brown plates and often appears pinkish-purple when sliced. The base of a larch trunk appears fluted because at ground level the corky bark becomes astonishingly thick, often 6 inches (15 cm) on old trees.

Ecological Role

Western larch's closest associate in Northwestern forests is lodgepole pine. These two shade-intolerant species dominate postburn communities across a broad range of forest habitats. Lodgepole pine trees have low resistance to fire and rely on seeds stored in closed cones to regenerate after severe fires. In contrast, larch is highly fire-resistant because of its thick bark; high, open canopy of non-flammable foliage; and ability to resprout and form new branches to replace those that are badly scorched. At least a few tall larch trees

A natural forest in western Montana in 1899 shows large western larch that survived a circa 1880s fire, as well as saplings of lodgepole pine (dark) and larch (light) that regenerated afterward. (U.S. Geological Survey photo)

areas bordering Seeley Lake retain many of the original, ancient larch trees, including the largest-known larch, which is more than 7 feet (2 m) in diameter, 162 feet (50 m) tall, and about 1000 years old (Van Pelt 2001). A study that dated tree ages and fire scars found that the big larch forest was maintained in open conditions for hundreds of years by low-intensity surface fires occurring at average intervals of about 25 years (Arno and others 1997). Archaeological and other evidence suggests that Native peoples camped here seasonally for at least 3500 years and set many of the fires. This unusually frequent burning for a moist, productive site allowed larch to predominate over competing and less fire-resistant Douglas-fir, subalpine fir, and Engelmann spruce. Many age classes of larch are present, dating from shortly after historic fires, but the most recent fire and the youngest larch date from the late 1800s.

Human History

The Salish and Kutenai peoples in western Montana prized the sweet syrup that they harvested from larch trees (Hart 1976). When the sap was flowing, they hollowed out a cavity, creating a basin in the trunk, and allowed perhaps a gallon of the sap to accumulate. After a while, evaporation concentrated the syrup. Certain trees produced a sweeter sap than others.

Several tribes made medicinal uses of larch. The gum was chewed for sore throat and applied on cuts and bruises, and a tea made of larch bark or foliage was drunk for relief from various diseases. In modern times, larch extracts are marketed as health-enhancing supplements. Larch contains a special water-soluble gum (arabinogalactan), about the consistency of honey, which is used in commercial printing, food, pharmaceuticals, paint, ink, and other industrial uses.

Larch wood—dense, strong, and durable—is used extensively for structural lumber. Tall, straight larch trees are processed into large utility poles. Larch wood also has many other commercial uses, and because of its density and ease of splitting, it has long been the premier firewood in the inland Northwest.

Considering the great size and fine form of the original larch trees on favorable sites, it may seem surprising that many of the largest trees were spared from logging. Early lumbermen recognized that the oldest larch trees often have extensive bole rot. The quinine conk (*Fomitopsis officinalis*), a cream-colored fungal growth or bracket fungus, is often seen high up on an old larch trunk, and it indicates the tree is so rotten that it is worthless for timber. That larch trees can survive at least a couple centuries despite a rotten bole makes them of great value for cavity-nesters including woodpeckers, owls, various songbirds, and flying squirrels.

Even trees without rot often have ring shake—complete separation of the wood along individual growth rings—which renders the base of the tree useless for lumber. This defect in old trees is thought to result from continual bending in strong winds that eventually breaks the bond between growth rings. To avoid some of the basal rot and ring shake, early-day loggers would cut larch trees high above ground, leaving 10-foot-tall (3-m-tall) stumps. These century-old arboreal relics still have the notches that held the springboards that fallers stood on while wielding the ax or pulling the two-man crosscut saw known as a misery whip. Another technique for discarding the base of big trees was to cut off or "long butt" a section, about 6 feet (2 m) long, from the base of the fallen tree.

While western white pine was historically the prime timber tree in humid northern Idaho, a combination of old-growth western larch and ponderosa pine filled that role in the drier climate of western Montana. The larch, most abundant in cooler, moist habitats, and "yellow pine" on adjacent drier sites codominated much of the landscape as a result of their ability to prosper under the influence of frequent fires. When growing in mixed stands, the cinnamon-colored boles of old larch and ponderosa look so similar that it is often necessary to look up into the canopy to distinguish them.

The Big Blackfoot River drainage northeast of Missoula, which includes the Seeley Lake country, produced vast quantities of larch and ponderosa pine. From 1885 until the 1920s, huge accumulations of logs were floated down the Blackfoot canyon to the sprawling sawmill at the river's mouth. (Later, logs were transported through the canyon by train and truck.) This was about when the young Norman Maclean was first introduced to the Blackfoot's exceptional fishery that he recounted in *A River Runs Through It*. Tree buffs beware: Maclean's story (University of Chicago Press, 1976) and Robert Redford's 1992 movie version of it omit the omnipresent lumber industry centered on the Blackfoot River in those days. Worse yet, the movie was filmed on the distant Gallatin River, which has none of the Blackfoot's beautiful larch or ponderosa pine.

By the 1980s, larch forests at Seeley Lake had been engulfed in ladder fuels—a dense understory of Douglas-fir, grand fir, and other conifers that promotes crown fire. The 1988 Red Bench fire torched a similar forest in Glacier National Park, Montana, killing most of the trees, including old larch, on 26,000 acres (10,500 ha). In previous centuries, the area had

Log drive on Big Blackfoot River in 1910. (Archives & Special Collections, University of Montana, Missoula)

experienced less-intense fires that larch survived (Barrett and others 1991). Land managers came to recognize that nearly a century of suppressing fires had created an unprecedented threat of crown fires. Also, many old larch trees were dying as a result of excessive competition from shade-tolerant trees.

During the 1990s, the Seeley Lake Ranger District initiated restoration projects that by 2005 had expanded to cover a few thousand acres of the historic big larch forest surrounding the Seeley Lake community (Arno and Fiedler 2005). Most understory trees and many midsized firs were removed carefully on snow-covered ground so as to prevent damage to the larch trees. Much of the treated forest was then "underburned" using low-intensity prescribed fire. In the thinned and burned areas, a new age-class of larch seedlings became established for the first time in a century.

In the old larch forests of Montana's Glacier National Park and the Bob Marshall Wilderness, managers have allowed many lightning fires to burn under surveillance since 1994. These fires have already begun to restore a pattern of variable-intensity burns on the landscape that promote regeneration and survival of western larch, a unique and venerable treasure of the inland Northwest.

ALPINE LARCH

Larix lyallii, Pine family—Pinaceae

In the 1890s, while surveying newly established federal forest reserves in the mountains of Idaho and Montana, U.S. Geological Survey employee John Leiberg described (1900) a remarkable tree he found dwelling among the highest peaks: "With a light and graceful foliage, offering slight resistance to the winter's blasts, a compact, strong trunk and a root system firmly anchored in the crevices of underlying rocks, it can bid defiance to winds of any violence . . ." This tree, alpine larch (also called subalpine larch), is a deciduous conifer that occupies some of the coldest and rockiest sites in high mountains of the inland Northwest. Many tree fanciers who have never seen alpine larch up close have viewed it from valleys below in autumn when it shimmers golden-yellow among the lofty crags.

Compared with its subalpine associates—subalpine fir, Engelmann spruce, and even whitebark pine—alpine larch has a very restricted geographic and elevational distribution. Within its limited range, however, this tree often ascends higher on the mountains than the evergreen conifers, forming pure stands on sites that would otherwise become alpine tundra. It also colonizes slopes deeply covered with coarse talus (boulders) and devoid of soil. On wind-sheltered sites in the timberline zone, venerable alpine larch often form the largest trees, with long, spreading branches that subalpine firs grow up through as if ascending a trellis.

Although alpine larch is well adapted to the harshest sites, it grows too slowly to compete for growing space in the dense subalpine forest, so it descends into that zone only on rock piles or in snow-avalanche chutes. Alpine larch shares a heritage of extreme cold-hardiness with Eurasian larch species, which form the highest tree lines in the European Alps and the towering Himalayas and grow northward in Siberia hundreds of miles beyond evergreen conifers.

Where It Grows

Like its close evolutionary relative, western larch, alpine larch is confined to the inland mountains of the Greater Northwest; however, unlike its lower-elevation cousin, alpine larch spreads east of the Continental Divide into the austere, desiccating climate of the Rocky Mountain Front Ranges in Montana and Alberta. In the Rockies, alpine larch's distribution extends in a patchy pattern from high peaks north of the Salmon River canyon (about 45½ degrees N latitude) in Idaho and western Montana to just beyond Lake Louise, Alberta (about 51½ degrees N latitude)—a distance of about 420 miles (675 km).

Within this distribution, alpine larch is notably abundant in Montana's Anaconda-Pintler and Bitterroot ranges—mostly between elevations of 7500 and 9500 feet (2300 and 2900 m), British Columbia's southern Purcell Range, and the crest of the Rockies in Banff National Park, Alberta—generally above 6500 feet (2000 m). It is reached by popular hiking trails and can be viewed from valleys below when it turns bright golden yellow in late September.

The Rocky Mountain and Cascades' distributions of alpine larch are separated by about 125 miles (200 km), across southern British Columbia, probably due to a scarcity of high-elevation habitat. In the Cascades, alpine larch can be found from central Washington's Wenatchee Mountains northward about 120 miles (190 km) just into the southern edge of

alpine larch and a subalpine fir

British Columbia. It is found mainly above 6000 feet (1800 m) and is notably accessible via hiking routes into Washington's Alpine Lakes Wilderness near Mount Stuart and by road at Harts Pass near the Pasayten Wilderness, as well as on the trail up Mount Frosty in Manning Provincial Park, British Columbia.

Appearance

Alpine larch trees are small compared to many trees of lower elevations, but they are often among the largest trees at timberline. They have open crowns covered with soft, light bluish-green needles, as opposed to the shiny yellow-green foliage of western larch; however, these color differences are subtle. Cones of alpine larch are slightly longer, 1½ to 2 inches (4 to 5 cm), than those of western larch, but the best distinguishing characteristic is fine, white, woolly hairs covering new twigs (only the most-recent year's growth) of alpine larch in contrast to western larch's virtually hairless new shoots. Trees 10 inches (25 cm) or more in diameter can be distinguished by bark near the ground, which is only about 1 inch thick

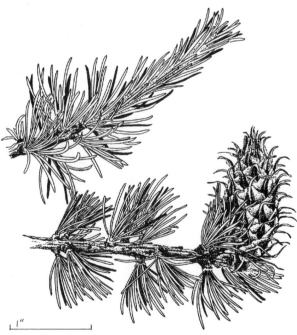

1″

alpine larch

(2.5 cm) in alpine larch and 2 to several inches (5 or more cm), as evidenced by deep bark ridges, in the fire-resistant western larch.

Alpine larch saplings have irregular-shaped canopies, a tendency that increases as the tree continues to grow under a hostile climate. Trees 150 to 300 years old tend to have a slender, straight trunk, supporting a spreading crown. Trees more than 500 years old, which are found in many stands, often have a stout trunk supporting a markedly irregular crown with large, spreading limbs and a storm-battered top. Eventually, the crown may be snapped off by violent winds, leaving the gnarled trunk supporting only a handful of lower branches. Such a living snag can survive for a century or longer.

Ecological Role

Alpine larch is a self-perpetuating, or climax, species in sites where competing evergreen conifers are scarce, stunted, or absent (Arno and Habeck 1972). Alpine larch can eke out an existence in places that are too cold, too snowbound, too avalanche prone, too rocky, and too boggy for other trees. It can colonize sites that have not been occupied by vegetation, such as fresh moraines at the foot of alpine glaciers. However, alpine larch is very intolerant of competition from evergreen conifers and also requires a continuous supply of soil moisture through the summer.

In their first twenty-five years, alpine larch saplings reach only about 12 inches (30 cm) in height but produce extensive root systems, apparently to access sufficient soil moisture before they begin to develop much canopy foliage (Richards 1981). Seedlings are difficult to cultivate under the warm conditions at lower elevations. Under natural conditions, seedlings and ground-hugging branches of small saplings have specialized leaves—"wintergreen" foliage—that survive through one winter and a second summer rather than being deciduous (Richards 1981). This wintergreen foliage makes up about one-fourth of the leaves on a small sapling. Physiological studies suggest that wintergreen foliage aids tree establishment because it is less susceptible to drought stress than fully deciduous leaves.

Even where open rock piles and avalanche chutes extend down north-facing slopes, alpine larch do not inhabit them very far down into the middle elevations—for instance, it remains above 5000 or 5500 feet (1500 to 1700 m) in such open habitats in the Cascades and Canadian Rockies and above 7500 feet (2300 m) at the tree's southern range limits in lofty cirque basins north of the hot, dry Salmon River canyon in central Idaho. At higher elevations—8500 to 9500 feet (2600 to 2900 m) in the nearby southern Bitterroot Range—squatty old alpine larch reminiscent of ancient bristlecone pines occupy some boulder-clad south-facing slopes; but in summer, water can be heard trickling beneath the big rocks.

Even-aged patches of alpine larch saplings or larger juvenile trees fill former snow-drift openings near timberline, probably as a result of warmer conditions since the late 1800s, as demonstrated by retreating glaciers (Arno and Habeck 1972). Groves of small, pole-sized alpine larch often develop on steep, snowy sites and in avalanche chutes. The strong, flexible larch trunks can survive flattening by snow slides and yet spring upright again undamaged when the snow melts in July. As the larch trees get too large to survive this flattening—about 5 inches (13 cm) in diameter—some of them snap off. Others are strong enough to survive and may eventually become stout trees that can withstand even a larger avalanche.

Alpine larch has a physiological advantage over its evergreen competitors in not having its fine, needlelike leaves exposed to ice-blasting winter storms nor to solar heating in late spring that dries out foliage while roots still encased in frigid soil cannot resupply lost moisture. Also unlike evergreens, buds on larch

trees are protected in woody spur shoots and tough, flexible branches are less vulnerable to snow damage. On the other hand, evergreens keep their foliage and so are ready to grow as soon as summer comes, while deciduous trees have to produce their frost-sensitive foliage in a hurry. The deciduous alpine larch, to take advantage of the short, cool growing season, produces its needles quickly by beginning to leaf out and initiate its pollen and seed cones in early June, despite several feet of remaining snowpack. By late June, hikers commonly encounter alpine larch with bright green new foliage standing in last winter's snow. Protected by the snowpack, the soil is probably not quite frozen in the rooting zone. Evergreen conifers, on the other hand, are unable to begin foliar development until the snowpack is gone and the soil begins to warm up.

Where soil and climatic conditions are less severe, subalpine fir, Engelmann spruce, or mountain hemlock form a closed subalpine forest, and alpine larch cannot compete, except that sometimes it regenerates on burned sites. Upslope in the timberline zone, where the forest becomes patchy with numerous openings, alpine larch trees of various sizes and ages form mixed, open stands with clusters of mostly stunted subalpine fir and scattered spruce and whitebark pine trees.

Alpine larch seems to have a more complementary than competitive relationship with whitebark pine, which is also shade-intolerant but is adapted to dry, sunny sites and exposed ridge tops. Moist timberline sites in cirque basins support an occasional "patriarch" alpine larch up to 1000 years old (and perhaps older yet) with a branch-free lower trunk 3 to 5 feet (90 to 150 cm) thick that supports a spreading but storm-battered crown. Ancient larch trees usually have a hollow trunk, and this often serves as habitat for cavity-nesting birds or mammals.

Larch hybrids. On mountain ranges where both larch species grow, alpine larch usually reaches its lower elevational limits 500 to 1000 feet (150 to 300 m) from the uppermost western larch. Occasionally, however, the two species overlap where alpine larch extends unusually far down in avalanche chutes and talus. Several of these overlaps occur along the east slope of the Bitterroot Range between Lolo and Stevensville, Montana. These sites are populated by an assortment of alpine larch, western larch, and a range of intermediate forms that represent hybrids and hybrids backcrossed to one or the other species (Carlson and others 1990). On a rocky outcrop in Carlton Ridge Research Natural Area, an observer in late September can see golden-yellow larch trees of short, spreading growth-form (alpine larch) adjacent to tall, pyramidal larch trees with green foliage (western larch) and all manner of intermediates in form and coloration.

Human History

Native Americans evidently made little use of this species. Alpine larch became known to science when Scottish naturalist Dr. David Lyall found it growing along the international boundary in the Cascades and the Rockies during his surveys (1858–61) with the North American Boundary Commission.

Modern societies have had little effect on it, in part because the tree has no commercial value. A few ski resorts have impacted alpine larch communities by cutting swaths of trees and damaging the fragile undergrowth and soil with equipment. A large ski area is proposed in the alpine larch stands on Carlton Ridge and Lolo Peak in western Montana. Accelerated global warming certainly could stress this high mountain tree.

This remarkable tree has inspired mountain travelers at least from the time of forest inspector Leiberg around 1900. Those who encounter it on a backcountry hike will take special notice and, when it is clothed in fall color, a lot of prized photographs. Camping under alpine larch is a special experience as a breeze stirs the wispy boughs overhead, setting them in eerie motion across a background of moon- or starlight.

SITKA SPRUCE

Picea sitchensis, Pine family—Pinaceae

During their encampment at the mouth of the Columbia River in 1805–06, explorers Lewis and Clark suffered through the dreary, wet, cold, and stormy winter characteristic of a Sitka spruce habitat. Even in midsummer, Sitka spruce seldom has to cope with significant drought.

The robust Sitka spruce is an icon of the rain-lashed North Pacific coast, where it provides a perch for bald eagles as they scan the beach and surf. Much as the giant redwood epitomizes California's coastal fog belt, Sitka spruce dominates the broader and colder wet belt that envelopes the coast from Oregon to Alaska. Another common name, "tideland spruce," denotes how this tree lines the shores and inlets. On storm-battered headlands and rock islands known as sea stacks, this irrepressible denizen of the salt air forms wind-sheared, stunted trees reminiscent of alpine timberlines. Along much of the ocean-side strip, Sitka spruce produces a dense forest of squat, limby trees. Farther back from the sea-wind onslaught, this tree attains gigantic proportions, equaling the largest coastal Douglas-fir. When not crowded, big spruce trees develop a thick canopy of long limbs extending nearly to the ground, the lower branches draped with hanging mosses.

Where It Grows

Sitka spruce lines 2000 miles (3200 km) of the North Pacific shore, but it seldom occurs more than a few dozen miles inland. Unlike several other coastal conifers, it does not spread east across the British Columbia Coast Range or the Cascades. Although small populations inhabit the northern coast of California, Sitka spruce gradually becomes much more abundant northward through Oregon, Washington, British Columbia, and Alaska. It reaches Kodiak Island, farther north and west along the coast into the maritime tundra than any other conifer. It dominates Alaska's coastal forest from sea level to timberline, which averages about 2500 feet (750 m) in elevation. In contrast to most conifers, which grow at progressively higher elevations to the south, Sitka spruce becomes restricted to a narrower band along the coastal lowlands southward from Alaska.

shoreline form of Sitka spruce

Sitka spruce on seastacks

From southwestern British Columbia to Oregon, this species seldom ascends above 1500 feet (450 m) in elevation, and it is abundant only in the oceanic environment along the western side of Vancouver Island and the western slope of the Olympics and other coastal mountains of Washington and Oregon. Sitka spruce forests are deluged with rain—averaging between 80 and 200 inches (2000 to 5000 mm) annually in different locations. The ocean's influence keeps the climate humid and cool year-round, with summer temperatures markedly colder and relative humidity higher than those in Vancouver, British Columbia; Seattle, Washington; or Portland, Oregon.

In the drier coastal region inland from the ocean, including the Strait of Georgia, Puget Sound, and the Willamette Valley, Sitka spruce is restricted to special, moist habitats. Stringers of spruce reach dozens of miles eastward along major rivers, including the Fraser and the Columbia, mostly in floodplains. They extend up the Snoqualmie River valley, along the route of Interstate 90, to within 5 miles (8 km) of the Cascade crest. Large second-growth Sitka spruce are seen where the highway crosses the Snoqualmie River at North Bend.

Appearance

Sitka spruce needles are stiff and prickly to the touch and about 1 inch (2.5 cm) long. They differ from needles of other Northwest spruces in being flattened so they do not readily roll between one's fingers. The tan-colored cones are 2½ to 4 inches (6 to 10 cm) long and are composed of thin, papery scales with jagged edges. The seeds are tiny—averaging 210,000 per pound (460,000 per kg) and can be carried long distances in the wind. Sitka spruce bark is thin and distinct from other coastal trees in that its surface consists of large, loose scales, which are easily pulled off to reveal the purplish or reddish brown inner bark.

Abundant moisture allows Sitka spruce to grow prodigiously. On favorable sites, it can produce a trunk 4 feet (1.2 m) thick and 170 feet (52 m) tall in 100 years. Under moderately open conditions, young trees support a thick canopy of long, spreading limbs. Big, open-growing spruce with huge, limby canopies, called "wolf trees," make good shelter from the rain, although it might be futile to wait out the rain in winter. The great, outreaching branches often have secondary branchlets hanging down in a weeping appearance. As trees in dense stands grow tall, lower limbs die out, eventually baring the smooth, round trunk.

Old Sitka spruce trees often have immense root buttresses and a swollen base extending up several feet above the ground. Even above butt swell, however, old-growth spruce in valley sites are commonly more than 7 feet (2 m) thick, and several record-sized trees 12 to 17 feet (3.7 to 5.2 m) in diameter inhabit coastal areas from the Queen Charlotte Islands to northern Oregon (Van Pelt 2001). Each of these behemoths contains between 9000 and 12,000 cubic feet (250 to 340 cubic meters) of wood—enough to build three or four average houses. The most accessible record-sized spruce are the Klootchy Creek Giant in a wayside park on US 26 a few miles west of Seaside, Oregon, and the "Big Tree" along the drive to the Hoh Rain Forest Visitor Center in Washington's Olympic National Park. On Vancouver Island, the giant San Juan spruce can be reached by road and is visible immediately upstream from the San Juan River bridge 12 miles (19 km) east of Port Renfrew (Stoltmann 1987).

The original tops of most record-sized Sitka spruce have been broken by winter storms, but in some wind-sheltered valleys the tallest spruces stretch 300 feet (90 m) into the humid air. Such a feat is achieved by only four other tree species in the world: coastal Douglas-fir, redwood, giant sequoia, and a species of Australian eucalyptus. The ability of some trees to pull water and nutrients up through microscopically thin capillary tubes to such heights has amazed physicists.

Along the exposed oceanfront, Sitka spruce's resilience and vitality are pitted against recurrent gale- and hurricane-force winds. Stout, gnarled, limby trees result. The most extreme of these is the Octopus Tree at Cape Meares State Park near Tillamook, Oregon—a single spruce with many great trunks that sprawl across the top of an oceanside bluff. Trunks of oceanfront Sitka spruce sometimes support huge bulbous burls, the cause of which remains unknown. One spruce on the Olympic Peninsula is 36 inches (90 cm) in diameter but has a burl 84 inches (213 cm) across.

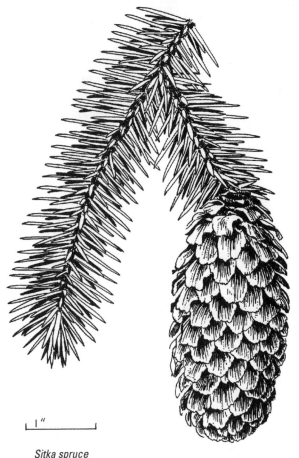

1"

Sitka spruce

Sitka spruce on coastal headland

Sitka spruce burls

Ecological Role

Much of Sitka spruce's range near the ocean supports thick stands of young conifers that have arisen after logging. Conversely, numerous parks and other preserves contain old forests. Sitka spruce is considered shade tolerant and would thus be an able competitor for growing space except that its principal associates—western hemlock and western redcedar—are very shade tolerant. Hemlock regenerates abundantly in shady places and gradually replaces Sitka spruce—except when a major disturbance intervenes.

Logging that bares sizable areas of ground, forest fires, and extensive windthrow provide spruce seedlings an opportunity to get established. Sitka spruce bark is thin and pro-vides little protection against forest fires that develop on the rare occasions when the luxuriant vegetation dries out and a fire is ignited. Dry lightning storms are unusual in Sitka spruce forests, but wildfires started by humans are more common. Sitka spruce has a shallow root system, and raging storms often wrench giant trees out of the ground or shatter their trunks. Even in areas that haven't experienced these disturbances in two centuries or longer, Sitka spruce has one advantage over hemlock: It grows larger and lives longer, and this allows spruce to persist in small numbers for prolonged periods.

An exceptional kind of old-growth spruce-hemlock forest graces broad valleys on the prodigiously rainy western slopes of Vancouver Island and the Olympic Peninsula. Although some vegetation scientists argue that true rain forests develop only in the tropics, these distinctive spruce-hemlock forests are commonly known as temperate rain forests (Franklin and Dyrness 1973; Kirk 1966). In Olympic National Park, they occupy river terraces and consist of massive Sitka spruce, western redcedar, and more numerous western hemlock growing in relatively open stands along with broad-crowned bigleaf maples half as tall and sprawling vine maples. Moss hangs from the maples and a thick carpet of moss and herbs blankets the forest floor. Foraging by herds of Roosevelt elk apparently prevents development of a dense shrub and hemlock understory. The rain forests are easily accessed by roads up the Hoh, Queets, and Quinault rivers. Recently, biologists have raised an intriguing question: Do the tons of spawning salmon that die along streams each year have a fertilizing effect in these riverside forests (Gende and others 2002)?

Most conifers cannot regenerate in moss-covered ground, but they can get established on rotting logs and stumps and even in the clods of soil clinging to roots of overthrown trees. Succulent new shoots on Sitka spruce saplings are a favorite food of elk and Columbian black-tailed deer, thus growing high atop a rotten log or stump affords saplings protection. Only in such an ultrahumid environment is it possible or necessary for conifer seedlings to grow on these elevated microsites, but many of the big spruce trees in the rain forest stand off the ground on stilted root systems that centuries ago spanned a log or stump. Often, large trees are lined up in a row or colonnade revealing their origin as seedlings on the same rotten log.

Human History

Native peoples of the North Pacific coast made many uses of Sitka spruce (Moerman 1998). Its fine, pliable roots were woven into baskets and rain hats. The roots were also heated, softened, and pounded to make cord. Spruce gum was chewed for pleasure and used medicinally for sore throat and cough. Spruce resin served as glue, sealer, and waterproofing agent. Natives and pioneer settlers split shakes from spruce for siding and roofs.

The wood of this species is light, stiff, soft, and easily worked and painted, but it is also exceptionally strong and resilient for its weight. Thus it is well suited for a myriad of purposes ranging from ladders to racing shells. Its most storied use came during World Wars I and II when it supplied much of the wood used in American and British air forces. Sitka spruce forests were heavily logged during the war years to obtain the very small percentage of flawless wood that could qualify for airplane frames and propellers. In those days, wooden aircraft could be produced in less time than was needed for fabricating, riveting, and welding metal planes, and spruce wood was generally less vulnerable to shock and serious damage in combat. (Howard Hughes' famous postwar *Spruce Goose* airplane was, however, framed in birch.)

Sitka spruce is highly resonant, and select-grade logs are of great value for musical instruments. Appropriately, Sitka spruce wood is used for the sounding boards that are mounted like billboards at strategic points along narrow navigation channels, which are themselves often lined with spruce trees. Boat captains determine their location in fog or darkness in hazard-strewn passages by the spruce sounding board's echo in response to blasts from the vessel's horn.

ENGELMANN SPRUCE

Picea engelmannii, Pine family—Pinaceae

Engelmann spruce is a lofty, impressive tree of moist habitats, like Sitka spruce. However, unlike its coastal relative, it inhabits high inland mountains subject to frigid winters. This spruce commonly forms the largest trees growing in the high country, where its luxuriant, pyramidal crowns commonly border lakes and streams.

Engelmann spruce occupies virtually all moist and cool forest habitats in the inland mountains. It also grows at the edge of the alpine tundra, often as wind-sheared *krummholz*. It becomes a towering tree in wet, subalpine basins and along streams in deep canyons that are conduits for cold air. Its adaptability is enhanced by extensive hybridization and back-crossing that mix its traits with those of white spruce (*Picea glauca*), whose genetically pure form inhabits northern and eastern Canada and Alaska (see the next chapter).

Where It Grows

Engelmann spruce is found from the headwaters of the Fraser River in central British Columbia south through the Rockies and isolated high mountains of the eastern Great Basin, Arizona, and New Mexico. In the Cascades, it extends south to southern Oregon. A few widely scattered groves occupy the northeastern Olympic Mountains and northern California's Klamath Mountains.

Engelmann spruce is abundant in the Rocky Mountains. Spruce bottoms extend along mountain streams, and this species also dominates moist, north-facing slopes at higher elevations, often accompanied by a virtually impenetrable undergrowth of tall shrubs. It is the principal tree at high altitudes in southern Colorado, where its upper limits reach 12,000 feet (3650 m), and it descends as low as 1700

wind-shaped Engelmann spruce at timberline

feet (520 m) in cool canyons of northern Idaho. Northward from northwestern Montana into British Columbia and Alberta, Engelmann spruce is replaced at lower elevations by hybrids and intermediate forms that increasingly resemble white spruce (see the next chapter).

In the Cascades, Engelmann spruce is found mostly between about 3000 and 6000 feet (900 to 1800 m). It can be seen along many high-elevation roads and trails east of the Cascade crest. It seems to be intolerant of the oceanic climate and seldom grows on the western slopes

of the Cascades or the British Columbia Coast Range. However, in the 1960s a few Engelmann spruce groves were discovered in canyons of the northeastern Olympic Mountains, in the relatively dry rain-shadow zone. Surprisingly, these small groves harbor record-sized trees, including one that is 7 feet (2.1 m) thick and 179 feet (55 m) tall (Van Pelt 2001).

Appearance

Engelmann spruce is distinguished by its tall, narrow, conical crown made fuller by thousands of tassel-like branchlets hanging down from the main limbs. Its canopy is broader than the narrow spires of accompanying subalpine fir. Open-grown spruce are heavily limbed down to the ground. The distinctive bark is very thin, with a dark purplish or reddish tinge and loose scales that flake off readily, a trait evident even on trees only a few inches in diameter.

Like most other North American spruces, Engelmann spruce has sharp-pointed, prickly needles. Horticulturists can choose spruce if they want to create a robust, impenetrable hedge. Engelmann spruce needles are flexible and not as stout and rigid as those of the commonly planted Colorado blue spruce (*Picea pungens*). The needles are about 1 inch (2.5 cm) long and vary in color from a dull gray-green on lower branches of trees in a thick forest to decidedly bluish on vigorous young trees growing in openings. Needles are four-sided and can be rolled between one's fingers. Like those of other spruces, the needles are attached to the twigs by small wooden pegs that remain after the oldest needles fall. Thus, old twigs appear as if they were densely covered with tiny warts. When crushed, the needles emit a strong, pungent odor.

Engelmann spruce often has two different kinds of conelike structures hanging from its boughs, but one of these is really an aphid gall. What appear at first to be pointed scales are dried-up needles protruding from the multichambered house of the Cooley gall aphid. While the galls

are still soft, several tiny white aphids live in each chamber. After the insects depart, the galls dry out, harden, and turn brown. Then they remain on the branches for several years.

Heavy crops of tan-colored seed cones are often seen in the upper crown. They are bright red when very small in spring and then turn purple in summer before maturing and drying out. Mature cones range from 1 to 2½ inches (2.5 to 6 cm) long and have wrinkled papery scales that narrow distinctly toward the ragged-edged scale tip. In late spring, plump purple pollen cones about ½ inch (1 cm) long appear on the branch tips. Watch an open-growing spruce in a spring breeze, and you may see a yellow cloud of pollen burst into the air with every gust of wind.

Ecological Role

One remarkable feature of Engelmann spruce is its propensity to grow taller than other high-mountain trees. Near timberline, scattered individual spruce crowns often rise up higher than all other species. Engelmann spruce stem wood is not as strong as that of associated whitebark pine or alpine larch, and its canopy seems more vulnerable to wind damage than that of the flexible whitebark pine, deciduous larch, or spire-shaped subalpine fir. Also, Engelmann spruce's shallow roots expose it to windthrow. While other species adapt to harsh conditions at high elevations by taking on a compact growth form, Engelmann spruce seems programmed to grow tall regardless of consequences—a battered or broken top or uprooted stem—but sometimes it succeeds.

Engelmann spruce is considered to be shade tolerant and thus, barring disturbance, able to eventually outcompete more shade-intolerant associates such as lodgepole, western white, and whitebark pines; western and alpine larches; and inland Douglas-fir. However, it is less shade tolerant than its principal competitor, subalpine fir. When a forest does not experience fire, blowdown, logging, or other

Engelmann spruce in a mountain landscape

major disturbance for a few centuries, subalpine fir tends to regenerate beneath mature Engelmann spruce trees and gradually replace them. Disturbances allow spruce saplings to get established and often outgrow (and outlive) the first generation of competing subalpine fir.

Despite their great age and magnificence, individual trees as well as stands of old-growth Engelmann spruce are not permanent features of the forest. Three record-size Engelmann spruce in different areas have died since the 1970s (Van Pelt 2001). Mature spruce, with their massive canopies, shallow roots, and moderately weak stem wood, are vulnerable to violent windstorms. Their thin bark and shal-

low roots also leave them highly susceptible to fire. Stands that survive 300 years or so become prime targets for a buildup of spruce bark beetles, which can kill mature trees over vast areas, especially in conjunction with a period of drought or other climatic stress. In high-mountain canyons, snow avalanches sometimes explode outside the usual tracks and mow down large swaths of spruce forest, leaving an awesome jumble of smashed trunks and limbs.

Fire-killed spruce forests, composed of standing and fallen snags with rich herb, shrub, and sapling communities, become highly productive habitats for wildlife. Like avalanche chutes, these disturbance-created communities provide an abundance of shrubs laden with berries and succulent shoots (browse) as well as grasses and broad-leaved herbs that are relished by black and grizzly bears, mule deer, elk, moose, and many bird species. This cornucopia contrasts with the scarcity of forage found in old spruce forests.

Human History

Native peoples made medicines for various ailments from Engelmann spruce resin and foliage (Moerman 1998). European Americans have utilized the creamy white spruce wood for many purposes. It is very lightweight, stiff, and moderately strong for its weight, suitable for lumber, finishing wood, shelving, and many of the purposes described for Sitka spruce, including select material for violins and pianos. Since it has no odor and very little resin, it has been used for food containers, including barrels. It also yields excellent pulp—with long fibers, light color, and absence of resin—suitable for paper, including high-quality writing stock.

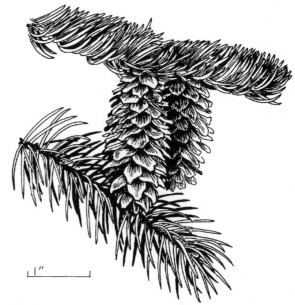

Engelmann spruce

Engelmann spruce is also associated with a major recreational pursuit and accompanying industry. Perhaps more than any other tree, it helps provide excellent habitat for mountain trout by sheltering and shading high-mountain streams and providing pools beneath its undercut roots.

BREWER SPRUCE *(Picea breweriana)*

The Northwest's other high-mountain spruce, Brewer spruce, is a small tree—seldom reaching 100 feet (30 m)—that contrasts in several ways from Engelmann spruce. Brewer spruce has an extremely restricted natural distribution and is little-known to most Northwest residents. However, it is prized by horticulturists for use as an ornamental—commonly called weeping spruce. This tree is native only to the Siskiyous and Klamath Mountains, where it occurs in widely scattered groves at elevations of 4000 to 8000 feet (1200 to 2400 m). Its Oregon distribution is primarily in the southern half of Josephine County, and it extends southward about 75 miles (125 km) into California.

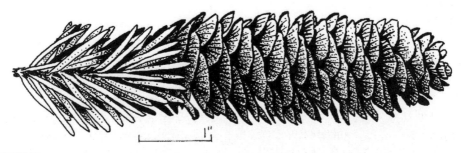

Brewer spruce

Brewer spruce is commonly limbed to the ground, its trunk swollen at the base and tapering rapidly upward. Its unique appearance is created by a multitude of stringlike branchlets that hang down 4 to 8 feet (1.2 to 2.4 m) from the main branches in the middle and lower canopy. Another feature that is unusual for a spruce is its needles, which are not sharp-pointed. The cones are also distinctive—3 to 6 inches (7.5 to 15 cm) long, with scales that are broad and rounded with smooth edges.

One of the more accessible groves lies along the secondary road from O'Brien, Oregon (located on US 199), to Happy Camp, California, near the road's summit just inside California.

WHITE SPRUCE AND ITS HYBRIDS

Picea glauca and *Picea glauca* x *P. engelmannii*, Pine family—Pinaceae

Typical white spruce has a natural range that extends more than 4000 miles (6400 km) across the North American boreal forest from Maine and Newfoundland to western Alaska. The species exhibits regional variation within this expansive distribution, but the most complex variation occurs along the Rocky Mountains in southwestern Alberta, southeastern British Columbia, and northern Montana, where it contacts Engelmann spruce. A narrow projection of white spruce reaches southward from the boreal forest along the eastern slope and low-elevation river valleys of the Rockies. This projection occurs in a region where Engelmann spruce is abundant at higher elevations. Detailed studies reveal that most of the spruce in the southern Canadian Rockies result from extensive interbreeding among white spruce, Engelmann spruce, and their hybrids (Habeck and Weaver 1969; Rajora and Dancik 2000).

Nevertheless, obvious differences in cones, foliage, form, and habitats separate some low-elevation trees that are comparable to the typical northern white spruce or have intermediate characteristics and can be considered as hybrid white spruce. Other trees, especially at higher elevations, resemble Engelmann spruce. Until taxonomists agree on how to classify trees within this genetic complex, the rest of us can simply identify them as resembling white spruce, Engelmann spruce, or hybrids (intermediate forms) based on a preponderance of indicators. This chapter describes the trees that have a majority of white spruce characteristics, recognizing that most of them in the Greater Northwest have some features of Engelmann spruce as well.

Where They Grow

North of the Banff–Lake Louise area (51 degrees N latitude), reasonably pure white spruce occupies the lowest valleys, hybrid forms occur between elevations of about 5000 and 5500 feet (1500 and 1700 m), and more typical Engelmann spruce grows higher up (Achuff 2006, pers. comm.). South of Banff and into northern Montana, typical white spruce is scarce, and hybrids occupy the lowest elevations, with Engelmann spruce in the higher country. These patterns are readily seen in the broad, glacial valleys of Banff, Jasper, and Kootenay national parks. Hybrid white spruce communities are also apparent in scattered, frost-prone valleys in northwestern Montana. Examples are readily seen in low-lying areas of the Flathead Valley along State Route 35 southeast of Kalispell. Hybrid white spruce also occupies rocky limestone sites at various elevations east of the Continental Divide as far south as northern Wyoming (Daubenmire 1974).

Appearance

Any tree enthusiast who has traveled through the boreal forest in Canada and interior Alaska becomes familiar with typical white spruce and its habitat: a small tree, commonly 60 to 80 feet (18 to 25 m) tall, with an irregular conical shape occupying a vast rolling landscape, from river floodplains to gravelly hills. The hybrid white spruce of the southern Canadian Rockies is of similar size and appearance—often having a narrow, rather sparse canopy that is uneven when seen in profile. New twigs of typical white spruce are generally without hairs; those of the hybrids have sparse hairs; and twigs of Engelmann spruce are densely hairy—best

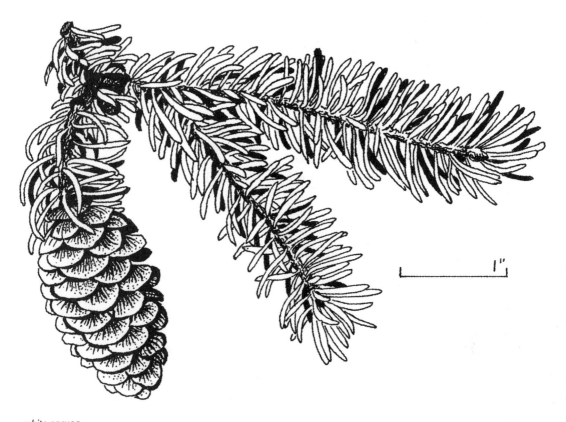

white spruce

seen with a magnifying glass (Achuff 2006, pers. comm.).

Cones provide the best characteristics for distinguishing white spruce, Engelmann spruce, and intermediate forms. Cone lengths are similar, averaging about 2 inches (5 cm), but the cone scales are very different. White spruce cones have scales that are somewhat triangular and broadest near the tip and have a leathery, firm texture; rounded tips; and a smooth margin (Achuff 2006, pers. comm.). Engelmann spruce cone scales are egg-shaped and broadest near the base and have a papery, crinkled texture; wedge-shaped tip; and a toothed margin. Hybrid spruce have cone characteristics that are intermediate or a mixture of those listed above. The seed and its wing makes a permanent impression on the upper (inside) surface of each cone scale, and the distance from the top of this impression to the scale tip is also diagnostic (Daubenmire 1974). In white spruce,

the distance is usually less than $1/8$ inch (3 mm), while in Engelmann spruce it is $1/8$ inch (3 mm) or more.

Ecological Role

White spruce and its hybrids occupy a broad range of habitats in the valleys and lower slopes of the southern Canadian Rockies, presumably because of their collective genetic diversity. They seem to be better adapted to warm and dry conditions than Engelmann spruce. In summer, these valleys often experience very warm days but frosty nights, as well as late-summer drought on upland sites. The gradation upslope from white spruce through hybrids to Engelmann spruce probably mirrors the change in climate and growing conditions that each is most adapted to.

In the southern Canadian Rockies, white spruce and hybrid spruce are part of a complex mosaic of forest communities that reflect variations in soil moisture and chemistry, microclimate (as influenced by slope angle and exposure), and disturbance history (Achuff 1989). The spruce are more shade-tolerant than most associates—lodgepole pine, Douglas-fir, quaking aspen, and cottonwood species—and thus, barring disturbance, are able to gradually regenerate in the understory and replace the other species, even though spruce grows slowly. However, even before the region was settled by European Americans, these valley forests were disturbance-prone, with mixed-severity fires every few decades killing many of the trees in a given area.

In the major valleys of Banff and Jasper national parks, hybrid white spruce forms distinctive communities on the river flats in areas subject to windblown deposition of calcium-rich dust (Achuff 2006, pers. comm.). This material originates from water-deposited glacial silt in the active floodplain, which is exposed during periods of low water. Other conifers don't seem to be able to tolerate these conditions, and the undergrowth species in these communities are different from those inhabiting adjacent sites not subject to heavy dust deposits.

Farther south, slow-growing hybrid spruce is one of the few trees able to colonize the droughty limestone mountains east of the Continental Divide in Montana and northern Wyoming—such as in the Little Belt, Big Snowy, Pryor, and Bighorn ranges. Here at middle elevations, spruce is associated with squatty Douglas-fir, shrubby junipers, limber pine, and a diverse undergrowth with species quite different from those that dominate most other mountain forests (Pfister and others 1977).

Human History

Aboriginal, historic, and modern uses of white and hybrid spruce probably parallel those of Engelmann spruce, except that the former do not attain the large size and produce the high-quality, clear lumber often associated with Engelmann spruce. On the other hand, wood from white spruce and its hybrids is denser and stronger than that of Engelmann spruce. In interior Alaska, white spruce was the most important tree used for dwellings and fuel by both Native peoples and frontiersmen, but that region is without lodgepole pine, which is abundant in the Canadian Rockies and there eclipsed white spruce and its hybrid forms for such uses.

twin flower

DOUGLAS-FIR

Pseudotsuga menziesii, Pine family—Pinaceae

Douglas-fir is the hallmark of the Northwest's timber industry, the State Tree of Oregon, and our customary wild Christmas tree. Most Westerners who know anything about native trees are familiar with Douglas-fir—but which Douglas-fir do they know? Throughout the Greater Northwest, Douglas-fir colonizes a broader range of habitats than do any of its associates. It could be considered nature's all-purpose tree.

In some forests, Douglas-fir is a pioneer (or early successional) species that depends on fires or other disturbances lest shade-tolerant true firs (*Abies* species) or western hemlock displace it. In other forests, Douglas-fir is the most shade-tolerant tree, and it supplants fire-dependent trees including ponderosa pine and western larch. Then again, in some cold, dry environments Douglas-fir alone makes up the forest.

West of the Cascade crest, Douglas-fir is the most common native evergreen in residential and rural areas. It is also the vigorous young conifer that regenerates after logging, a magnificent old-growth colossus in the rain forest, the predominant conifer in dry areas including the San Juan Islands, and often the small misshapen tree clinging to rock cliffs. In humid northern Idaho, Douglas-fir colonizes and grows rapidly following disturbance; but it typically dies by age 80 or so and is replaced by other species. Conversely, in the dry mountains of southwestern Montana, Douglas-fir grows slowly but can produce a bulky, heavy-limbed giant that survives 500 years.

Thus, our challenge is to comprehend the many faces of Douglas-fir and the various ecological roles it plays in different habitats. However, comprehending the Northwest's most common tree requires confronting the paradox about its identity:

Identification difficulties. Botanical explorers were impressed but also perplexed when they first encountered this species. The huge, corky-barked coastal trees were first reported in 1793 by the Scottish physician and naturalist Dr. Archibald Menzies, who encountered them on Vancouver Island while accompanying Captain George Vancouver. Three decades later, botanical explorer David Douglas described this tree in Oregon. At first, botanists classified it as a pine, and it was commonly called Oregon pine. However, this magnificent conifer does not bear needles in clusters as pines do, nor does it have pinelike cones. Bark on the young trees is smooth and pocked with resin blisters like that of the firs (*Abies*). The pointed, inch-long needles somewhat resemble spruce (*Picea*) or yew (*Taxus*), but the cone with its long, three-pronged bracts is unique. One botanist called it a fir with a yewlike leaf—in other words, *Abies taxifolia*—while John Muir and some others named it Douglas spruce.

Later in the nineteenth century, botanists exploring the mountains of China and Japan brought back samples of other similar trees that also had three-pronged cone bracts. The genus name *Pseudotsuga*, meaning "false hemlock," was proposed for this distinctive group. For a long time, our tree was called *Pseudotsuga taxifolia*; however, that name had not been recorded properly under the rules of plant nomenclature. Consequently, the official name became *Pseudotsuga menziesii* based upon the next-oldest name. Thus, the botanical name now acknowledges the original discoverer, while the common name, Douglas-fir, is applied to all the members of the genus *Pseudotsuga*. (The only other *Pseudotsuga* in the western hemisphere is a small tree bearing large cones that grows in

the mountains of southern California, and it is called bigcone Douglas-fir, *P. macrocarpa*.)

The common name should be hyphenated or run together as a single word (Douglasfir) because these trees are not actually firs (*Abies*). Loggers often call this tree red fir in recognition of its light reddish brown heartwood, apparent on cut logs and stumps. Naturalist Donald Culross Peattie (1950) advanced the name Douglastree, to clearly differentiate it from firs, and John Worrall and some of his colleagues at the University of British Columbia call it common douglas.

Where It Grows

Douglas-fir extends north along the Pacific coast nearly to the northern tip of Vancouver Island, in central British Columbia to about 55 degrees N latitude (vicinity of Smithers), and in Alberta to Jasper. It occupies nearly all of southern British Columbia, western Washington, and western Oregon from sea level to 5000 feet (1500 m) elevation and sometimes higher. It inhabits all inland forests in the Greater Northwest except for the driest ponderosa pine types, juniper woodlands, and highest subalpine habitats. Along the eastern slope of the Continental Divide in northern Montana and southern Alberta, Douglas-fir, sometimes accompanied by limber pine, replaces ponderosa pine in forming low-elevation dry-site forests, in a climate that is apparently too cold for

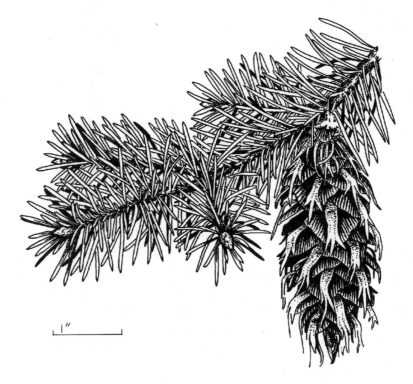

1"

Douglas-fir

inland Douglas-fir high-lined by elk

ponderosa. Southward, Douglas-fir grows in nearly all the higher mountain ranges from Utah and Wyoming well into Mexico. It also spreads southward along the coast and Sierra Nevada to central California.

Two geographic varieties are recognized, which probably reflect genetic and ecological differences more than physical distinctions. Coastal Douglas-fir, *P. menziesii* variety *menziesii* inhabits the Cascade–Sierra Nevada and British Columbia Coast Range and lands to the west. Areas farther east are occupied by the Rocky Mountain or inland Douglas-fir, *P. menziesii* variety *glauca*.

Appearance

A healthy young Douglas-fir typically has a full canopy of long, outward-projecting limbs with abundant branchlets. Limbs near the treetop sweep upward. The branches and twigs are arranged irregularly, unlike the more symmetrical branching pattern of true firs. As trees mature in fairly dense stands, their lower branches die and eventually fall off, so that live foliage occupies only the upper 30 to 40 percent of the main stem.

Douglas-fir has needlelike leaves about 1 inch (2.5 cm) long that are attached to all sides of the twigs and are not sharp or prickly to touch. The leaves are green on the upper surface and have two white bands (of microscopic pores) on the underside. Distinctive buds aid identification; they are brown, sharp-pointed, and covered with overlapping scales that flex backward and remain after bud-burst in late spring. In contrast, buds of Northwestern true firs are blunt and covered with wax.

Douglas-fir cones have a unique diagnostic feature: three-pronged pitchfork-shaped bracts that project from between the scales. The cones are tan when mature and 2½ to 4 inches (6 to 10 cm) long in coastal Douglas-fir versus 1½ to 2¾ inches (4 to 7 cm) long in the inland variety. Some of the bracts on cones of inland Douglas-fir are bent backward.

The bark on small trees is smooth and has resin-filled blisters like true firs, but once the trunk is about 12 inches (30 cm) thick, the bark starts to grow furrowed and corky. Bark continues to accumulate, becoming dark brown and deeply furrowed. It often thickens to 9 inches (22 cm) at the base of old coastal Douglas-firs and 5 inches (13 cm) on inland trees. This corky material is dense and durable, and chunks of it can still be found near ground line on stumps cut a century ago. The bark aids identification of Douglas-fir, since when cut with a knife it shows well-defined, wavy bands and lenses of light tan and dark brown, somewhat like the pattern in a pile of sliced bacon.

Coastal Douglas-firs up to 8 feet (2.5 m) thick and 250 feet (75 m) tall grace many parks and natural areas in southwestern British Columbia, western Washington, and western Oregon. Occasional trees in sheltered valleys tower 300 feet (90 m) in height, but the largest trees have often lost part of their crown to raging windstorms during their 600- to 1000-year existence. The 12- to 15-foot- (3.5- to 4.5-m) thick trunks of record-sized coastal Douglas-fir are equaled in volume only by Sitka spruce and exceeded only by giant sequoia, redwood, and western redcedar among the world's arboreal behemoths (Van Pelt 2001). Hulking old sentinels of inland Douglas-fir with enormous limbs, perched on grassy ridges at about 7000 feet (2100 m) elevation, are also impressive. Some of them—4 to 5 feet (1.2 to 1.5 m) thick and up to 90 feet (27 m) tall—can be seen along the road near Tower Junction in Yellowstone National Park.

Ecological Role

Douglas-fir is classed as intermediate in shade tolerance, which means it has the ability to regenerate and grow up beneath other trees and eventually displace them. (This process of vegetation change is called forest succession.) As a result, Douglas-fir may be either an early successional species subject to replacement by other trees or a late successional species that deposes its associates. Additionally, a third situation arises in some habitats where Douglas-fir is the only forest tree. Below, each of these roles is described in detail:

Douglas-fir is an early successional species in humid regions such as the coastal Northwest and in moist inland areas including northern Idaho. Here it depends on occasional disturbances that kill patches of forest. Otherwise shade-tolerant trees such as grand fir and western hemlock will eventually replace it. Huge old Douglas-fir trees once dominated much of the landscape west of the Cascades, largely as a result of fires sweeping through drier areas (including the Puget Sound valley) every few decades and burning moist mountain habitats every few centuries. Because of its thick bark, deep roots, and lofty crown, coastal Douglas-fir is able to survive fire better than its competitors do, and it readily colonizes burned areas. Even today, char from long-ago fires can be seen on the bark of great old Douglas-firs. Although veteran Douglas-firs still occupy large areas of

Douglas-fir seedlings from rodent seed cache

parks and forest reserves west of the Cascade crest, fire suppression is so successful here that very few of these forests experience the disturbances that helped create and sustain them. The age-old process of survival and regeneration in an old-growth Douglas-fir forest swept by fire (in 1986) can be witnessed along the Skokomish River trail a short way above Staircase Ranger Station in Olympic National Park.

In many inland areas, Douglas-fir is a late successional species that, barring disturbance, will replace its associates—ponderosa pine, lodgepole pine, western larch, and quaking aspen. Similarly, it will displace native prairies and Oregon white oak woodlands in coastal lowlands. Historically, fires favored the shade-intolerant trees or prai-

dwarf mistletoe in inland Douglas-fir

rie vegetation and controlled the abundance of Douglas-fir. Large old ponderosa pine and larch commonly grew in open stands with Douglas-fir as a result of frequent low-intensity fires that killed most Douglas-fir saplings, whereas saplings of ponderosa pine and larch are more fire-resistant. After the pattern of historic fires was interrupted in the early 1900s, Douglas-fir saplings filled the understory and developed into thickets of small trees, susceptible to epidemics of insects and disease and more-severe crown fires.

A third situation, wherein Douglas-fir is essentially the only tree, occurs in cold, dry mountain habitats especially in southwestern Montana and eastern Idaho. Historically, scattered open stands of Douglas-fir were mixed with mountain grasslands, and periodic grass fires killed most saplings. By the 1930s, livestock grazing had removed much of the grass that served as fire fuel, and human suppression efforts had largely prevented fire. As a result, Douglas-fir saplings were able to colonize grasslands and proliferated in open forests, eventually growing into thickets of small, drought-stressed trees. This greatly diminished forage values in these formerly productive wildlife and livestock habitats (Gruell and others 1986).

Although Douglas-fir plays different roles in a myriad of forest types, most of these communities were shaped through past millennia by patterns of fire. Efforts to exclude fire have often led to undesirable consequences in Douglas-fir communities. People interested in native forests are now beginning to recognize these problems and in some cases seek remedies using knowledge of the historical ecosystem (Arno and Fiedler 2005).

Human History

Native peoples, including the Bella Coola tribe of British Columbia, had many medicinal uses for Douglas-fir, such as mixing the tree's resin with dogfish oil as a virtual panacea (Moerman 1998). Several tribes used Douglas-fir foliage as a body freshener in conjunction with sweat

Felling a coastal Douglas-fir, Mason County, Washington, in 1899. (U.S. Forest Service photo)

baths. The leaves were used by some peoples as a substitute for coffee. (Starbucks beware!) The wood and resin were widely used, and then as now, Douglas-fir was preferred firewood. The bark of coastal Douglas-fir was especially favored, possibly because this thick, corky material makes long-lasting hot coals.

Douglas-fir's wood is relatively heavy, hard, strong, and resilient under stress and is therefore broadly useful. By the turn of the twentieth century, it had replaced white pine as the prime industrial timber, since coastal Douglas-fir grew in vast forests of very large trees. It made an excellent structural material also because it was available in high-grade lumber in large sizes. Gigantic timbers of virtually any length could be cut from these trees. A 299.5-foot-long (91-m-long) Douglas-fir flagpole was part of Oregon's exhibit at the 1915 Panama-Pacific Exposition in San Francisco. Douglas-fir became a prime material for plywood and is used for a variety of other forest products as well. Today, large old trees are not widely available or needed for most lumber and other products, and there is high demand for the smaller Douglas-fir. Much of this is obtained from plantation forests in coastal areas and from thinning the overly dense stands in inland areas.

WESTERN HEMLOCK

Tsuga heterophylla, Pine family—Pinaceae

Western hemlock's distinctive appearance is a product of its short, delicate needles; abundant little cones; drooping branch tips; and the bent-over leader at the treetop. This tree is smaller, slower-growing, and often shorter-lived than its majestic associates, including Sitka spruce near the coast, Douglas-fir west of the Cascades, western redcedar along northwestern rivers and streams, and western white pine in northern Idaho. However, a closer look at the mature forest reveals that young hemlocks far outnumber regeneration of the other species. When the lofty spruce, coastal Douglas-fir, redcedar, or white pine lose vigor and die, a dense stand of smaller hemlocks will replace them. Root competition from hemlocks may even hasten the demise of their larger associates.

Where It Grows

Western hemlock is one of several trees whose main distribution follows the North Pacific coast, west of the Cascades and the British Columbia Coast Range. It extends from the redwood forest in northernmost California to south-central Alaska's Kenai Peninsula. From northwestern Oregon to the Alaska Panhandle, western hemlock will, barring disturbance, eventually dominate all but the driest forest habitats. It is abundant in western Washington from sea level to elevations of at least 3500 feet (1070 m) and is designated as Washington's State Tree.

Like numerous other coastal Northwest species, western hemlock also inhabits the wettest area of inland mountains—the region historically dominated by western white pine. Here—in southeastern British Columbia, northeastern Washington, northern Idaho, and northwestern Montana—western hemlock occupies moist

habitats, especially north-facing slopes, up to about 5000 feet (1500 m). The valleys it occupies generally receive at least 32 inches (800 mm) of precipitation in the average year. Still, western hemlock is less prevalent across this inland area than it is west of the Cascades due to many intervening dry valleys and to more frequent fires, which favor its competitors.

Appearance

The small needles and cones and drooping branch tips and leader give young western hemlocks a graceful appearance. As the trees grow, they develop a long, thick canopy that casts a dense shadow. Despite western hemlock's modest size by Northwest standards, it is thought to be the largest of the ten or so hemlock species

western hemlock

found in the northern hemisphere. At middle elevations in the coastal mountains, very old hemlocks sometimes attain diameters of 6 to 8 feet (1.8 to 2.4 m) and heights of 200 feet (60 m) or more (Van Pelt 2001). In inland areas on sites with minimal moisture stress, old hemlocks can reach a diameter of 4 feet (1.2 m).

Western hemlock's fine foliage and branching arrangement give the boughs a delicate spraylike appearance unlike other needle-leaved conifers. The flat, blunt needles range from about ¼ to ¾ inch (0.5 to 2 cm) long on any given branch. The species name *heterophylla* means "variable leaves." Needles have white bands (of microscopic pores) on the underside and grow in a somewhat two-ranked pattern, from opposite sides of the twigs. Western hemlock cones, also small and delicate, are borne in large quantities on the branches throughout most of the canopy. They are tan and papery and less than 1 inch (2.5 cm) long when mature. They are borne in such plenty that they often cover the forest floor.

Near its upper elevational limits on mountain slopes, western hemlock commonly mingles with its high-elevation relative, mountain hemlock (see the next chapter). Occasionally trees have foliage or cones that appear intermediate between the two species—for example, denser leaf arrangement on twigs and larger cones than normal for western hemlock. However, little evidence of actual hybridization between these species has been confirmed, and it seems that trees that appear intermediate are probably western hemlocks that acquired some characteristics similar to mountain hemlock's.

The bark on large western hemlocks is dark brown and heavily furrowed, superficially resembling Douglas-fir. This can be confusing in the dim light of an old hemlock forest, which may contain relict Douglas-firs. However, these species are easily distinguished by examining the bark. Douglas-fir bark is several inches thick and when sliced reveals bands of light tan and

dark brown, whereas hemlock bark is only about 1 inch (2.5 cm) thick, and the inner layers are dark red to purple.

Ecological Role

While faster-growing and larger associates depend on fire, blowdown, or other disturbances to perpetuate themselves, western hemlock employs a different strategy. It is amazingly well adapted to achieving dominance over all other species in the dense forest when there is no major disturbance for a long period of time. For one thing, hemlock yields seed in abundance. Eight million seeds averaging roughly 260,000 per pound (570,000 per kg) were produced per acre (20 million per ha) in an Oregon forest one year. The seeds can germinate and grow on a variety of seedbeds, beneath shrubs or other trees. This tree begins to yield cones at age twenty-five or thirty and then outproduces all its associates. The seeds have a membranous wing, allowing them to travel 0.5 mile (1 km) from the parent tree in just a light wind. Small wonder that western hemlock saplings are commonly found growing in places far from any seed-bearing hemlocks.

Because of intense competition from established vegetation under a forest canopy, conifer seedlings are often most successful getting established on a rotten log. One of these logs in the coastal rain forest may support hundreds of western hemlock seedlings accompanied by only a few of the less shade-tolerant Sitka spruce and rarely a Douglas-fir seedling, despite the presence of spruce and Douglas-fir in the overstory.

Hemlock seedlings can survive at a very slow rate of growth for many decades, until a favorable event such as toppling of a large tree gives a few of them the opportunity to grow more rapidly and perhaps even reach into the forest canopy. Many seedlings on rotten logs succeed in extending roots down into underlying mineral soil, and as the log disintegrates, the developing trees display a stilted root system. A small western hemlock tree is sometimes seen perched atop a broken-off rotting snag more than 15 feet (4.5 m) above the ground; inspection will reveal that one or more roots extend down the stump into the damp soil.

Although individual hemlocks grow more slowly than do their shade-intolerant competitors, they can accumulate more biomass or wood volume per acre than coastal Douglas-fir, Sitka spruce, or other species do, because they are able to sustain good growth at higher densities (U.S. Forest Service 1990). However, dense old hemlock forests are prone to heavy damage by fungi that cause root or stem rot, defoliating insects such as hemlock looper and black-headed budworm, and the parasitic plant dwarf mistletoe. At lower elevations, western hemlock seldom attain 300 years of age before they succumb to

western hemlock seedling on a western redcedar stump

disease or weather damage such as breaking off or uprooting in high winds. (Trees at higher elevations may live longer.) Their shallow roots and thin bark also make them highly vulnerable to fire.

Partially because of the dense shade and root competition, old hemlock forests support only sparse undergrowth. In contrast, young forests that arise after fire, windthrow, or some forms of logging have a profusion of herbaceous plants and shrubs that provide forage and fruits favored by wildlife. Similarly, a variety of tree species commonly gets established in a burned hemlock forest. On burned or heavily logged sites, western hemlock seedlings do not compete in initial height growth with red alder, coastal Douglas-fir, western white pine, western larch, or other shade-intolerant tree species, and they may be damaged by excessive exposure to the drying sun. But after other species become well established, the shade they cast is favorable for western hemlock, which then increases in the understory.

In recent years, ecologists have discovered that concepts of disturbance and succession in western hemlock forests are actually more complex than previously thought. Studies reveal that much of today's western hemlock forest was historically subject to mixed-severity fires that killed most hemlocks and other fire-susceptible trees but allowed many shade-intolerant trees to survive or to regenerate in abundance (Arno 2000). Principal beneficiaries of fire were Douglas-fir in coastal forests and western larch, white pine, and lodgepole pine in inland forests. Fire-resistant survivors became important old-growth features in the ecosystem—for instance, as habitat for cavity-nesting birds and mammals. With the general success of fire suppression in old forests, especially west of the Cascades, there is no mechanism for perpetuating historic conditions, including large, fire-resistant trees.

Human History

Native peoples had many uses for western hemlock (Moerman 1998). Several tribes cooked bark to make extracts for treating tuberculosis, rheumatic fever, or hemorrhage. The inner bark served as a survival food in winter. Boiled bark made reddish brown or darker dyes for fish nets and lines that rendered them invisible to fish. Some coastal tribes submerged hemlock trees and anchored them underwater to collect

salmonberry in western hemlock habitat

herring eggs that would stick on the foliage and could then be gathered for food.

Until about 1920, lumber mills regarded western hemlock as a weed tree, apparently because they assumed that the wood had poor qualities similar to eastern hemlock (*Tsuga canadensis*). Later, they learned that western hemlock wood is superior to its eastern kin from almost all standpoints. Today's forest industry makes extensive use of western hemlock wood. It absorbs preservative treatments well and is used for pilings, poles, and railroad ties.

It is suitable in strength and nailing characteristics for construction lumber and is made into flooring for gymnasiums. It provides excellent wood pulp for various types of paper and serves as a source of cellulose fiber used in the manufacture of rayon and many plastics. The bark is rich in tannin and has a long history of use in tanning leather.

Thus, just as western hemlock's biological importance in Northwest forests is well established, it has proven to be a Cinderella tree from the commercial viewpoint.

MOUNTAIN HEMLOCK

Tsuga mertensiana, Pine family—Pinaceae

Mountain hemlock is a handsome tree with luxuriant foliage that inhabits the high country of the Pacific Coast mountains and some of the snowiest inland ranges. Its picturesque form attracts photographers at mountain recreation areas including Whistler, British Columbia; Mount Baker, Washington; and Mount Hood and Crater Lake, Oregon. It develops into a medium-sized tree in the dense subalpine forest and ascends to the alpine tree line as a multistemmed, stunted tree or huge sprawling shrub (*krummholz*). In the coastal mountains, abundant snow and humid conditions protect mountain hemlock from desiccation and extreme cold, allowing it to occupy a broad zone at high elevations. In drier, inland mountains, it is restricted to moist, protected sites.

Where It Grows

Mountain hemlock is plentiful in the high Cascades, the Olympic Mountains, and British Columbia's Coast Range. It extends northward to Alaska's Kenai Peninsula. Farther south, it occurs in isolated populations on high peaks in the Siskiyous and California's Cascades and Sierra Nevada. From northwestern Oregon to southwestern British Columbia, it grows mostly between elevations of 3500 and 6000 feet (1100 to 1800 m), while at Crater Lake it occurs mainly at 6000 to 8000 feet (1800 to 2400 m).

Mountain hemlock also grows in the wettest inland mountains, about 200 miles (325 km) east of the Cascades. However, it is widespread and abundant only in the snowy Selkirks of southeastern British Columbia and the northern Bitterroot Mountains of Idaho and northwestern Montana, north of Lolo Pass on US 12. Northeastern Oregon's Wallowa Mountains support a good-sized outlier population well to

the south of the Bitterroots and east of the Cascades (Johnson 2004).

Overall, mountain hemlock's regional distribution is remarkably similar to that of western hemlock, which is, however, confined to lower elevations. The one major geographical difference is that mountain hemlock extends south of Crater Lake in the Cascades and Sierra Nevada. In this region, summers are evidently too long and dry for western hemlock, whereas at high elevations, mountain hemlock is sustained by lingering snowpack and cool temperatures.

Appearance

Rugged mountain hemlocks with their bushy foliage, irregular canopies, and slightly drooping leaders are a highlight of the subalpine parkland—a mosaic of tree groves, heatherlike mountain heath (species of *Phyllodoce* and *Cassiope*), flowery meadows, rocky areas, and ponds. Hemlock trunks are clad in dark purplish brown, furrowed bark about 1¼ inches (3 cm) thick. In the forest proper, mountain hemlock's canopy is so dense that it may have inspired the logger's common name black hemlock.

Mountain hemlock's needles—½ to ¾ inch (1 to 2 cm) long—project from all sides of the twigs and also radiate from little spur shoots, somewhat as in larches, giving branchlets a brushlike appearance. This contrasts with western hemlock's flat needles arranged in flat, open sprays. Mountain hemlock foliage is often bluish green, while western hemlock is yellowish green.

Quantities of cones, changing from purple to tan to brown as they ripen, enhance the decorative appearance of mountain hemlock boughs. The cones are generally 1½ to 3 inches (4 to 8 cm) long, in contrast to those of other hemlocks,

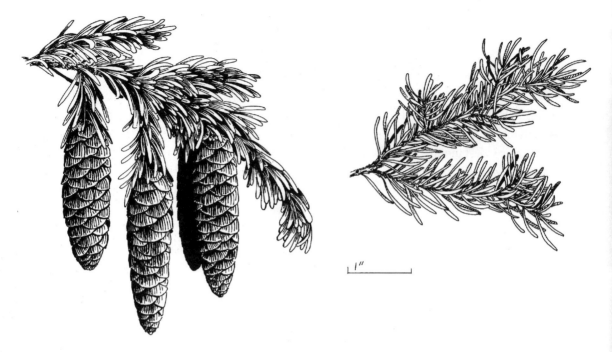

mountain hemlock: cone-bearing foliage; twig from lower branch

which are 1 inch (2.5 cm) or less long. Mountain hemlock cones somewhat resemble spruce cones, and some early naturalists, including John Muir, referred to this species as Hemlock Spruce. In 1949 a French botanist theorized that mountain hemlock was actually a hybrid of spruce and hemlock, but more recent genetic studies confirm it is a hemlock.

Ecological Role

Mountain hemlock is highly tolerant of shade, and thus in a closed forest it can eventually displace less shade-tolerant associates such as lodgepole pine and noble fir. However, mountain hemlock itself can be crowded out in the closed subalpine forest by the even more shade-tolerant Pacific silver fir. Occasional fires, blowdowns, snow avalanches, and insect and disease epidemics allow a mixture of species to prevail across the high-mountain landscape. In the parkland zone, above the limit of contiguous forest, open areas and harsh conditions allow a variety of species to persist if they are sufficiently cold-hardy.

Mountain hemlock assumes different growth forms induced by high-mountain conditions. In the subalpine forest proper, it grows in dense, dark stands; in coastal mountains, it grows with Pacific silver fir and other species and in inland areas with subalpine fir and others. The crowded trees are straight and tall, and only the upper third of the trunk supports a live canopy. Higher up the mountain, where excessive snow, wind, and rugged terrain break up the forest, mountain hemlocks often grow as stout, isolated trees, with wind-battered crowns and thick, gnarled trunks. At the limit of trees, a dwarfed but vigorous hemlock sometimes produces many upturned branch-trunks and appears like a small grove. On exposed ridges, some *krummholz* hemlocks have wind-pruned surfaces as if clipped by a gardener.

Mountain hemlock seedlings are often the first trees to colonize heathland and other openings at timberline in response to climatic warming (Arno and Hammerly 1984). Although its seed crops tend to be ample, this species also regenerates extensively through

mountain hemlock: wind-sheared alpine scrub

layering—that is, lower branches of established trees in contact with the ground (perhaps weighted down by snow) take root and then grow erect to become new trees. Small, pyramidal hemlocks often surround the weather-scarred 400-year-old veterans. Layering is an effective means of regenerating at timberline since layered saplings are sheltered by the adjacent parent tree and receive nutrients through its root system.

Mountain hemlock occupies the snowiest forest zone in North America. Average annual snowfall ranges from about 32 to 50 feet (10 to 15 m). Weather stations in the mountain hemlock zone on both Mount Baker and Mount Rainier in Washington have measured yearly (July 1 to June 30) record snowfalls of more than 90 feet (27 m). This is not light powder but heavy, wet snow. Groves of small, slender mountain hemlocks colonize slopes where they

are flattened each winter by sliding snowpack. On July afternoons as the snow melts, hikers witness these trees popping up out of their winter tombs.

These snowpacks yield massive quantities of runoff when they melt in late spring and

young, limber mountain hemlock under heavy snowpack

summer, often washed down raging streams with copious rain. Average annual precipitation is 100 inches (2500 mm) or more in much of the area dominated by mountain hemlock. In coastal mountains, this species can grow on the rockiest soils, including lava flows or pumice (such as around Crater Lake) if winter snowpack lingers well into summer. One study found that mountain hemlocks emerging through several feet of snow were transpiring, and presumably photosynthesizing, while nearby whitebark pines did not transpire until the soil was snow free (U.S. Forest Service 1990). The southernmost grove of mountain hemlock—at 10,000 feet (3050 m) in Sequoia National Park, California—is situated on fractured bedrock but has springs flowing all through it in midsummer. On the other hand, the notoriously wet and snowy Olympic Mountains have a dry, rain-shadow climate in their northeastern corner, and here mountain hemlock becomes scarce.

Experimental tests of mountain hemlock and other coastal conifers show that they are significantly less cold-hardy than are Rocky Mountain trees. The distribution of mountain hemlock seems to verify this conclusion. In the Rocky Mountain chain, mountain hemlock is common only among the snowiest, most humid western ranges, where it is probably encased in snow and rime ice when lethal winter frosts occur—at temperatures of perhaps −20 degrees F (−29 C) or so.

Mountain hemlock's winged seed is relatively light, averaging 114,000 per pound (250,000 per kg), and can be carried long distances by stiff mountain updrafts. This is demonstrated by the common occurrence of isolated hemlocks 10 miles (16 km) or more downwind from the nearest mature, cone-bearing trees. Such isolated individuals growing far to the east of existing groves in the Bitterroot Mountains are almost invariably stunted by repeated frost damage, despite no such injury to associated lodgepole pine, subalpine fir, and Engelmann spruce. The frost-stunted hemlocks are found in a rain-shadow zone receiving much less snow and more frequent Arctic cold waves than do hemlock groves occurring farther west.

A root rot (*Phellinus weirii*) causes the most conspicuous damage in mountain hemlock forests. In pumice soils on the Cascade crest near Waldo Lake, Oregon, this fungus spreads from centers of infection along tree roots, killing all trees in circular areas (Dickman and Cook 1989). Fires occasionally burn some stands, which may then regenerate to lodgepole pine that resists root rot but eventually is displaced by mountain hemlock.

Human History

Native peoples evidently made less use of mountain hemlock than the more accessible western hemlock. Recorded uses are generally similar to those for western hemlock, except that the bushy, fragrant mountain hemlock boughs served as sleeping mats and bath brushes (Moerman 1998). Beginning in the mid-1900s, mountain hemlock has been harvested for lumber occasionally in the Northwest near its lower elevational limits. Its wood is generally mixed with western hemlock in marketing.

Mountain hemlock parklands in the high Cascades are coveted for their beauty by sightseers, especially during hiking and backpacking trips. Parklands that feature mountain hemlock resemble a Japanese garden, and not by accident. Hemlocks from Asian mountain forests have long been a favorite of Japanese horticulturists. Moreover, mountain hemlock is often chosen for landscaping in parts of the Northwest that have relatively moist, mild climates—where it performs well, gracing gardens with its attractive foliage and form.

Opposite: mountain hemlock along a hiking trail

PACIFIC SILVER FIR

Abies amabilis, Pine family—Pinaceae

Pacific silver fir, whose scientific name means "lovely fir," is a distinctive, major tree of the Northwest coastal mountains that, nevertheless, can easily go unrecognized. Unlike lower-elevation trees, it isn't seen in or near most places that people frequent, and unlike trees that stand out in high-elevation parklands, its form and foliage are obscured amid dense, dark forests. This tree is an artist's delight, with its smooth, whitish trunk; symmetrical branching pattern; and foliage that is dark glossy green above and silvery below. It is well adapted for success in dark, snowy forests that allow it to dominate the middle elevations in Northwest coastal mountains.

Where It Grows

Pacific silver fir occupies forests along the western slope and crest of the Cascades northward from the vicinity of Crater Lake, Oregon, to southern British Columbia. It is abundant on north-facing and other moist slopes between about 3300 and 5000 feet (1000 and 1500 m) in Oregon and 2000 and 4300 feet (600 and 1300 m) in Washington. It is a major species in the Olympic Mountains and in the coastal mountains of British Columbia, where it sometimes descends to sea level. However, outside of this core area, silver fir quickly becomes scarce. A few isolated populations are found in the northern Oregon Coast Range, the Klamath Mountains just inside northern California, and the southern panhandle of Alaska. Unlike several other coastal conifers, silver fir is absent from even the wettest mountain ranges east of the Cascades.

Appearance

Saplings and small silver fir trees growing in open areas have regular, conical crowns made up of horizontal branches. Mature Pacific silver firs tend to be straight, slender, and tall. Mature trees are commonly 24 to 42 inches (60 to 105 cm) in diameter and 150 to 200 feet (45 to 60 m) in height. They have a dome-shaped top made up of horizontal branches. Silver fir grows in dense stands, where only the upper third or so of the trunk supports canopy foliage.

Trees up to 36 inches (90 cm) in diameter have relatively smooth, thin, ashy gray bark with large, chalky-colored blotches due to lichens. On the largest trees, the bark breaks up into small flakes that turn purplish. Young silver firs and other true firs as well as Douglas-fir have resin-filled blisters protruding from their smooth bark. These blisters contain a clear resinous liquid that solidifies when exposed to air and is used as a fastening agent (balsam), especially for microscope slides. Thus, anyone cutting or handling the trunks of these trees is advised to wear gloves!

Silver fir branches are covered with flattened, blunt, 1-inch-long (2.5-cm-long) needles that are dark glossy green on top and silvery white on the bottom. The needles are neatly arranged, projecting horizontally from opposite sides of the twig and bending forward along the top, giving the foliage a ruffled appearance. The result is a decorative, flattened spray that is lustrous deep green above and silvery on its underside. This tree, like all true or balsam firs (genus *Abies*), produces a different kind of foliage at the treetop on cone-bearing branches. Here, the needles are stout, curved, and very sharp; thus, they often confuse the beginning botanist who finds a broken treetop lying on the forest floor.

Like other true firs, silver fir's cones sit stiffly erect on horizontal branches near the

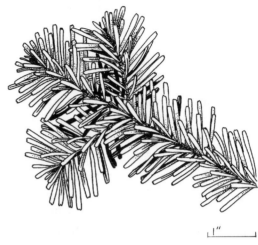

Pacific silver fir: cone; lower foliage

treetop. Silver fir cones are cylindrical, purple, and covered outside with smooth scales—without protruding bracts. They are 3½ to 6 inches (9 to 15 cm) long. All true fir cones disintegrate on the tree as they mature and dry out, leaving only the cone axis like a vertical spike. Because silver fir commonly grows as a tall tree in dense stands, it is difficult to see its cones even with binoculars. However, during the day, squirrels fell many cones, which then lie on the ground for a few hours before the furry harvesters stash them away. (One morning I came across some of the fresh-cut cones on a trail and hid a few of them under a boulder, planning to retrieve them on the return trip, but the squirrel tracked down this stolen food and hauled it to its cone cache before I returned.)

Pacific silver fir cone debris

Ecological Role

Pacific silver fir is one of six true fir species in the Greater Northwest. Silver fir and noble fir are the two specialists among this group that are adapted to a comparatively narrow range of habitats. The other four fir species show considerable genetic variation—as well as morphological variation—from place to place, which allows them to succeed in a broader geographic area and a wider range of habitats.

The unique structure of a mature Pacific silver fir forest reflects the species' ecology and its relationship to other trees. Hundreds of miles of hiking trails thread their way through these midelevation forests, where there is a closed canopy high overhead and no direct sunlight reaches below. The tall trees have branch-free trunks extending high above ground, and hikers walk within a somber but rather open understory as the intense shade permits only sparse, lanky shrubs. Like ants beneath tall grass, hikers see several different kinds of tree trunks. Smooth whitish trunks (Pacific silver fir) and rough, dark ones (western hemlock) are most common. Occasionally, there is a fluted butt covered with stringy, fibrous bark (western redcedar). Here and there stands a gigantic veteran (Douglas-fir), its thick, corky bark tinged with charcoal from the fire centuries ago that killed most of the other trees and gave rise to this forest.

Only one kind of small tree grows in any abundance beneath this forest. It occurs in scattered patches and is shaped somewhat like an umbrella. Generally 3 to 7 feet (1 to 2 m) tall, it has a straight, erect stem with swollen nodes and closely spaced whorls (layers) of long, flat branches projecting horizontally from near the top of the stem. These silver fir saplings, 70 to 200 years old, exist in a holding pattern and are able to initiate vigorous vertical growth if the tall trees above them die. Silver fir saplings survive better than those of the equally shade-tolerant western hemlock because their stiffly erect form resists being flattened by tree litter and heavy, wet snow. This characteristic seems critical for silver fir's success, since it is slow-growing compared to most of its associates. Moreover, its heavy seeds average 11,000 per pound (24,000 per kg) and do not disperse very far, so they do not become abundant in large burns, blowdowns, or other disturbed areas. Although other species outgrow silver fir on disturbed sites, it is able to grow up among and beneath them.

Silver fir has thin bark and is easily killed by fire, but after a few centuries without major disturbance, it begins to displace the fire-resistant Douglas-fir and other more light-demanding (shade-intolerant) species. Pacific silver fir is considered very tolerant of shade and thus it and western hemlock are self-perpetuating in old stands at middle elevations. Near its lower elevational limits, silver fir seems to have a competitive disadvantage against faster-growing western hemlock.

At high elevations, silver fir and mountain hemlock are self-maintaining, but the fir generally does not extend very far up into the subalpine parkland. Evidently silver fir is not as frost-hardy as mountain hemlock or the other timberline dwellers. This differential hardiness was demonstrated in early July 1969 when a snowstorm and hard frost killed the succulent new growth on silver fir at a parkland site in the North Cascades but caused no damage to mountain hemlock, subalpine fir, whitebark pine, or alpine larch (Arno 1970).

Pacific silver fir is a moderately long-lived tree, often surviving 400 years or more, especially at higher elevations, but then beginning to deteriorate due to advancing root or heart rot. Silver fir is also susceptible to damage from many other diseases as well as insects, the most serious being the imported balsam woolly aphid (*Adelges piceae*). This tiny insect feeds on the bark and injects a chemical that causes swelling of branch nodes and death of the tree, but since a major outbreak in the 1950s its spread has been slowed. Foresters imported and cultured populations of some of the parasites that keep the aphid in check in European fir forests.

Human History

Native peoples occasionally made use of the rather remotely situated tree, most commonly as a remedy for various ailments. Although David Douglas discovered this species in 1825 near Mount Hood, Oregon, and it was cultivated from seed he brought back to England, later field naturalists failed to locate it. Some botanical authorities questioned Douglas's finding, believing it to be a misidentified grand fir, and consequently did not include it in their tree books. Finally in 1880, three prominent botanists who had doubted its existence (George Engelmann, Charles Sargent, and Charles Parry) rediscovered Pacific silver fir in the mountains above Fort Hope on the lower Fraser River in British Columbia.

Another case of mistaken identity still attends Pacific silver fir, since West Coast loggers call it and noble fir "larch" to distinguish them from other true firs, whose wood is considered inferior. Pacific silver fir produces good-quality wood that is marketed with western hemlock and widely used for framing lumber, plywood, and other purposes where strength and decay-resistance are not so important. Silver fir's wood is light in color and lacks odor, gum, or resin, making it suitable for numerous applications. It also yields highly valued wood pulp for paper making.

Because of Pacific silver fir's beautiful foliage, gardeners have long wanted to cultivate it. It often does well when grown west of the Cascades and in the cooler parts of Great Britain, but elsewhere the results have frequently been disappointing. Many a horticulturist has lamented that this species is more lovely in the wild than in the garden.

GRAND FIR AND WHITE FIR

Abies grandis and *A. concolor* var. *lowiana* or *A. lowiana**,
Pine family—Pinaceae

Grand fir, white fir, and their hybrid forms collectively occupy low- and midelevation forests throughout most of the Northwest, west of the Continental Divide. They can be distinguished by differences in their foliage, bark, and the chemical makeup of their resin, and hybrids are intermediate in these characteristics. Grand firs often stand out in woodland pastures as solitary trees limbed nearly to the ground with down-swept, flattened branches. Both grand fir and white fir are also abundant in moist mountain forests east of the Cascade crest. Crowded thickets of these firs with stiff horizontal branches fill many a forest understory. Some grand fir and white fir forests have suffered epidemics of insects and diseases that killed most of the trees, leaving whitened snags.

------

*Note: White fir's scientific name is not agreed upon (see *www.conifers.org*).

Where They Grow

Grand fir grows in coastal lowlands from northern California's redwood belt through Oregon and Washington and along the east side of Vancouver Island and the British Columbia mainland to the latitude of Campbell River. In western Washington, grand fir is usually confined to valleys below 1500 feet (450 m) in elevation. Grand fir is more abundant and broadly distributed in moist forests on the eastern slope of the Cascades southward to northern Oregon. Also, it is plentiful between 1800 and 5500 feet (550 and 1700 m) in moist areas of eastern Washington, northern Idaho, northwestern Montana, and southern British Columbia in the vicinity of Kootenay Lake. East of the Cascades, habitats supporting

grand fir usually receive an average of 25 inches (640 mm) or more of annual precipitation but are too dry for or beyond the range limits of western hemlock and western redcedar.

The white fir found in the Greater Northwest is more drought-tolerant than grand fir and is able to occupy a broader range of forests. Its stronghold is the mountains of California, but it extends north into southern Oregon inland from the coast. Hybrid forms of grand fir and white fir predominate in the mountains of central and eastern Oregon and west-central Idaho, south nearly to Boise. The Rocky Mountain white fir (*A. concolor* var. *concolor* or simply *A. concolor*, depending upon the botanical authority), native to the middle and southern Rockies, is the most commonly cultivated form of this tree, prized for its light blue-green foliage. Contrary to some published range maps, this tree does not extend north into southeastern Idaho (Little 1971; Johnson 1995).

Comparative Appearance

Saplings and young trees of grand fir, white fir, and their hybrids have conical crowns composed of regular whorls of stiff, horizontal branches. These trees retain lower branches longer than accompanying Douglas-fir, and even in a mature forest they often support a live crown extending at least halfway to the ground. Trees in openings retain a thick, full-length canopy. Dominant old trees in the Cascades and inland Northwest often attain diameters of 30 to 40 inches (75 to 100 cm) and heights of 100 to 150 feet (30 to 45 m). Grand firs in coastal river valleys grow larger. Some of them scattered among giant Douglas-firs in northern and eastern valleys of Washington's Olympic

grand fir

National Park are 5 feet (1.5 m) thick and well over 200 feet (60 m) tall.

When the tip of an old grand fir or white fir dies, the tree unlike many other conifers readily sprouts new leaders. A conspicuous forked top develops, sometimes resembling a candelabrum. Two to several leaders of similar size arise from upper branches and stand erect, side by side. The visual effect is even more interesting when the multiple tops are loaded with upright cones. Similarly, grand fir and white fir readily sprout large quantities of epicormic branches from dormant buds if light and space suddenly become available, thus replacing live limbs that were broken or sawed off or died due to shading. This phenomenon is often seen where tall firs are trimmed along a powerline or roadway.

The bark on mature trees can be used to differentiate grand fir and white fir. Grand fir bark is about 2 inches (5 cm) thick, furrowed and divided into narrow, flat plates. It is gray or reddish brown outside but purple when sliced. Mature white firs have very thick bark—4 inches (10 cm) or more. It is hard and heavily furrowed and has a texture similar to that of old Douglas-fir trees. White-fir bark is ashy gray on the surface and has light- and dark-brown layers inside. Hybrid trees are intermediate in bark and foliage characteristics.

Grand fir foliage is easy to identify, except for foliage near the treetop. The lower boughs have flat, blunt needles, the longer ones

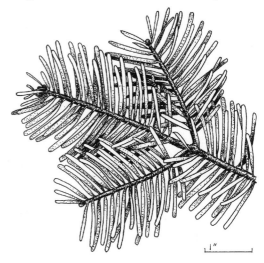

grand fir needle detail, from lower branch

forked crown of a grand fir

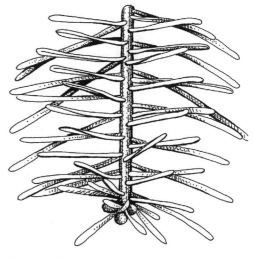

white fir needle detail, from lower branch

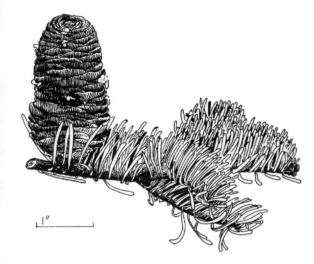

grand fir: cone and upper foliage

being 1½ to 2¼ inches (3.5 to 6 cm) long. These spread in two regular, comblike rows from opposite sides of the twig, producing flat branches. The needles and branches are shiny dark green above and whitish on the underside.

White fir foliage is also distinctive. The longer needles on lower boughs are 2 to 3 inches (5 to 7.5 cm) long. They are only somewhat two-ranked, and many are upturned so the branchlets aren't flat, although they may appear V-shaped. White fir needles have a whitish bloom on both upper and lower surfaces that makes them appear pale grayish green. The scientific species name, *concolor*, means "of the same color," which applies to the needles.

Cones of grand fir and white fir are similar, averaging about 4 inches (10 cm) long, green to reddish and covered with smooth scales. They sit upright in the trees except that they sometimes bend the branch tips as much as 90 degrees with their weight before they dry out and disintegrate.

Ecological Role

Grand fir and white fir are more shade tolerant than Douglas-fir (and thus able to displace it) but less shade tolerant than western hemlock or western redcedar. West of the Cascades from the Willamette Valley north-

ward, grand fir is most common in river valleys on deep soils where it grows rapidly and faces less competition from hemlock. In these sites, its growth rate sometimes exceeds that of coastal Douglas-fir, although the tree is relatively short-lived and therefore doesn't attain the mammoth size of old-growth Douglas-fir (Van Pelt 2001). One exceptional grand fir on Vancouver Island attained a height of 140 feet (43 m) at an age of only fifty years.

East of the Cascade crest, grand fir occupies vast areas of moderately moist forestland. When historical fire cycles were interrupted by fire suppression, grand fir proliferated in forests formerly dominated by more fire-resistant species such as ponderosa pine, western larch, inland Douglas-fir, and western white pine. Grand fir and white fir saplings are capable of surviving under shady conditions and grow very slowly for decades until larger trees die or are cut, creating openings that allow some of the saplings to grow fast and take over the vacant space.

In these east-side forests, grand fir is susceptible to a number of defoliating insects and rotting fungi. Under historic conditions, grand fir often attained 250 to 280 years, but in modern stands, crowded, stressed grand fir often succumb within 100 years. In the late 1980s and early 1990s, large areas of dense grand fir and hybrid fir forests in the eastern Cascades and Blue Mountains suffered massive mortality from epidemics of western spruce budworm (*Choristoneura occidentalis*) and other defoliators. Some mountainsides had a light gray cast for many years due to the predominance of weathered, dead trees.

Dead branch stubs or scrapes from falling trees provide a point of entry for fungi, partially because grand fir (unlike pines) does not exude pitch over wounds, nor does it contain decay-inhibiting properties in the wood (as does western redcedar). One study found that rot readily entered 90 percent of the grand firs that were scraped during a logging operation.

Historically, rot entered through scars caused by low-intensity fires.

East of the Cascade crest, grand fir is heavily infected by the trunk-rotting Indian paint fungus (*Echinodontium tinctorium*). This fungus is detected by sighting "conks" or fruiting bodies, which are large brackets or hoof-shaped growths attached to the trunk, often high above ground. The conk of Indian paint fungus can be identified by the grayish spines that make up its lower surface. The interior of the conk is rust-red and was used by native peoples as a pigment. The presence of an Indian paint conk indicates that the tree has a rotten core, and in some areas most grand firs are infected by age sixty or so. Large, rotten grand firs are often saturated with water, and during subzero weather (–18 C or colder), this freezes and produces a vertical frost crack running up the trunk.

White fir differs ecologically from grand fir, and hybrids tend to be intermediate in their attributes. Wherever grand fir grows east of the Cascades, it is associated with inland Douglas-fir, which also occupies drier and colder sites and is more fire-resistant. In contrast, inland Douglas-fir is absent from California and southern Oregon, and white fir seems to expand its range to occupy habitats where inland Douglas-fir might be expected. White fir inhabits both drier and colder sites than grand fir. It is also more resistant to heart rot and generally lives longer than grand fir. White fir has much thicker bark than grand fir and is fire-resistant. However, without occasional understory fires to thin out saplings, both white fir and grand fir tend to develop thickets that constitute a fuel ladder, promoting crown fires.

Human History

Grand fir, white fir, and their intermediate forms were used by Native peoples primarily for diverse medicinal purposes (Moerman 1998). Most often mentioned were compounds using powdered bark or pitch for treatment of tuberculosis or dermatological problems. Thompson River tribes of southwestern British Columbia used the bark to cover lodges and to make canoes. The flat branches provided bedding and floor mats that were changed every two to three days. Lewis and Clark also mention this use of boughs among the tribes at the mouth of the Columbia River where the Corps of Discovery spent the winter of 1805–06.

Grand fir was first described scientifically by David Douglas and was cultivated in 1830 from seeds he brought back to Great Britain. Both grand fir and white fir are handsome trees with luxuriant full-length canopies when cultivated in a favorable climate. Both do well when planted west of the Cascades and in other moist areas of the Northwest. White fir are commonly used as wild Christmas trees in California. Grand fir also makes a beautiful Christmas tree but is not favored commercially because the long, stiff, horizontal branches do not allow it to be packed economically. Because of grand fir's fine symmetry and beautiful foliage, some communities west of the Cascades (for example, Tracyton and Silverdale, Washington) have maintained living grand fir Christmas trees that are up to 100 feet (30 m) tall.

The soft, white wood of grand fir and white fir makes pulp suitable for high-quality papers and is also used in construction applications where strength is not a major concern. Grand fir and white fir also provide habitat for wildlife. Pileated woodpeckers make impressive excavations in search of larvae and ants and for nesting sites. Large firs with rotten centers serve as home sites for many species of birds and mammals, including black bears. Hikers also find that the large, spreading canopy of a grand fir serves as a splendid rain shelter, since the flat, down-swept boughs shed water as a tent would. However, one shouldn't utilize such a lightning-prone site during an electrical storm!

SUBALPINE FIR

Abies lasiocarpa and *A. bifolia*, Pine family—Pinaceae

Subalpine firs are the trees shaped like narrow cathedral spires that adorn high-country parklands throughout the Greater Northwest. Their short, stiff, horizontal branches extend to the ground and produce such a slender, conical form that only a limited amount of winter snow can pile up on them. Clusters of these sylvan pinnacles beautify our most popular subalpine parklands, including Paradise and Sunrise on Mount Rainier, the Beartooth Scenic Highway near Yellowstone National Park, Going-to-the-Sun Road in Glacier National Park, and the Icefields Parkway in Banff and Jasper national parks.

Casual visitors who recognize subalpine fir only in high-mountain settings might conclude that it is a scarce, highly specialized tree. Actually, it is a generalist that takes on many growth forms and has adapted remarkably well to a broad range of forest habitats in western North America, including some at relatively low elevations. Although this species is the smallest fir, it is an effective competitor in the inland mountains and can displace most other species in the absence of fire or other major disturbances.

Where It Grows

Subalpine fir grows atop some of the isolated peaks that rise high above the deserts of Arizona and New Mexico, and it colonizes the lofty terrain of the Rockies northward to the Yukon Territory. It occupies nearly all the high inland and coastal mountains of the Northwest; however, except for a couple of spots in the Siskiyous, this tree doesn't extend southward into California.

West of the Cascade crest, subalpine fir becomes most abundant near timberline and is mostly found between elevations of 4000 and 6500 feet (1200 and 2000 m). East of the crest and in many of the inland ranges, it doesn't have to compete with more shade-tolerant hemlocks or Pacific silver fir. Perhaps as a result, it expands to occupy a broad zone at mid- and high elevations. For instance, in western Montana it is common between about 5000 and 8800 feet (1500 and 2700 m) and extends much lower in frost-prone valleys. In the U.S. Northern Rockies, subalpine fir occupies more forest habitat types than any other tree except inland Douglas-fir (Pfister and others 1977). Subalpine fir is abundant in coastal mountain habitats receiving more than 150 inches (3800 mm) of annual precipitation, including a deluge of snowfall, but it also occupies inland sites that get only 25 inches (650 mm) of precipitation yearly, including just a modest snowfall. Although its high-elevation haunts have cool summers, it also inhabits some inland valleys where summer maximum temperatures approach 100 degrees F (38 C).

Identification difficulties. Considering the remarkable array of habitats it occupies and its sprawling geographic range, one might wonder if there are grounds for dividing subalpine fir into two or more species. The form of subalpine fir found in Arizona and New Mexico, commonly known as corkbark fir because of its distinctive thick bark, has long been recognized as a separate variety or even a species (*A. arizonica*). However, morphological differences among subalpine firs from Colorado to the Yukon and the coastal Northwest seem minor.

During the 1990s, a taxonomist proposed splitting these populations into two species— one in coastal mountains (*A. lasiocarpa*), and the other (*A. bifolia*) occupying inland areas (see *www.conifers.org*). The principal differences are in chemical constituents and a microscopic

subalpine fir on the flanks of Mount Rainier

characteristic. Perhaps the only feature readily distinguished by nonspecialists is the color of scars left when the oldest needles are removed: red in the coastal form and light brown in its inland counterpart. Time, perhaps aided by additional evidence, will tell if the split into two species will be universally accepted.

Appearance

Subalpine fir's exceptionally slender, spire-like profile can be recognized from afar; from somewhat closer, the very short, stiff, horizontal branches are apparent. In all but the densest stands, the canopy or at least some live limbs extend nearly to the ground. In the timberline zone, and on exceptionally wind-exposed or rock-pile sites, subalpine fir develops a skirt of luxuriant, long lower limbs within about 3 feet (1 m) of the ground. It also takes on a variety of stunted, multistemmed, and shrublike forms—more than any other Northwest tree. On relatively moist, sheltered sites at moderate elevations, subalpine fir, often accompanying the larger Engelmann spruce, can grow straight and tall, often exceeding 24 inches (60 cm) in diameter and 100 feet (30 m) in height by age 200 or so, when further growth becomes negligible.

Subalpine fir's bark is thin, smooth, and light gray with conspicuous resin blisters. Near the base of old trees, the bark develops shallow vertical fissures. The tree's foliage is rather deep green and the needles have fine white bands of microscopic pores on all surfaces. The blunt needles are about 1 inch (2.5 cm) long and grow out from all sides of the twig, making a brush-like bough. Heavily shaded lower branchlets have sparser foliage more like that of Douglas-fir. Most true firs (genus *Abies*), however, have small, blunt, wax-covered buds, unlike Douglas-fir's large, brown pointed ones.

Subalpine fir's cones are easily viewed on the stunted trees near timberline. They are 2½ to 4 inches (6 to 10 cm) long and deep purple, and they stand upright on the short, rigid boughs in the pointed treetop. The cones are often covered with an icing of glistening resin. They are pretty to look at but not worth touching, as anyone who has gotten the sticky pitch on their hands can attest!

Ecological Role

The most obvious characteristics of subalpine fir are those that adapt it to survival in cold, snowy environments. Its slender, conical shape and dense foliage make its crown like an A-frame ski cabin that prevents accumulation of heavy snow loads. Still, a moderate quantity of snow collects on the branches, which helps protect them from high winds, intense radiation, and temperature extremes in winter. The apparent effectiveness of this tree's growth form is illustrated by its success in snowy timberline habitats despite having wood that is lightweight and weak compared to other conifers.

Subalpine fir's ability to take on different growth forms also allows it to succeed under extremely harsh growing conditions. Climbing upward through the timberline zone, an observer witnesses a continuum of change in the

subalpine fir groves in a mountain landscape

1"

subalpine fir

height and shape of subalpine firs. At the lower edge of this parkland, the trees are tall, symmetrical cones. Ascending the slope, the firs become shorter, are more confined to clusters, and develop skirts of lower limbs that extend out several feet beyond the conical canopy. The skirts lie sheltered in snowpack throughout the long winter and are protected from damaging winds. In summer, they occupy a warmer, sheltered microclimate near the ground.

Climbing higher up the slope, the hiker will note that fir trunks are smaller and closer together in tight clusters, and some of the skirts seem to have upright "sprouts." When the lower boughs become compressed against moist, duff-covered ground, some will take root and then send up a vertical leader, which can become a new trunk. Subalpine fir does this vegetative reproduction, called layering, extensively at timberline. Layering allows new trees to get

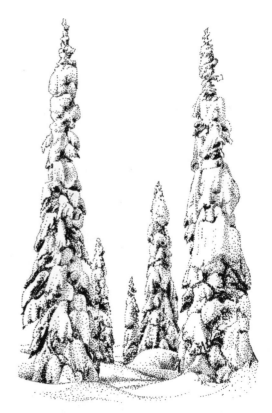

young, snow-laden subalpine fir

high-elevation subalpine fir: clusters (timber atoll); exposed, windswept forms (flagged krummholz)

established while connected to and benefiting from the root system of the parent tree.

At timberline, a single subalpine fir occasionally gets established from seed. If it succeeds against long odds and becomes an erect tree, its skirt of lower limbs may be able to produce a cluster of younger trees through layering. As these mature, the original tree in the center will die and decay, leaving a hollow center in the cluster, which is then called a timber atoll—because its appearance is likened to atolls in the South Pacific, which are ring-shaped coral islands. Often a hardier tree such as whitebark pine serves as the progenitor of a subalpine fir timber atoll. Higher yet on the slope, firs grow mostly as cushion *krummholz* (the low, shrubby form described in the whitebark pine chapter). Occasional erect stems manage to survive in a wind-battered form called flagged *krummholz*.

Some species have adapted to the adverse conditions at timberline by developing extreme hardiness—for example, whitebark pine and alpine larch, which are able to grow erect on sites where subalpine fir forms cushion *krummholz*. In contrast, subalpine fir demonstrates a mastery of adaptation by exhibiting different life forms and means of reproduction to succeed where cold, wind, and snow prevent normal tree growth. Subalpine fir has weaker wood and is shorter lived than whitebark pine, alpine larch, mountain hemlock, or Engelmann spruce at timberline, but its many growth forms and propensity for vegetative reproduction help it prevail anyway.

Subalpine fir's success in the dense middle- to high-elevation forests east of the Cascades may also seem surprising, since this tree is slow growing, short lived, and highly susceptible to fire. When intense fire or logging removes a forest, subalpine firs often seed in along

subalpine fir intergrowing with alpine larch

with faster-growing species such as lodgepole pine, western larch, Douglas-fir, and Engelmann spruce. These other species attain dominance, but subalpine fir perseveres and slowly increases in the forest understory. Without another disturbance in the next couple centuries, subalpine fir will begin to displace its competitors. The other species fail to establish a new generation of trees in the dense forest, while subalpine fir can do so because it is highly tolerant of shade and crowded conditions. When the other trees succumb in old age, hastened by crowding, young subalpine firs grow up and control the vacated space. Historically in the inland mountains, fires were frequent enough to favor lodgepole pine, western larch, and the other competitors, but now that most fires are suppressed, subalpine fir is able to dominate larger expanses of mountain forest.

Subalpine fir clusters and *krummholz* are used by many animals, ranging from grouse to mountain goats, for shelter from the elements and protection from predators. Firs act as a snow fence, accumulating snow that then melts gradually into summer, providing soil moisture that may sustain small meadows where otherwise there would be only dry, rocky habitats.

Human History

Native peoples made many uses of subalpine fir (Moerman 1998). They burned the needles in their lodges for incense or curative vapor. They used needles as a deodorizer, solutions of powdered bark or other fir components as a cold remedy, gummy resin as a wound dressing or chewed for pleasure or to sweeten bad breath, and boughs as bedding and floor mats.

Explorers Lewis and Clark made note of this species during their perilous journey across the snow-covered Bitterroot Mountains in September 1805. On their return trek over this rugged route, on June 25, 1806, Lewis described how their Nez Perce guides set fire to trees that almost certainly were subalpine firs, which when mature have highly flammable foliage and lichens:

> *last evening the indians entertained us with seting the fir trees on fire. they have a great number of dry lims near their bodies which when set on fire creates a very suddon and immence blaze from bottom to top of those tall trees. they are a beatifull object in this situation at night. this exhibition reminded me of a display of fireworks. the natives told us that their object in seting those trees on fire was to bring fair weather for our journey (Moulton 1993, vol. 8, p. 50).*

Because of its weak wood, small limby trunks, and frequent heart rot, subalpine fir is seldom used for lumber. It is suitable for wood pulp, although it is harvested only incidentally when growing with other more-valuable species.

This species is a favorite of horticulturists because of its pinnacle shape and brushlike foliage. It tends to do well in cultivation west of the Cascades and in irrigated and moderately cool places in the inland Northwest. It can be grown as a bonsai, but a dwarfed tree transplanted from a wild setting is likely to either die or respond with vigorous growth.

One remarkable subalpine fir tree has both a wildlife and a human connection. In 1963 my small party was hiking cross-country through a remote, high basin in Olympic National Park when we encountered a subalpine fir so outsized that we could hardly believe our eyes. This tree, nearly 7 feet (2.1 m) thick and 129 feet (39 m) tall, has reigned ever since as the largest known of the species. But equally surprising, the tree's base looked like an elf's house. A neatly fashioned little door sealed off a cavity in the trunk, evidently for use as a cache site. It turned out that the couple who a decade earlier made the pioneering Walt Disney documentary *The Olympic Elk* stored food or equipment in this tree while they backpacked through the subalpine fir parklands, capturing this enchanting habitat and its animal life on film.

noble fir

NOBLE FIR AND SHASTA RED FIR

Abies procera and *A. magnifica* var. *shastensis*, Pine family—Pinaceae

In the early 1800s, botanical explorer David Douglas discovered a tree in the Cascade Range that was so impressive he called it "noble fir." Virtually all tree enthusiasts since then have agreed with Douglas's assessment. Noble fir is the largest and tallest of the world's forty or more species of true firs (*Abies*), its growth rate and productivity rivaling coastal Douglas-fir. It produces the finest wood of any true fir—largely defect-free, light, and relatively strong. Young noble firs have foliage and form so beautiful that they are the most sought-after native species for Christmas trees.

In the mountains of southern Oregon, noble fir apparently hybridizes and intergrades with Shasta red fir, which is a variety of California's common, high-elevation fir (*Abies magnifica*). Noble fir, intermediate forms, and Shasta red fir have subtle but recognizable differences in foliage, cones, bark, resin composition, and ecological characteristics—notably that noble fir is intolerant of shade, or competition, while Shasta red fir is shade tolerant.

Where They Grow

Noble fir grows at middle elevations in the Cascades and coastal mountains—like Pacific silver fir—but it has a more restricted distribution. Small communities of noble fir occur mostly above 2000 feet (600 m) in elevation in the low coastal mountains from the Willapa Hills in southwestern Washington to Saddle Mountain near Astoria, Oregon, and Marys Peak near Corvallis, Oregon. Noble fir has not been found in the Olympic Mountains or in any of the ranges east of the Cascades.

Noble fir is abundant between 2500 and 5000 feet (750 and 1500 m) along and west of the Cascade crest from Stevens Pass

(US 2), Washington, to McKenzie Pass near Sisters, Oregon. Scattered populations, including intergrades with Shasta red fir, occur southward in the Oregon Cascades and perhaps in the Siskiyous, although there is disagreement about the presence of noble fir in southern Oregon (Franklin and Dyrness 1973; Parker 1963, 1998; Van Pelt 2001). From Crater Lake National Park southward, Shasta red fir is abundant between 5500 and 7500 feet (1700 and 2300 m).

Comparative Appearance

Noble firs have an almost regal appearance. Young trees in relatively open stands are conical and limbed to the ground with regularly spaced whorls of stiffly horizontal branches. Large old trees in a closed forest have towering, clear trunks that support a short, open, dome-shaped canopy composed of spreading branches. The trunk is

noble fir

smooth, pillarlike, and covered with ashy-brown bark divided by vertical seams into narrow, flat ridges. These ridges of bark are broken into long plates that flake off readily to reveal the reddish inner bark.

Mature trees on good sites commonly attain diameters of 45 to 60 inches (115 to 150 cm) and heights of 150 feet (45 m) or more. The largest-known noble firs are 8 to 9 feet (2.4 to 2.7 m) thick and (those with unbroken tops) about 260 to 280 feet (80 to 85 m) tall (Van Pelt 2001). Shasta red firs are also big, impressive trees, but they do not attain dimensions comparable to the record-size noble firs.

Noble fir's foliage is distinctive. On young trees with relatively full canopies, the needles are stiff, closely crowded on the twigs, and upturned, producing a beautifully formed "hairbrush" appearance. In contrast, the undersurface of the twig has a flat, combed appearance. The foliage ranges from a pale, almost silvery color to deep bluish green. The needles contrast with those of other true firs in having two whitish bands (of microscopic pores) on their upper as well as their lower surfaces. By comparison, subalpine fir has one broad band of pores above and two below, while Pacific silver and grand firs have only the two lower bands. White fir needles are more uniformly whitish and much longer. Un-

like other true firs, noble fir needles on young, open-grown trees are plump rather than being noticeably flattened in cross section. Shaded foliage on old noble fir trees consists of flat needles that are two-ranked.

Identification should prove easy in summer when the ornate cones are visible. Sometimes they can be seen in the treetops by using binoculars. They stand out atop the relatively small trees that colonize old clear-cuts, burns, and the Mount Saint Helens blast zone. On summer days, they may be found temporarily lying on the ground when squirrels are felling and gathering them. The cones stand erect and are barrel-shaped and somewhat larger than those of other Northwestern firs—4½ to 8 inches (11 to 20 cm) long and 2½ inches (6 cm) thick. The key to identification is their "shingled" surface covered with papery bracts that extend out and down from between the cone scales. Even after the cones disintegrate in early fall, the scales with their longer, protruding bract still attached can be found lying on the forest floor.

In southern Oregon, some trees have the "typical" noble fir features as described above, while others have features more like Shasta red fir or appear intermediate. Eugene Parker (1963, 1998) studied these species and their

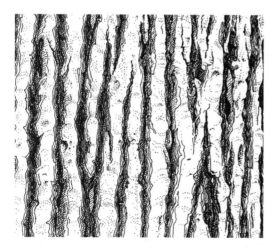

noble fir bark

Shasta red fir bark

intermediate forms and lists some distinguishing features.

The surface of a noble fir cone consists of purple scales at least half covered by the yellow-green papery bracts, while cones of Shasta red fir are less than half covered by bracts. Noble fir needles densely clothe and virtually hide the twig, while Shasta red fir leaves are less closely packed, allowing the twig to be seen through them. The upper surface of noble fir needles has a groove, while Shasta red fir needles have a ridge on top. Noble fir's bark has prominent vertical ridges, while Shasta red fir bark has both vertical and horizontal breaks, creating plates resembling old ponderosa pine. Moreover, noble fir bark is usually less than 2 inches (5 cm) thick, while old Shasta red firs generally have 4 to 6 inches (10 to 15 cm) of bark protecting them.

Ecological Role

In addition to being superlative, noble fir is the most specialized of the six Northwestern true firs, and it has the smallest natural range. This species requires a cool, moist habitat, similar to that of Pacific silver fir, but it differs from all other American true firs in being relatively intolerant of shade. Thus its great, cylindrical trunks ascend to lofty heights free of branches (being shaded out).

Noble fir requires periodic disturbances in order to perpetuate itself. In this sense, it is like coastal Douglas-fir but adapted to a cooler, wetter habitat than is optimum for Douglas-fir. Unlike Douglas-fir, noble fir seldom survives forest fires. However, fires are very infrequent in its cool, wet habitat.

The high-elevation environment changes southward in the Cascades as summer drought becomes more prominent and fire more frequent. In the southernmost Cascades, fires historically occurred every few decades, favoring the fire-resistant and drought-tolerant Shasta red fir (Taylor and Halpern 1991). Unlike the "specialized" noble fir, Shasta red fir is a generalist, well suited to prospering in a broader range of high-elevation habitats with or without disturbances.

Noble fir seeds are moderately heavy, averaging 13,500 per pound (29,750 per kg), and viable seeds are produced only every few years; consequently, its natural regeneration is sporadic even on burned, logged, or other disturbed sites. Still, sometimes noble fir regenerates on large, disturbed areas with remarkable efficiency. This situation can be seen along the scenic drive into the Mount Saint Helens blast zone south of Randle, Washington. Thousands of acres of forest were destroyed by the 1980 eruption, and young (posteruption) noble firs are abundant, thriving, and often producing cone crops. Shasta red fir bears somewhat heavier seeds, but it is able to regenerate on both shady and open sites.

Seeds of noble fir and Shasta red fir are sometimes cast on snow in the fall and then germinate on the slowly melting snowpack the following spring, with no chance of rooting into the soil and surviving. Even on good sites, noble fir seedlings often grow slowly for the first several years, typically requiring 3 to 5 years to attain 12 inches (30 cm) of height. However, after saplings reach a few feet of height, they begin vigorous growth that may continue for 200 years and allows them to overtop most other species. At middle elevations, noble fir grows mixed with equally tall Douglas-fir and smaller western hemlock. At higher altitudes, it is primarily accompanied by smaller Pacific silver fir and mountain hemlock.

Noble fir is long-lived for a true fir, and it resists damage by insects and diseases more than other true firs or western hemlock. It is relatively wind-firm and resists breaking under heavy snow loads. Still, once a forest gets to be 300 to 400 years old, the noble fir component begins to decline and give way to shade-tolerant hemlocks or Pacific silver fir.

noble fir in a mountain landscape with Pacific silver fir and mountain hemlock

Noble fir grows surprisingly well on the rockiest soils if they remain moist throughout the summer. This situation is demonstrated at about 6000 feet (1800 m) in elevation on the loose, pumice-covered slopes of Mount Hood in Oregon. Here, in the subalpine parkland, the droughty surface restricts the development of herbs and other ground cover, but noble fir and other trees are able to tap ample subsoil moisture. Soil moisture is especially critical for regeneration because the roots of noble fir seedlings grow slowly.

Human History

Little is known about aboriginals' use of noble fir or Shasta red fir, except that Paiute peoples used the foliage as a remedy for colds and coughs (Moerman 1998).

Historically, loggers recognized the superior qualities of noble fir's wood. To avoid the lumber industry's prejudice against true firs, whose wood was of little value, they called this tree "larch." Two Larch Mountains on opposite sides of the Columbia River east of Portland are named for the noble fir that covers their summits. Because of its high strength-to-weight ratio, noble fir wood has been used for specialty products such as ladders. During World War II, it was reportedly used for the frames of the Royal Air Force Mosquito bombers. Shasta red fir's wood is softer and weaker than that of noble fir.

Horticulturists were first introduced to noble fir as a result of seeds that David Douglas sent back to Great Britain in 1830. Douglas's accompanying letter to botanist William J. Hooker stated: "I however transmit one bundle of six species, exceedingly beautiful. . . . Among these, *A. nobilis* [noble fir] is by far the finest. I spent three weeks in a forest composed of this tree, and day by day could not cease to admire it . . . " (Davies 1980, 153). This species has been a favorite in northern temperate gardens ever since.

INCENSE-CEDAR

Calocedrus decurrens, Cypress family—Cupressaceae

Northwesterners tend to think of cedars as big trees growing in wet places. People from the Southwest and Southern Plains envision cedars as small, bushy trees growing on dry sites, although these trees are actually junipers (*Juniperus* species). Incense-cedar encompasses both these images as well as situations in between. On wet or even moderately dry sites, incense-cedar becomes a large tree with a fluted base. On hot, dry, rocky sites, it forms small trees and is second only to ponderosa pine and junipers in drought tolerance among Northwestern conifers. Rarely dominating a stand, incense-cedars grow scattered among other trees in many different habitats at low to middle elevations in forests and woodlands of southwestern Oregon and California. Young incense-cedars growing in openings produce luxuriant, pyramidal canopies. The wood is valued for its aromatic odor and rot resistance.

Where It Grows

Incense-cedar is a common constituent of the foothill and midelevation forests of northern California and the Siskiyou region of southwestern Oregon. It reaches as far north as Coos Bay but remains several miles inland from the ocean. At the lowest elevations, it is principally associated with ponderosa pine and oaks, but it also extends upslope into mixed-conifer forests. It is found in diminishing numbers northward to the Santiam River on the west slope of the Cascades and in small amounts nearly to Mount Hood on the east slope. It even inhabits some of the semi-arid mountains in central Oregon east of Bend. Southeast of Mount Hood, pyramidal young incense-cedars can be sighted along the Wapinita Cutoff (State Route 216), at Bear Springs and eastward.

West of the Cascades, incense-cedars dot the rolling hillsides and old pastures along Interstate 5 south of Cottage Grove, Oregon. The species also grows at lower elevations in Crater Lake National Park.

Appearance

Incense-cedar can appear to be two different species. Young, healthy trees often look like well-pruned ornamentals, while in stark contrast, old trees often have sparse, tattered canopies supported by fire-scarred or otherwise damaged trunks. When growing naturally or cultivated in a moist place, incense-cedars grow vigorously, producing a stout, rapidly tapering trunk and a dense, pointed canopy much like a young giant sequoia. Also like giant sequoia, native only to California's Sierra Nevada, the bark on old incense-cedars is thick, orange-brown, and fibrous, with deep, irregular, vertical furrows. Confusion with giant sequoia arises because these two species are common ornamentals west of the Cascades, where they achieve impressive size within half a century.

Naturalist John Muir described incense-cedar as a tree that in its prime is densely thatched with beautiful fernlike plumes, thus shedding rain and snow and making a fine shelter. He recounted that as the tree gets old, it responds to top damage by producing large special branches that form "big, stubborn elbows, and then shoot up. . . . Very old trees are usually dead at the top, the main axis protruding above ample masses of green plumes, gray and lichen-covered . . . " (Muir 1894, 132).

In southwestern Oregon and California, old incense-cedars often stand 100 feet (30 m) or more tall, with a trunk 4 feet (1.2 m) thick. Record-sized trees (Van Pelt 2001) attain diameters of 9 feet (2.8 m) or more and heights of about 140 feet (40 m). North of the Siskiyou region, incense-cedars tend to be smaller. Although little is known about age limits of this species, some of the big trees have survived more than 500 years.

Incense-cedar's foliage is superficially similar to that of other cedars, but closer inspection reveals distinct differences. Approaching an incense-cedar, an observer notices something unique. Many of the flat, fanlike "sprays" (lacy branchlets) have a peculiar orientation; they are twisted so as to align vertically at right angles to the branches. In contrast, other Northwestern cedars have flattened sprays that slant downward in a horizontal plane.

Incense-cedar has small, blunt, scaly leaves, generally like those of our other cedars and junipers. Giant sequoia's leaves differ in being distinctly sharp-pointed. Incense-cedar's

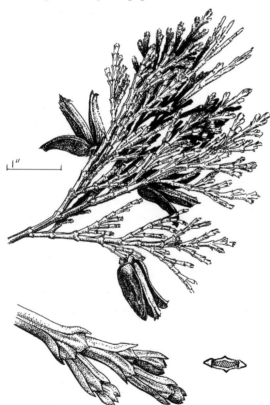

incense-cedar foliage and cones: close-up and cross section

scalelike leaves are pressed tightly against the twigs, which are flattened as if ironed. The more-conspicuous lateral leaves are up to ½ inch (12 mm) long, much longer than those of our other cedars. Copious crops of tiny pollen-bearing flowers ripen at an unusual time of year, tingeing the incense-cedar with golden yellow in winter and early spring.

The seed-bearing cones often hang in profusion from the tips of sprays and could hardly be confused with those of any other species. Compared to cones of other Northwest cedars, they are relatively long—about 1 inch (2.5 cm). Also, they have a unique structure and shape. When green, they are smooth and vase-shaped. As they ripen, they turn brown and two large scales bend back at right angles from the central axis, giving the impression of a duck's bill wide open with the tongue sticking straight out. Seeds are of average size for a Northwestern conifer—about 15,000 per pound (33,000 per kg), but they have a very large wing and can be transported long distances by the wind.

In the summer following a good seed year, curious-looking little seedlings are found on the forest floor. These new incense-cedars, just a few inches high, have several types of leaves: a pair of 1-inch-long (2.5-cm-long) needlelike seed-leaves (cotyledons) at the base, then shorter needles giving way above to sharp-pointed, scaly leaves. Then the customary blunt, scaly leaves are found at the top.

Ecological Role

Incense-cedars can regenerate under a wide range of light intensities on mineral soil or thick needle litter. Often seedlings grow up beneath shrubs. This species is relatively tolerant of shade and competition—more so than Douglas-fir but less so than grand fir and white fir. In crowded stands, it is commonly overtopped by other species and persists by growing very slowly and maintaining sparse foliage.

Seedlings of incense-cedar grow more slowly than those of its common associates, ponderosa and sugar pines. Its roots reach down about 12 inches (30 cm) the first year versus 20 inches (50 cm) or more for the pines. Incense-cedar's stem develops even more slowly, often attaining only 6 inches (15 cm) in height after three to five years. Unlike the pines, however, its seedlings can succeed in a seedbed of needle litter. On especially dry sites or beneath a dense forest canopy, saplings may be only 36 inches (90 cm) in height after thirty years. Nevertheless, even under these stifling conditions, they can eke out an existence and then, if an opening arises, respond by growing faster.

Incense-cedar is well adapted to the mountain climate of southwestern Oregon and California and is widely distributed across most geological types and elevations there. This "Mediterranean climate" is characterized by two dominant seasons: a relatively mild, wet winter and a warm, very dry summer.

However, even in southwestern Oregon, incense-cedar is seldom abundant enough to dominate a patch of forest. Instead, it is usually a secondary species in stands dominated by larger and faster-growing pines, Douglas-fir, and white fir. Still, it is able to tolerate a broad range of site conditions from hot, dry lava flows to cold, water-logged sites. The gigantic incense-cedars described by Robert Van Pelt (2001) occupy soggy soils in cirque basins high up in the Siskiyous. He maintains that one of the secrets of incense-cedar's success is its ability to tolerate more stressful sites than many of its competitors. Consistent with this theory, incense-cedar is also one of the few tree species able to occupy the extremely infertile serpentine bedrock in the Siskiyous, described in the sidebar on Jeffrey pine (see the ponderosa pine chapter).

The thick basal bark on mature incense-cedars protects them from surface fires, an advantage over grand fir and some other competitors. Still, fire commonly leaves large scars on the surviving trees, and these scars become ports of entry for pocket dry rot (*Tyromyces amarus*) that eventually honeycombs the wood with small cavities. A high percentage of very old incense-cedars in southwestern Oregon is fire-scarred and riddled with this rot, which seems ironic considering that incense-cedar heartwood lumber is highly resistant to decay. However, this particular decay organism seems relatively resistant to protective substances in the heartwood that are toxic to other rotting fungi.

The canopies of stressed trees tend to be sparse and irregular, often with scattered, clumpy growths called witch's brooms. Most of this is the result of a parasitic mistletoe plant (*Phoradendron*) or a foliar rust disease (*Gymnosporangium*), which commonly infect and weaken incense-cedar but seldom kill it. Some mistletoe infections in living incense-cedars are estimated to date back a few hundred years.

Human History

Native peoples had several uses for incense-cedar (Moerman 1998). One northern California tribe used the lacy branchlets for spreading water gently over acorn meal to prevent sand from mixing with it during the leaching process. Incense-cedar foliage also served as a flavoring for the meal. The Klamath peoples used branches of this tree for twirling sticks to produce fire by friction. They were also among several tribes that used the wood, roots, and bark in making baskets.

Explorer John C. Frémont discovered incense-cedar in the northern Sierra Nevada in 1844, and specimens he collected were used in the species' original botanical description. Until late in the twentieth century, incense-cedar was grouped into the diverse genus *Libocedrus*, composed of species growing in both the northern and southern hemispheres. Later investigation revealed that cones of the three species growing north of the equator differ markedly in structure from the others. Thus, our incense-cedar and one each from China and Taiwan were re-classified in the new genus *Calocedrus*, meaning "beautiful cedar."

The common name "incense-cedar" acknowledges the aromatic wood, which is used for making "mothproof" hope chests, and the leaves, which give off a pungent odor when crushed. The wood is soft, lightweight, and very rot-resistant. Incense-cedar has been used extensively for exterior siding because it doesn't shrink or warp and holds paint well, in addition to being durable. Rich color, sound knots, and fragrance make the wood popular for interior paneling and woodwork. "Pecky cedar" boards from trees with pocket dry rot have been favored for decorative paneling and backyard fencing. Incense-cedar wood is ideally suited to the manufacture of pencils because it is soft and easily whittled without splintering, and it has straight grain. Top-grade incense-cedar lumber once supplied much of the world's pencils.

Incense-cedar is a popular ornamental tree in temperate regions of the northern hemisphere, including western and central Europe. In cultivation, free from drought stress and competition, it is fast-growing, attractive, and trouble-free.

WHAT IS A "CEDAR"?

North Americans use the name "cedar" for various trees of the cypress family that have lacey foliage made up of small, scalelike leaves. In contrast, true cedars, genus *Cedrus*, are needle-leaved trees that belong to the pine family and are native to the Old World, including the cedar of Lebanon *(C. libani)* and Himalayan cedar *(C. deodara)*, a common ornamental west of the Cascades. Because our "cedars" are not true cedars, their common names require prefixes—for example, incense-cedar and western redcedar. One similarity between our "cedars" and true cedars is that both are valued for their durable and fragrant wood.

WESTERN REDCEDAR

Thuja plicata, Cypress family—Cupressaceae

Western redcedar is an icon of the Northwestern forest, beloved for its majesty, beauty, and excellent wood. This tree's sturdy trunk, covered with fibrous bark, supports the distinctive, light-green canopy made up of drooping, fernlike sprays. It is the Northwest's common cedar and is native only to our region. It is abundant west of the Cascades as well as in moist inland areas. It achieves gargantuan proportions through tenacity, by surviving longer than its competitors even while much of its trunk and crown is dying.

To Native peoples of the Northwest coast, this was the revered tree that provided shelter, clothing, and the means for obtaining and preparing food and whose spirit was addressed as "Long Life Maker" (Stewart 1984). Explorers Lewis and Clark were delighted to discover this tree, so suitable for dugout canoes, when they finally reached the headwaters of the Columbia River in what is now northern Idaho. They recognized it as "arbor vitae"—Latin for "tree of life"—by the similarity to its smaller eastern relative, northern white-cedar (*Thuja occidentalis*). It became known as "giant arborvitae," appropriately, since it forms the largest trees in coastal and inland forests of the Northwest.

Where It Grows

Western redcedar inhabits all but the driest areas west of the Cascade crest and north of Oregon's Rogue River drainage. It extends southward along a narrow coastal strip about 100 miles (160 km) into California. It spreads northward through coastal British Columbia and into the southeastern tip of the Alaska Panhandle. It also occupies the moist inland region west of the Continental Divide from the vicinity of Grangeville in north-central Idaho to Prince George in central British Columbia, including northeastern Washington and northwestern Montana. It is designated as British Columbia's official tree. In the coastal Northwest, it grows mainly between sea level and 3500 feet (1100 m) elevation but extends somewhat higher in southwestern Oregon and up to about 5000 feet (1500 m) in Idaho.

Western redcedar is characteristically a tree of moist habitats and areas with a cool, wet climate. It is usually found where annual precipitation averages well over 30 inches (750 mm), and it thrives in valleys receiving 60 to 120 inches (1500 to 3000 mm). In relatively dry areas west of the Cascades, western redcedar becomes abundant only in wet sites such as in ravines, along streams, or on poorly drained bottomlands. Near its range limits in inland mountains, it grows almost exclusively in narrow canyons where its roots are irrigated all summer by a mountain stream.

Appearance

Young western redcedars grow straight and tall but are conspicuously lighter green than associated conifers. The oldest branchlets turn orange-brown before being shed in autumn, giving the trees a mottled, two-toned appearance. The young tree develops a broad, pyramidal canopy consisting of long, spreading branches supporting a profusion of lacy sprays. The flattened sprays droop gracefully from lower limbs that sweep out and down nearly to the ground. As a tree matures, its lower trunk swells and its buttresses connect to large, shallow roots. As centuries pass, the original top is damaged by windstorms, and branches ascend like upswept arms to take its place, eventually forming a multiforked crown of living and dead leaders. The trunk,

damaged by fire and decay, becomes hollow; but still the tree survives.

Ancient western redcedars in moist valleys west of the Cascades and British Columbia Coast Range often stand 8 to 10 feet (2.4 to 3 m) thick and 200 feet (60 m) tall. Trees in sheltered valleys of northern Idaho are nearly as large. Record-sized redcedars 18 to 19.5 feet (5.5 to 5.9 m) in diameter grow along the western coast of Washington and Vancouver Island (Van Pelt 2001). They have broken, many-forked, living and dead tops, and most are 150 to 180 feet (45 to 55 m) tall. Because of their great bulk and heart rot, these behemoths are virtually impossible to age, but they are estimated to be 1,000 years old or older. These gigantic redcedars differ in growth form from record-sized trees of other northwestern conifers, which often have a broken top but not the complex, many-branched trunk.

The trunk of a mature western redcedar is covered with gray-brown bark, ridged and

western redcedar in low-elevation moist forest habitat

western redcedar foliage and cones: close-up and cross section

fissured into an interlacing network of vertical fibrous strips. The bark is very thin but tough and can be peeled in long, narrow strips. The foliage consists of flat, lacy branchlets made up of scalelike leaves only about ⅛ inch (3 mm) long and pressed tightly against the twigs. Redcedar boughs give off a pleasant aromatic smell.

The fernlike sprays droop gracefully from long branches and often bear great quantities of tiny brown cones. These are about ½ inch (12 mm) long, stand upright, and are shaped like miniature roses in bud. The cones bear seeds so small—averaging roughly 400,000 per pound (880,000 per kg)—that rodents seldom bother to eat them. Western redcedar seed crops can be prodigious—up to 1 million seeds per acre (2.5 million per ha)—in mixed coastal forests containing this species.

Ecological Role

In coastal lowland forests, western redcedar seeds can germinate in fall, winter, or spring, producing an immense crop of new seedlings. Still, fungi, birds, insects, strong sunlight (lethal heating), surface soil drought, and smothering by fallen leaves of deciduous shrubs and trees take a heavy toll. Partial shade is considered beneficial for successful seedling establishment.

Western redcedar also reproduces vegetatively via three methods. Layering occurs when lower branches of existing trees are pressed against the ground (for instance, by a fallen trunk) and take root. Uprooted, fallen trees can produce a row of new trees arising from their branches. Also, live branches that break off and land on moist ground can take root. These vegetative saplings, termed "veglings," are more abundant in mature Idaho redcedar groves than is seed-produced regeneration (Habeck 1978).

Western redcedar is more tolerant of shade than its principal associates except western hemlock and Pacific silver fir. Because of its greater size and longevity, it can persist indefinitely in undisturbed old forests despite competition from hemlock. However, western redcedar seldom dominates stands except those on very wet soils where hemlock and most other conifers do poorly. In mucky soils along mountain streams, redcedar reigns supreme, forming majestic groves of giant trees with fluted butts accompanied by a luxuriant undergrowth of sprawling vine maple, tall shrubs, robust lady ferns (*Athyrium filix-femina*), devil's club (*Oplopanax horridum*), and, sometimes, skunk cabbage (*Lysichitum americanum*). Devil's club, frequent in redcedar groves and well known to hikers, has stout stems and huge maplelike leaves armed with vicious, easily detached spines. Splendid redcedar groves occupy isolated wet habitats as far inland as Glacier National Park, Montana.

Unlike giant sequoias, redwood, and coastal Douglas-fir, veteran western redcedars do not owe their long-term survival to thick bark that insulates them from surface fires. Giant redcedars often escape fire, as do Sitka spruce, by occupying sodden habitats that rarely burn, but redcedars also extend into drier, fire-prone territory, especially in the Rockies. There, despite thin bark and shallow roots, ancient redcedars survive surface fires by their remarkable tenacity and decay resistance. In northern Idaho, many old redcedars have scars from two or more fires that girdled part of their circumference. Sometimes a tree several feet thick remains alive, nurtured by only a narrow strip of bark and underlying cambium that survived fires and fungi. The heartwood owes its legendary decay-resistance to a natural fungicide.

Many kinds of animals, including hibernating bears, reside in hollow redcedars. In the Rockies, any redcedar foliage within reach is eagerly devoured in winter by deer, elk, and moose.

Human History

Hillary Stewart's (1984) book, *Cedar*, explains how this tree provided a bountiful life for Na-

tives of the Northwest Coast. When a baby was born, it was placed on a cradle of firmly woven cedar roots, with a mattress and diapers of soft, shredded cedar bark. The mother wore a cedar-bark hat, cape, and skirt to protect her from rain and cold. The people used baskets woven from long, slender cedar twigs and roots. They boiled fish, clams, and other foods by placing fire-heated rocks in water-tight boxes fashioned from steamed, bent cedar "planks." Large cedar-wood boxes or root baskets were used to store foods for winter. Western redcedar also served many medicinal needs and has the most extensive catalog of uses by Native peoples among all North American plants (Moerman 1998).

Planks of various sizes and thicknesses were split by expert insertion of wedges into trunks of living or dead redcedar trees. Planks, poles, posts, and logs of cedar were used to

Oceangoing western redcedar dugout canoe at the American Museum of Natural History in New York.

construct their houses. In 1808 explorer Simon Fraser described a cedar-plank longhouse near present-day Vancouver, British Columbia, as being 650 feet (200 m) long by 60 feet (18 m) broad, under one roof, and containing apartments for families (Stewart 1984). Outside the house would stand a tall carved cedar memorial pole (totem pole) chronicling the family lineage and spiritual symbols.

Native peoples fashioned dugout canoes of many sizes from the trunk of a western redcedar. Cedar canoes would carry the people along rivers and out into the salt water to fish for salmon or even whales. Cedar was also used to make the nets and harpoons. A gigantic ocean-going cedar canoe housed at the American Museum of Natural History in New York is 64 feet long (19.5 m) and 8 feet wide (2.4 m), with a bow over 7 feet high (2.2 m) for throwing off high waves (Stewart 1984).

Pioneer settlers soon recognized many values of western redcedar as well. A few made temporary dwellings out of gigantic stumps. In 1898 Thomas Stringham, a settler in the Elwha River valley west of Port Angeles, Washington, made a family home and U.S. post office (McDonald, Washington) out of a redcedar stump on his property. The tree, which had been hollowed out by decay and fires, had been logged to a very tall stump. Stringham cut a doorway on one side and built a roof of cedar shakes.

Another traditional and modern use of redcedar is for kindling. In the rain-soaked Northwest, firestarter is often a critical need, which cedar fills easily and abundantly. Many a wet, cold camper has been thankful to find a fallen redcedar and the surefire kindling that its trunk offers. The ease of splitting redcedar wood along flat planes continues to make hand-split cedar shakes prized for a durable, natural roof. A major caveat attends such an application, however. The roof is in effect made of kindling that can burn rapidly if a firebrand (from a woodstove or nearby forest fire) lands on it! Demand for western redcedar shakes and rot-resistant fence posts and rails is so great that partially rotten butt-sections left in logging slash command a good price, and "cedar poaching" of scattered live trees or even of marketable logging slash has long been an illicit trade.

Western redcedar's wood is prized for many special uses. It is soft, weak, and brittle but quite resistant to decay; it is also fragrant and lightweight and has an attractive orange-brown color. It is easy to carve and work with tools. Used as paneling indoors or outside and sheltered from rain and sun, it requires no stain or finish, although it takes stain readily. Redcedar is also used for utility poles, house logs, decking, picnic tables, clothes closets, and clothes chests. Redcedar leaf oil is used in perfumes, insecticides, deodorants, and many other products.

Western redcedar is a handsome tree in cultivation, limbed to the ground, with long, sweeping boughs. Unlike many conifers, when pruned it sprouts new foliage (epicormic branches) along the trunk, and thus when it is trimmed properly, it can make an excellent hedge.

Although Native people regarded western redcedar as a gift from the creator, Euro-American society has often taken it for granted. Unlike other associated valuable trees such as coastal Douglas-fir and western white pine in Idaho, western redcedar is not easily propagated by planting it in logged areas. It often seeds in and regenerates naturally among the planted species, but in recent decades, more foresters want to ensure that it gets reestablished after logging. There is also a growing trend to spare and protect old redcedars in harvesting operations on public and commercial forestlands. This practice can retain an important feature in the ecosystem and provide an additional seed source for regenerating the "tree of life."

YELLOW-CEDAR

Xanthocyparis nootkatensis or *Callitropsis nootkatensis*,
Cypress family—Cupressaceae

Yellow-cedar is the tree with a graceful, drooping form that inhabits the snowbound subalpine terrain of the Northwest's high coastal mountains, including the western Cascades. In contrast to western redcedar, which it replaces at high elevations, yellow-cedar's foliage is dark bluish green and hangs limp, giving the tree a weeping appearance. But this species is not fragile. It colonizes exposed, rocky summits at the limit of trees, where it forms sprawling, shrublike *krummholz*. In cold, wet subalpine basins, it sometimes develops into a large tree over the course of a millennium or longer. Although it occupies remote mountain sites, yellow-cedar can also be seen growing as an ornamental in cities west of the Cascades. No doubt it is chosen for its interesting appearance and conveniently slow growth, which is nevertheless faster in cultivation than in its native habitat. Its wood is prized for many special purposes, including boat-building.

Identification difficulties. Both the common and scientific names of the tree we call "yellow-cedar" are debatable. It wasn't always so. For more than 150 years, yellow-cedar was considered to belong to the genus *Chamaecyparis*, commonly known as false cypress. Suddenly, with the dawn of a new millennium, its identity is in tumult. In 2000, genetic evidence indicated that it belongs with true cypresses—genus *Cupressus*. The following year, a new conifer similar to it was discovered in Vietnam. This triggered further analysis of species' characteristics and historical nomenclature. It now appears that yellow-cedar will be in a new genus called either *Xanthocyparis* or *Callitropsis*, but that won't be decided until the International Botanical Congress convenes in 2011.

Meanwhile, the common name is also in flux. The U.S. Forest Service calls it Alaska-cedar, while Canadians refer to it as yellow cypress, yellow-cedar, or Nootka cypress—the latter in recognition of its discovery at Nootka Sound on Vancouver Island. Its cones are like those of cypress, but its large size and flattened, lacy foliage fits a Northwest concept of cedar. Moreover, cypresses are primarily found in warm, seasonally dry climates, whereas this tree is restricted to cold, wet environments. Yellow-cedar is a historic name used in the lumber trade, based on the color of the wood, and it seems as appropriate as any.

Where It Grows

Yellow-cedar is abundant in the coastal mountain ranges of southeastern Alaska and British Columbia, in the Olympic Mountains, and in the Cascades as far south as Mount Rainier (Antos and Zobel 1986). It is only intermittently common southward as far as the headwaters of the Willamette River in Oregon's west-central Cascades. Widely dispersed groves can be found farther south in the western Cascades, but the species is rare along the Cascade crest in southern Oregon, apparently because of the droughty, deep pumice soils. Small yellow-cedars are also found in some exceptionally rocky sites in the Siskiyous on both sides of the Oregon-California border.

This species thrives in a cold, wet maritime climate where annual precipitation exceeds 60 inches (1500 mm), winter snowfall accumulates to great depths, and trees are seldom exposed to temperatures much below 0 degrees F (−18 C). In the northern part of its range in coastal Alaska, it grows from tidewater to

timberline, which is only 2000 to 2500 feet (600 to 750 m) in elevation. However, south of Juneau, it occurs at increasingly high elevations. From southwestern British Columbia to western Oregon, it is usually found between 2500 and 6500 feet (750 and 2000 m). However, in southern Oregon it seems to require wet, sheltered sites and rarely ascends to the highest ridges and peaks.

Yellow-cedar is one of the few Northwestern conifers that is restricted to the Pacific coast mountains and does not occur even in the wettest ranges east of the Cascades. However, there are a couple of interesting exceptions to this pattern. A small grove of yellow-cedar occupies a cool ravine at 5500 feet (1700 m) in the semi-arid Aldrich Mountains near John Day in central Oregon. Also, the species is reported near Evans Lake northwest of Nelson, British Columbia, about 150 miles (240 km) east of the Cascades. These remarkably isolated groves may be remnants of more extensive yellow-cedar populations that occupied the inland mountains during the last major Ice Age, when a cooler, wetter climate prevailed (Frenkel 1974).

Appearance

Young yellow-cedars, including most of those planted horticulturally, have a slender, lanky form. The sparse branches support lacy sprays that droop; the tree's leader also droops. As the trees mature, they develop a denser pyramidal canopy. After a few centuries, many trees suffer dieback of the tip and upper crown branches and then exhibit a ragged appearance. In all growth forms, the limp foliage remains a distinguishing characteristic.

Yellow-cedars are commonly small to medium-sized trees, as a result of their slow growth rate and the cold, unproductive habitat. Occasionally, however, in sheltered subalpine ravines and basins, this species attains astounding dimensions over the course of 1000

years or more. Four record-sized yellow-cedars on Vancouver Island and the Olympic Peninsula measure 11 to 13.5 feet (3.5 to 4 m) in diameter and 130 to 200 feet (40 to 60 m) tall despite dead, broken tops (Van Pelt 2001).

Yellow-cedar saplings are covered with thin purplish bark that is relatively smooth. Mature trees have shaggy gray bark that hangs in loose, rough pieces or flakes but will not peel off in long strips as does western redcedar bark.

The flat, fernlike sprays of yellow-cedar are made up of tiny scalelike leaves—about $\frac{1}{8}$ inch (3 mm) long—that are commonly dark bluish green. In contrast to the smooth, scalelike leaves of western redcedar, yellow-cedar's leaves have sharp, spreading tips that make them seem prickly when stroked backward. The leaves survive for two years and then turn yellow to rusty brown. Since they are not shed for another year, they often give the tree a yellowish or brownish tinge.

Yellow-cedar cones are easy to identify. They are round and about $\frac{1}{3}$ inch (8 mm) in diameter. The first year, they are green and berrylike with a bumpy surface. They mature at the end of the second growing season,

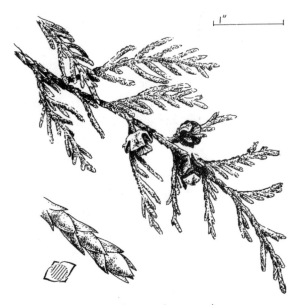

yellow-cedar foliage and cones: close-up and cross section

yellow-cedar cone   *western redcedar cone*

becoming tan and woody and separating into four to six shield-shaped scales with fissures in between that harbor the seeds. Each scale has a knob or horn on top. The woody cones cling to the sprays long after they shed seeds. The seeds are small but also have small wings and thus do not disperse very far from the parent tree. A small percentage of seeds is viable, and vegetative reproduction of yellow-cedar is also rather limited, except near tree line.

Ecological Role

Yellow-cedar is relatively shade tolerant but apparently less tolerant than its principal competitors, mountain hemlock and Pacific silver fir. It is very slow growing and is unable to colonize as broad a range of habitats as the above competitors or subalpine fir. As a result, yellow-cedar has a limited distribution in the Northwest's mountains, becoming common only where competition from other species is less intense: in very cold and wet sites, in bogs, in avalanche chutes, on rocky crags, and at the upper limit of trees.

Although yellow-cedar and western redcedar have many similar growth characteristics and site preferences, in southernmost British Columbia, Washington, and Oregon, they seldom grow together to any extent (Antos and Zobel 1986). Instead, the lower limit of yellow-cedar corresponds closely with the upper limit of western redcedar, which appears to be controlled by cold temperatures. The most consistent characteristic of yellow-cedar populations in the Northwest is their proximity to

higher-elevation sites that lack a closed forest. Yellow-cedar is abundant in southeastern Alaska on extensive areas of swamp and bedrock.

The species' flexible and drooping branches may be advantageous for preventing damage from heavy accumulations of snow and for surviving snow slides without breaking, unlike the more brittle firs. Even as *krummholz* above the limit of erect trees, the flexible branchlets may be less likely to be scoured off in ice-blasting gales than the stiff twigs of subalpine fir.

Yellow-cedar *krummholz* is quite remarkable. One circular *krummholz* cushion on Mount Angeles in Washington's Olympic National Park is about 50 feet (15 m) across and barely 3 feet (1 m) tall. This elfin tree has a hollow center, like a "timber atoll" of subalpine fir, and it undoubtedly has survived many centuries in this hostile environment. A large, living root, partially exposed by erosion, leads 75 feet (22 m) across the steep mountainside from another *krummholz* yellow-cedar before this anchor and lifeline submerges into the rocky substrate.

The extreme durability of yellow-cedar wood allows *krummholz* as well as erect trees of this species to survive longer than other species. At least three different chemical components of yellow-cedar's heartwood are toxic to fungi, allowing many of these trees to achieve ages of 1500 years or more, as confirmed by counts of annual growth rings (Van Pelt 2001).

Yellow-cedars sustain relatively little damage from insects and diseases, although over their prolonged life span, large trees may become hollowed out by heart rot. Since the late 1800s, large expanses of this species on boggy ground in Alaska have suffered dieback and outright mortality, evidently due to some unknown factor of climate or the physical environment.

The durability of the wood is exemplified by the old fire-killed snags along the road to Paradise in Mount Rainier National Park. Some of these were cut early in park history and milled into fine lumber for building desks, tables, and other features inside Paradise Inn and the Administration Building at Longmire. The snags furnished beautiful, light yellow wood even though they had weathered in the cold, wet climate for almost fifty years.

Human History

Native peoples who lived along the coast of what is now northwestern Washington, British Columbia, and Alaska used yellow-cedar wood for many purposes, including canoe paddles. It is fine-grained, even-textured, easy to carve, harder, and stronger than western redcedar and not so prone to splitting. However, south of the Queen Charlotte Islands, it was nowhere near as abundant and accessible as redcedar or as available in large sizes suitable for dugout canoes. The inner bark of yellow-cedar is tougher than that of redcedar and was highly valued for making baskets and clothing. Hilary Stewart (1984) describes the painstaking preparations, including repeated soaking and beating, of the inner bark so that it could be processed into thread used in weaving fine blankets and capes. Both yellow-cedar and western redcedar were first described in 1793 by the Scottish naturalist Archibald Menzies, who accompanied Captain George Vancouver.

Besides being rot resistant and durable, yellow-cedar wood has other admirable qualities. Its fine, even grain makes it excellent for woodworking. It is lightweight but relatively strong and stiff, and it shrinks very little upon drying. It polishes nicely and has long been prized for ornamental carpentry in Japan, where most of today's limited harvest of high-quality logs, from Alaska and British Columbia, is shipped.

In 1955, as a youngster growing up on the shores of Puget Sound, I asked a traditional Norwegian boatbuilder in our neighborhood to make me a small, swift rowboat. For this little craft, the old artisan had me order clear boards of yellow-cedar at the local lumberyard. Beautiful yellow-cedar boards were available at a modest price, which I doubt would be the case today!

PORT ORFORD-CEDAR

Chamaecyparis lawsoniana, Cypress family—Cupressaceae

Port Orford-cedar is a paradox. Although it has a very small geographic distribution, within that limited area it occupies wet and dry habitats from sea level to high in the mountains. Along Oregon's southern coast, it was once the pride of the lumber industry, but today some sleuthing is necessary to find it. On the other hand, its more than 200 horticultural varieties grace parks and gardens throughout much of the world.

This species is a beautiful cedar with a pyramidal form and lacy, feathery foliage. On good sites along the Oregon coast, it was part of a mixed forest described by nineteenth-century observers as having no equal in variety of magnificent trees and luxuriant undergrowth. Its highly valued wood spurred exploitation of the most accessible and productive stands, but since the 1950s an introduced disease has decimated much of the remaining Port Orford-cedar. Still, some of these highly prized trees survive, and today better understanding of the disease gives us the opportunity to begin restoring this special feature of the northwestern forest.

Where It Grows

Port Orford-cedar occupies the Pacific coast from Coos Bay, Oregon, to northern Humboldt County, California, a distance of only 200 miles (320 km). In Oregon, it grows from near sea level to about 5000 feet (1500 m) in elevation. It is most abundant on uplifted terraces a few miles inland from the ocean and in the coastal mountains of southern Coos County and northern Curry County, Oregon, particularly in the South Fork of the Coquille River drainage. A secondary concentration is found at high elevations in the Illinois and Klamath river drainages near the Oregon-California border. Throughout the rest of its range, it is found in small, scattered populations in mountain forests as far inland as Oregon Caves National Monument and Interstate 5, south of Weed, California.

Appearance

Vigorous, young Port Orford-cedars have a regular conical form composed of thick foliage extending to the ground. Their fine, lacy branchlets droop just at their tips, giving the canopy a distinctive feathery appearance. Large old trees have silvery brown, fibrous bark 6 to 10 inches (15 to 25 cm) thick at the base and divided into wide, vertical ridges separated by deep, uneven furrows. The historic five-story chateau at Oregon Caves National Monument is sided with Port Orford-cedar bark. This species' occasional associate, incense-cedar, has thick orange-brown bark while another companion, western redcedar, has very thin bark. Large old Port Orford-cedars have branch-free lower trunks, irregular crowns, and, often, dead tops. The largest known living trees are mostly 8 to 9 feet (2.4 to 2.7 m) thick and more than 200 feet (60 m) tall (Van Pelt 2001), but many trees this size or larger were no doubt cut long ago. Very large trees attain ages of 500 to 600 years.

Port Orford-cedar's foliage differs in several ways from associated western redcedar and incense-cedar. Its twigs and lacy sprays are much finer, its scalelike leaves being barely $1/16$ inch (1.5 mm) long, only half as long as other Northwest cedars. The tips of these tiny leaves are pressed against the twig, not flaring out like those of yellow-cedar. Leaves on the underside of sprays often have a distinct and unique white X pattern. The sprays are very flat and horizontal, unlike the vertical sprays

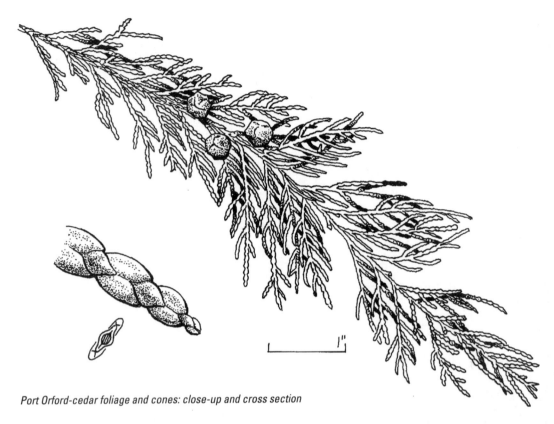

Port Orford-cedar foliage and cones: close-up and cross section

of incense-cedar, but feathery and drooping at the tips. In sunlight, the foliage appears shiny bright green on the upper side, unlike the yellow-green of western redcedar.

Port Orford-cedar cones are round and with shield-shaped scales like cones of yellow-cedar, but they mature in just one season. The tiny seeds, despite having small wings on both sides, apparently fall more rapidly than many larger conifer seeds. The seed wings appear to aid flotation on water, an interesting characteristic for a tree commonly found along streams in dry mountains inland from the ocean.

Ecological Role

Few North American trees have natural distributions anywhere near as small as that of Port Orford-cedar. Usually, other trees that are confined to small areas are also limited to cer-

tain habitats, such as bogs, subalpine areas, or particular geologic substrates. In contrast, Port Orford-cedar occupies a broad range of habitats, comparable to coastal Douglas-fir, and yet it is abundant in very few of them.

We can understand this species better by looking at the place where it grows best. Historical accounts describe the largest, most productive populations of Port Orford-cedar extending southward about 50 miles (80 km) from Coos Bay to the community of Port Orford and spreading 12 miles or so (20 km) inland. The area consists of uplifted terraces and low hills along the lower, western slopes of the Coast Range. Huge old Port Orford-cedars grew here on deep soils weathered from sedimentary rocks. They were mixed with Sitka spruce, western hemlock, western redcedar, white fir, and Douglas-fir. Remaining old Port Orford-cedars

Opposite: Port Orford-cedar in Curry County, Oregon, from American Lumberman, November 11, 1911. (Supplied by Robert Van Pelt)

often have multiple fire scars, suggesting that, like coastal Douglas-fir, thick bark allowed them to survive repeated surface fires in past centuries. The species also regenerates in abundance on logged or burned forest land. It is considered shade tolerant, but less so than accompanying western hemlock and white fir, which can outcompete and eventually replace it. Outside of the lowlands from Coos Bay to Port Orford, this species is widespread but occurs mostly in small, scattered populations.

Insufficient water appears to be a very important factor limiting the Port Orford-cedar's distribution (Zobel and others 1985). It is abundant and productive only where climate is consistently moist and soils are deep and well-drained. Near the ocean, where there is a persistent flow of moist air, it can occupy relatively dry soils. In the drier climate farther inland, it can also survive if its roots can tap a shallow water table that supplies moisture throughout most of the growing season. To complicate matters, the underground water may need to be fresh—or at least not stagnant.

Port Orford-cedar's regional restriction seems also related to a mild year-round temperature regime (Zobel and others 1985). One theory has it that as climate has generally dried over the last 60 million years, the species range has become restricted to a small area with the best remaining combination of climatic moisture and temperatures. If its narrow moisture and temperature requirements are met, the species can tolerate virtually any kind of soil or substrate, from sand dunes to bogs, deep productive soils, and marginally toxic serpentine rocks.

But why does Port Orford-cedar's optimal development occur at the northern edge of its distribution? Also, why can this species, which has such exacting habitat requirements, prosper in much of the world in countless cultivated forms? Clearly, there are more questions than answers about Port Orford-cedar.

The fabled old-growth Port Orford-cedar forest south of Coos Bay fell to concentrated logging and severe wildfires in 1867 and 1868 (Zobel and others 1985). A 1936 wildfire and a devastating root disease killed much of the second growth. Individual big old Port Orford-cedars still stand in the Coquille River drainage south of Powers, Oregon, and in several scattered locations southward into California (Van Pelt 2001). Untouched small groves inhabit draws in the Kalmiopsis Wilderness, which stretches along 30 miles (50 km) of the Coast Range east of Gold Beach and Brookings, Oregon.

Port Orford-cedar is little affected by native insects and diseases, but a root rot caused by the fungus *Phytophthora lateralis* has plagued the tree since the fungus was accidentally introduced into the forest in the early 1950s after having arrived in the Northwest on nursery stock. The root rot attacks only Port Orford-cedar, which has no known genetic resistance, and it kills most trees of all sizes. The disease has spread through most of the tree's natural range, but some isolated groves in the Coast Range seem to have escaped infection so far. The disease spreads via spores transported in water or in mud on machinery or on the feet of people or animals. Further expansion of the root rot on public lands is being fought by limiting and regulating vehicles and equipment, including the cleaning of equipment before entry. Detailed recommendations for control of root rot in forest settings are available at a U.S. Forest Service website (*www.fs.fed.us/r6 /nr/fid/fidls/poc*).

Human History

Probably because Port Orford-cedar is restricted to such a small area, whereas associated western redcedar and incense-cedar are widespread and abundant, there is little record of aboriginal use of this species. This situation changed dramatically after European Americans discovered the forest of Port Orford-cedar near Coos Bay in the 1850s (Peattie 1950). Excellent properties of the wood soon propelled a booming export market. Early on, schooners anchored off the rocky, wind-battered coast that had no harbors. Cedar logs were then hauled along a high-line cable from the cliffs to the ship's wave-tossed deck—surely a dramatic scene!

The wood has a pungent, gingerlike odor caused by a volatile oil that renders it highly resistant to damage from decay or insects, including termites. Its oil was used as an insecticide. Remarkably, untreated pilings and posts of this species exposed to salt water have remained sound for several decades. The outstanding wood qualities are similar to those of yellow-cedar, but Port Orford-cedar was readily available in much larger, branch-free stems. It was highly valued for boatbuilding, and Sir Thomas Lipton (a tea magnate and America's Cup challenger) ordered all his racing yachts built from this species (Peattie 1950). It became the principal wood used to separate cells in storage batteries because of its electrical and acid resistance. It was used for Venetian blinds and many other special purposes. Eventually, nearly all better grades of logs were shipped to Asia, where *Chamaecyparis* is highly valued for caskets and temples.

The species' scientific name *lawsoniana* honors Sir Charles Lawson, a Scot who raised the first nursery seedlings from seeds sent him in 1854. In the ornamental trade, the tree is still known as Lawson cypress, and it is available in a myriad of showy ornamental varieties, including columnar forms with golden-tipped foliage. For all their popularity, however, these cultivated forms pale in comparison to the luxuriant and mysterious Port Orford-cedars growing in the wild.

JUNIPERS

Juniperus, Cypress family—Cupressaceae

Junipers include about sixty species of small trees and shrubs that populate some of the harshest sites throughout the northern hemisphere. From the scorching hills of North Africa to the Arctic tundra in Greenland, junipers make up in rugged hardiness what they lack in arborescent grandeur. Three species of arboreal juniper are native to the Greater Northwest; they are bushy little trees, typically 15 to 30 feet (5 to 9 m) tall on dry sites, with irregular canopies made up of foliage with tiny, scalelike leaves. Their branches radiate foliage from all sides rather than forming flat sprays like our "cedars" (western redcedar, etc.). Our western juniper (*J. occidentalis*), Rocky Mountain juniper (*J. scopulorum*), and Utah juniper (*J. osteosperma*) are adapted to the cold desert, being highly resistant to drought and extreme temperatures. They colonize parts of the sagebrush-grasslands on the Columbia Plateau and eastward beyond the Rockies, and they spread into the driest ponderosa pine and Douglas-fir forests.

In addition to the tree junipers, two species of shrubby juniper also inhabit the Greater Northwest. Matlike common juniper (*J. communis*), with small, prickly, needlelike leaves in whorls of three, is widespread in Northwest forests and woodlands, while the ground-hugging horizontal juniper (*J. horizontalis*), with small, scalelike leaves, is found mostly on stony sites along the east slope of the Rockies.

Where They Grow

Western juniper makes up the dwarf woodland that covers much of central and eastern Oregon. It extends north into the arid canyons along the Columbia and Snake rivers in southern Washington and eastward into the Owyhee Uplands of southwestern Idaho, and it is abundant southward in northeastern California.

Rocky Mountain juniper is the native juniper tree commonly found in most other dry regions of the Northwest. This species is widespread from New Mexico north through Idaho and Montana to central British Columbia and southwestern Alberta. However, it is scarce in

common juniper

Oregon and sporadic in Washington, noted locally near the Columbia River from Chelan to Vantage. Perhaps surprisingly, this arid-land tree inhabits one area of the Northwest Coast: scattered dry sites in the rain shadow formed by the Olympic Mountains, including the San Juan Islands, and northward along the Strait of Georgia.

Utah juniper is a Southwestern tree that extends north into eastern Idaho, overlapping with the more common Rocky Mountain juniper south of the Snake River and northward in the vicinity of Arco.

Comparative Appearance

All three of these junipers typically form ragged, bushy trees with canopies extending near the ground and commonly less than 40 feet (12 m) tall. The trunk is often divided into two or more stems near the base. On better sites, they can grow bigger, occasionally more than 30 inches (75 cm) in diameter and 50 feet (15 m) tall. Some junipers on rocky sites that have escaped fire live for several centuries. (A different variety of western juniper that grows high in the Sierra Nevada can live more than 1000 years and attain diameters of more than 6 feet [1.8 m].) The irregularly shaped trunks are covered with thin, fibrous bark that is divided into flat, interlacing ridges. The bark is reddish brown or grayish and hangs in loose vertical strips.

Juniper foliage is at first confusing, since individual trees have two kinds of leaves. Mature trees have mostly tiny, overlapping, scalelike leaves, but juvenile shoots and especially saplings are largely covered with prickly, ½-inch-long (12-mm-long) awl-like leaves. The scalelike leaves are best for identification. Juniper "berries" are technically berrylike cones. Although they are fleshy, they have the vestiges of cone scales etched into their surfaces. Immature juniper berries are green with a white, waxy bloom.

Western juniper. The scalelike leaves are arranged in whorls of three on the twigs. Foliage of western juniper is thick and stiff. Mature berries of western juniper are silvery blue and about ¼ inch (6 mm) in diameter.

Rocky Mountain juniper. The scalelike leaves are arranged opposite each other in pairs. Foliage (ultimate branchlets) of Rocky Mountain juniper is very fine. Like western juniper, mature berries of Rocky Mountain juniper are silvery blue and about ¼ inch (6 mm) in diameter.

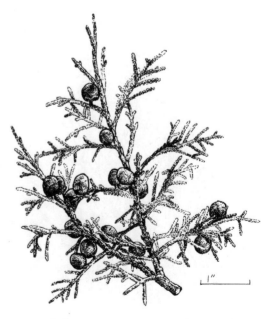

western juniper

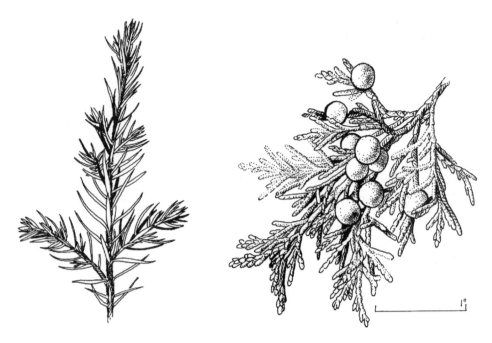

Rocky Mountain juniper: juvenile shoot; mature foliage and cones

Utah juniper. The scalelike leaves are arranged opposite each other in pairs. Foliage of Utah juniper, like that of western juniper, is thick and stiff. Mature berries of Utah juniper are silvery brown and ⅜ to ½ inch (9 to 12 mm) thick.

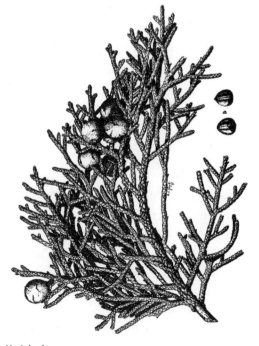

Utah juniper

Ecological Role

Juniper trees are abundant on rocky sites in some of the driest areas of the inland Northwest. Like ponderosa pine, they readily establish deep root systems among the rocks, where they also avoid having to compete with extensive fibrous root systems of grasses and other herbs. Western juniper can survive in places receiving as little as 8 inches (200 mm) of precipitation in the average year, such as the Sahara-like Juniper Dunes Wilderness, administered by the Bureau of Land Management, northeast of Pasco, Washington. Rocky Mountain juniper requires only about 10 inches (250 mm) of rainfall, and this tree occupies dry ravines in arid badland topography, including the Missouri River Breaks in central Montana.

Junipers can form contiguous woodland on sites too dry for ponderosa pine or interior Douglas-fir. Southward in the Great Basin and Southwest, juniper woodland covers more area than pine and fir forests, and it contains several additional species of juniper as well as pinyon pines and a variety of desert shrubs. Northwest junipers also occupy open stands of ponderosa pine and Douglas-fir on especially dry sites, but they are unable to compete with these forest trees on better sites. Junipers can endure shade in early life, but they become very intolerant of shade as they mature and are quickly over-topped by faster-growing forest trees.

Retakes of early landscape photographs and age analysis of juniper stands demonstrate that many juniper woodlands in Oregon colo-nized former grass and sagebrush communi-ties in the late nineteenth and early twentieth centuries. Two factors underlie this expansion. Heavy livestock grazing starting in the 1860s removed native grasses and left bare soil re-ceptive to establishment of junipers. Removal of grassy fuel and, later, organized fire sup-pression kept fire out for prolonged periods. The oldest junipers, dating to before 1850, are largely restricted to extremely rocky sites where fires were very patchy or infrequent because of sparse fuel. Junipers are commonly killed by surface fires that have little effect on ponderosa pines or larger Douglas-firs.

Stands with scattered junipers or patches of them can provide diverse and productive habitat for wildlife. However, many juniper woodlands have become so extensive and dense that they greatly reduce the forage produced by native grasses and shrubs, including bitter-brush (*Purshia tridentata*). A juniper's root sys-tem radiates far beyond the tree's canopy and is able to suppress nearby grasses. Also, juni-pers produce chemical compounds that inhibit growth of surrounding vegetation, a phenom-enon called allelopathy.

The juniper's rich berries cling to the tree all winter and are attractive to a wide variety of birds, which eat them for their pulp. The seeds pass unharmed through birds' digestive tract, scarified and ready to germinate. Birds are ap-parently the principal agent for dissemination of juniper seed across the landscape. One sci-entist found that 900 Rocky Mountain juni-per berries passed through a single bohemian waxwing in five hours. Junipers are often found growing along fence lines as a result of seeds having been deposited there by perched birds.

Although juniper berries serve as food for wildlife, the foliage is normally eaten only as a last resort. Thus, thickening woodlands produce scant forage for wildlife or livestock. These find-ings have spurred interest in use of fire to thin out juniper woodlands and stimulate grasses and shrubs. This is challenging because today's stands with sparse grass are difficult to burn except un-der conditions that would produce a severe wild-fire. One alternative is to fell some of the trees (and let the foliage cure) in a pattern that creates a receptive fuel bed for prescribed fire.

Human History

Native peoples throughout the Greater North-west made extensive use of the resinous ber-ries and foliage of junipers as medicine—for instance, to treat colds, coughs, fever, pain, rheumatism, diarrhea, upset stomach, dia-betes, pneumonia, and venereal disease; to induce vomiting, aid child birth, and serve as a sedative; and as a poultice for sores (Moerman 1998). Some tribes used the berries as food, generally cooked or roasted. The fibrous bark was employed as kindling and woven into a rope that would smolder and be used for carry-ing fire when traveling. Bark and roots served in basket-making, and the tough, dense wood was used for bows and firewood.

Pioneer settlers recognized juniper's po-tential, since they were very familiar with a juniper species in the Midwest and East: *Juni-perus virginiana*, commonly called eastern red-cedar. Rocky Mountain juniper is so similar to this Midwestern kin that Lewis and Clark did not distinguish it as a new species when they encountered it while approaching the Rockies in the spring of 1805.

Juniper wood is very dense and rot resis-tant and was used extensively for fence posts and firewood. Most trunks are so small, limby, and irregular in shape that juniper wood is not sought for conventional wood products. However, some stands produce trunks large enough to provide high-value specialty wood. The outer band of sapwood is creamy white, and beneath lies the fragrant heartwood that is purplish or rosy red when freshly cut and has lovely grain patterns. This makes beautiful "cedar" chests and woodcrafts, which are available in a few localities.

Rocky Mountain juniper is widely planted in windbreaks and horticulturally in dry, rocky soils where irrigation may not be possible. Certain groves of Rocky Mountain and western juniper have trees with dense, spirelike growth forms. Horticulturists have propagated some of these attractive forms through cuttings and made them available for landscaping.

MODOC CYPRESS
Cupressus bakeri, Cypress family—Cupressaceae

Modoc or Baker cypress is a rare and intriguing tree found in small numbers at a few widely scattered sites in the inland portion of Oregon's Siskiyou region. It is slightly more common in northeastern California, ancestral home of the Modoc people. Cypresses (genus *Cupressus*) are trees of warm climates, and the Modoc cypress in Oregon appears to be the northernmost cypress in the world. Cypresses generally have foliage similar to junipers but are taller and lanky. Modoc cypress commonly has a single trunk and narrow crown 30 to 80 feet (9 to 25 m) tall. The foliage is sparser than most junipers, and trees on better sites have a narrow, pyramidal form like that of a young fir. On poor sites, the canopy is scraggly. The small, rounded, woody cones resemble those of false-cypresses—Port Orford-cedar and yellow-cedar—but are somewhat larger. On young trees, the bark is cherry red and peeling, but it becomes blocky and grayish as the tree matures.

Modoc cypress is especially interesting from an ecological viewpoint since it is adapted to and dependent on fire, much like knobcone pine. It has thin bark and is easily killed by fire, but the heat opens the closed cones on the tree and releases viable seeds onto the burned site. Also like knobcone pine, Modoc cypress is slow growing and mainly inhabits poor, rocky sites at moderately high elevations, often on serpentine rocks or lava flows. The best-known groves in Oregon are an accessible one at Miller Lake near Steve Peak in southeastern Josephine County and a more remote grove at Flounce Rock west of Prospect in Jackson County.

Tree enthusiasts traveling US 101 between Port Orford, Oregon, and the California border may by surprised at the sight of many great spreading cypress trees among the forestland and pastures. These are planted Monterey cypresses (*C. macrocarpa*), often marking old homesteads. They thrive here even though they are small and scrubby in their native home on Monterey Bay south of San Francisco.

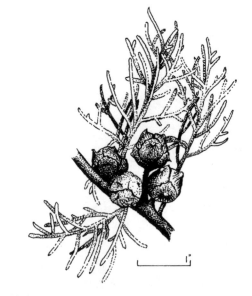

Modoc cypress

PACIFIC YEW

Taxus brevifolia, Yew family—Taxaceae

Pacific yew is unique among Northwest conifers in being an *understory* specialist, adapted to prosper in the dim light that manages to penetrate a closed canopy of spruce, redcedar, hemlock, true fir, or coastal Douglas-fir that towers high overhead. Yew is a small, spreading tree or gangly shrub that inhabits understories of moist forests in the coastal and inland Northwest, sometimes forming formidable thickets of "yew brush." It also shows up unexpectedly here and there as a result of bird-transported seeds.

Although it may seem insignificant compared to the associated forest giants, yew has some unusual connections to people and animals. Native peoples preferred the wood of Pacific yew for bows, arrows, canoe paddles, and tools because it is especially hard and resilient—just as primeval societies of Europe, and Robin Hood, employed the fabled English yew (*T. baccata*). During the 1980s and 1990s, the promise of a yew substance, Taxol, as a cancer inhibitor propelled this little tree into fame and triggered a controversial yew-bark harvest.

Yew foliage is a legendary poison, but in some Rocky Mountain forests, moose feed heavily on yew in winter, and this potent diet produces bright orange splotches in the snow where the animals urinate. Perhaps equally bizarre, and disconcerting to students in tree identification classes, yew foliage closely resembles one other western tree: the giant coastal redwood (*Sequoia sempervirens*)! (See the redwood sidebar.)

Where It Grows

Pacific yew inhabits the coastal lowlands and mountains, including the Cascades, from the southern tip of the Alaska Panhandle to the San Francisco Bay area. It is also widespread in the wettest inland mountains of southeastern British Columbia, northern Idaho, northeastern Washington, northeastern Oregon, and northwestern Montana. Small, open-grown yew trees with spreading, limby crowns and weeping branches are scattered about in rural areas west of the Cascades. West of the Cascade crest, shrubby yews sometimes occupy dry, rocky sites and avalanche chutes, where their foliage usually has an orange tinge suggesting drought stress. Very small, treelike, shrubby yews occupy the understory of moist forests at low to middle elevations west of the Cascades and in north-central Idaho. Near the species' range limits on the east slope of the Cascades, in western Montana, and the southwestern corner of Alberta, it is mostly confined to the wettest canyons and valleys at low elevations.

Appearance

I have always found it hard to consider Pacific yew as a scrubby little tree, although it often is, because as a small boy in the Puget Sound area, the first yew I came to know was stout, limby—perhaps 36 inches (90 cm) thick and 50 feet (15 m) tall—hung with 2-inch (5 cm) ivy vines and harboring my tree house. However, spindly yew trees and tall shrubs with long, irregular branches populate many forest understories. This species can be identified easily by several characteristics.

The foliage consists of flat, two-ranked needles about ²/₃ inch (17 mm) long, deep yellow-green on top and pale green underneath. (Redwood's foliage is similar, but its needles are whitish underneath.) Yew needles have slender points at their tips but are not sharp to touch. They narrow at the base into a petiole or leaf stem that then extends as a ridge along the twig. New twigs of Pacific yew remain green year-round, unlike other Northwestern conifers, but like the California redwood. Also like redwood and unlike most of our conifers, Pacific yew can grow permanent sprouts from cut stumps. The shrubby "yew brush" form spreads vegetatively through layering, the process in which lower branches take root. Yew can also be propagated from cuttings.

Pacific yew has a showy, bright-red, berry-like cone. However, they are often hard to find since birds gobble them up, which is no doubt part of a grand design for spreading this species.

This pea-sized morsel, technically called an aril, has a single seed surrounded but not enveloped by a cup-shaped, fleshy pulp. Arils and pollen cones are borne on separate female and male trees. Yew's seeds, foliage, and bark are considered poisonous, but the fleshy aril is edible and tastes like mild cherry Jell-O (Hartzell 1991; Johnson 1995). Interestingly, chipmunks and squirrels often eat the seeds and discard the reddish pulp. These rodents and some birds cache the seeds, which results in clusters of seedlings seen in some areas.

Pacific yew's bark is also distinctive. It is

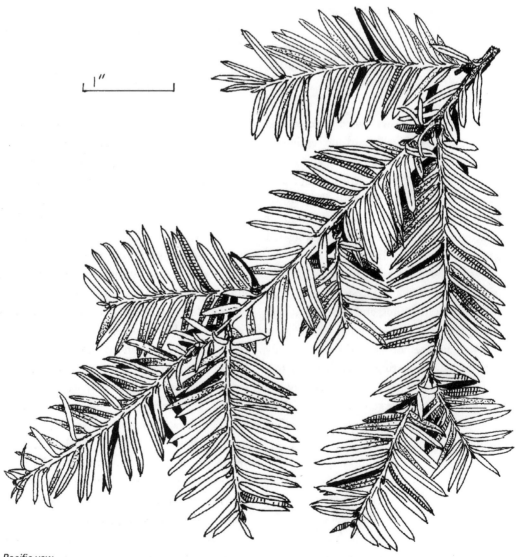

Pacific yew

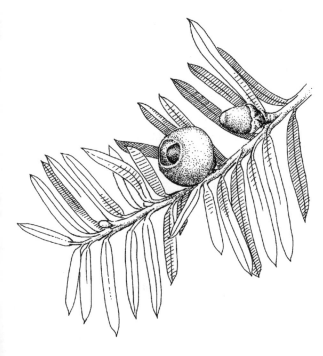

Pacific yew close-up with fruits

true fir can succeed amid the yew and become tall trees.

Pacific yew also plays the role of an opportunist, especially west of the Cascades. As birds spread its seeds in pastures or other disturbed sites in rural areas, it occasionally finds an open niche and is able to become a bushy tree, somewhat like tree junipers spread in the inland Northwest. In moist coastal mountains, shrubby yews also become established in open sites such as avalanche chutes and rocky outcrops as high as 4500 feet (1400 m) elevation in western Washington.

Human History

Even though Pacific yew, especially in tree form, is not particularly common, Native peoples sought its foliage and bark for a variety of medicinal purposes. Yew wood was highly prized for hunting equipment and tools and was traded to tribes of the interior Northwest, where it was scarce or mostly a shrub. The heartwood is bright orange to rose red when freshly cut, very fine textured, heavy, very hard but elastic, and very strong in bending and shock resistance. This exceptional wood carves fairly easily and finishes smoothly. It is also very durable when exposed to decay organisms.

Pacific yew is called "bow plant" in a number of Indian languages (Turner 1979). In addition to its well-known use for bows, arrows, and canoe paddles, yew wood was made into harpoon shafts, halibut and other fish hooks, wedges for splitting logs, digging sticks, clubs for battle and killing sea lions, pry bars, spoons, drum frames, snowshoe frames, and even arrowheads (Moerman 1998; Turner 1979). Top-grade Pacific yew logs have fetched high prices from Japanese and Taiwanese buyers, but they are not easy to locate among the small, often misshapen, limby trees. Contemporary artisans who make longbows of Pacific yew report that less than 1 percent of yew trees have the straight, knot-free grain they need.

very thin and reddish purple, and it flakes off in long, papery scales, while the new bark is rosy red.

Ecological Role

Unlike most conifers, yew thrives in the shady understory as a small tree or shrub and often suffers when the overstory canopy is removed, as in the case of clear-cut logging. The sudden exposure to full sunlight causes yew to turn yellow and die back. Then, as a new canopy of forest trees develops, yew gradually reestablishes beneath it.

West of the Cascade crest, yew propagates more slowly in the understory than many of its conifer associates. However, in some inland forests, notably in north-central Idaho, it can increase and dominate the understory (Cooper and others 1991). Occasionally, patches of tall forest die and give way to a tangle of yew that is maintained by vegetative reproduction. However, yew's constrained height growth restricts its ability to dominate any sizable area of forest. Occasional saplings of hemlock, redcedar, or

Aboriginals backed their yew bows with sinew to help absorb stress and prolong bow life, while modern bow makers laminate yew bows with layers of fiberglass to enhance durability.

Longbows made from the related English yew were a major factor in English warfare for more than 1000 years, but by late in the seventeenth century, archery was no longer viable because the natural stands of yew had been plundered (Hartzell 1991). English yew, widely planted as an ornamental in Northwest gardens, is distinguished from Pacific yew by its more luxuriant foliage and larger leaves.

In the 1990s, the specter of excessive exploitation suddenly loomed over Pacific yew, which became known as the prime source for a unique and highly valuable substance called Taxol, known in the chemical industry as paclitaxel, which inhibits ovarian and breast cancer. Soon Taxol was being extracted from the thin bark of Pacific yew stems harvested across thousands of acres of Northwestern forests and sold by the ton to pharmaceutical buyers. Forest biologists shuddered at the consequences of continuing this scale of exploitation of a small, slow-growing tree, but compelling demand was driven by a pharmaceutical giant, aided by testimony from desperate cancer patients!

Suddenly, by the year 2000, the volatile Taxol supply chain was abandoning use of wild Pacific yew. It had become clear to pharmaceutical companies that other sources were needed, and proprietary patents had run out, opening the market to worldwide competition. By 2003 Taxol was being produced from agricultural plantations of various yew species in different parts of the northern hemisphere, and the drug was also being synthesized. Thus, it appears that after a decade in the limelight and in peril, Pacific yew will drift back into safe semi-obscurity as the Northwest's little understory conifer.

REDWOOD
Sequoia sempervirens, Cypress family—Cupressaceae

Any tree spotter who travels coastal US 101 southward crossing into California will suddenly notice a new kind of giant tree scattered among the pastures and woodlands. Magnificent redwoods grace more than 400 miles (650 km) of the California coast but barely, and almost unnoticeably, extend into the southwestern corner of Oregon. Redwoods have branchlets with flat, two-ranked needles, much like Pacific yew, but with white bands on the bottom. The bark is extremely thick, fibrous, and reddish brown to cinnamon red. The trees grow rapidly to such large size that their identity becomes increasingly obvious.

The very restricted appearance of redwood north of the California border is puzzling, since some of the finest redwoods inhabit the Jedediah Smith Grove only 15 miles (24 km) southward into California. A few miles north of the border in Oregon, two redwood groves are located on the Chetco River. Here, a small grove is reached by trail from just beyond the entrance to Loeb State Park.

Redwood's distribution suggests it is not suited to the northwestern environment, but reasons behind this are unclear. In the vicinity of its northern limits, redwood no longer occupies the coastal strip but is restricted to sites a few miles inland and is typically found on slopes rather than in river bottoms (Franklin and Dyrness 1973). Redwood is closely associated with California's coastal fog belt, where its gargantuan crowns are bathed in moisture-laden air and both killing frost and drought are rare. As an example, Eureka, California, in the redwood belt has remarkably mild all-time record temperatures of 20 and 87 degrees F (–6 and 30 C).

redwood

This mild, humid environment is consistent with climates linked to redwood forests in fossil records from millions of years ago.

Conversely, lowland forests of western Washington and Oregon are exposed to harsher climatic conditions. One vivid example was the mid-November 1955 cold wave that sent temperatures plunging to near 0 degrees F (−18 C) in the Puget Sound region and Willamette Valley and began a stretch of more than 100 days of frost at Astoria on the Oregon coast. This event killed many redwoods planted north of their natural range. Similarly, in January 1972, severe frost in southwestern Oregon's Rogue River valley killed tender tops of planted redwoods and entire trees where the ground froze.

PART II BROAD-LEAVED TREES

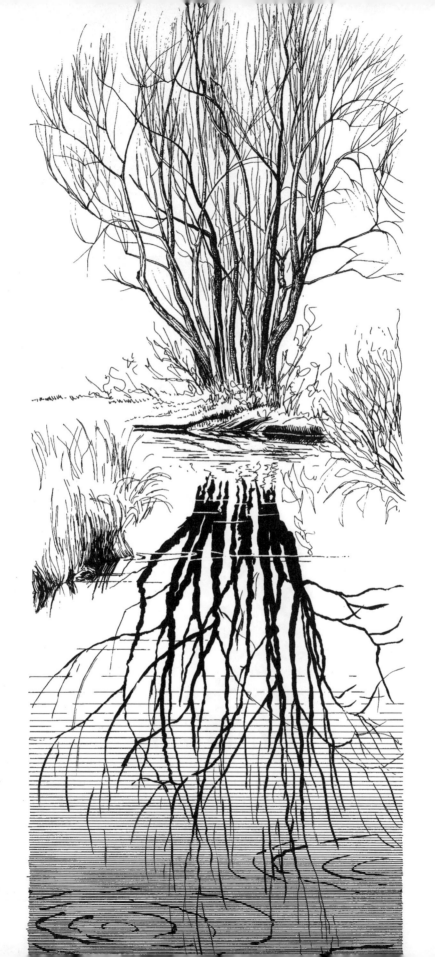

WILLOWS

Salix species, Willow family—Salicaceae

Willow is a cosmopolitan group (genus) of trees and shrubs, with about 300 species collectively inhabiting most regions of the world, but willows are particularly abundant in the north temperate and arctic zones. The Greater Northwest hosts about three dozen species of willows, ranging from fair-sized spreading trees along lowland rivers to prostrate shrubs above timberline that grow as a lawnlike mat.

Where They Grow

Willows typically form thickets of tall shrubs and small trees bordering streams and wetlands throughout the Greater Northwest. In late winter, masses of yellow, orange, or reddish willow twigs brighten an otherwise monochromatic scene. One species of willow also occupies most of our upland forests.

Comparative Appearance

Only about seven or eight of our willow species commonly exceed 20 feet (6 m) in height and thus are described here as "trees." Even these species often grow primarily as tall shrubs with clumps of slender stems less than 5 inches (12 cm) in diameter at maturity.

Willows as a group have narrow leaves, or at least the leaves are longer than broad. The leaves are simple and not lobed. They are attached in an alternating pattern along the twigs. Northwestern willows have leaves that have smooth or finely toothed edges. Leaves on vigorous new shoots or sprouts can be very confusing since they often have an unusual shape or large size. Additionally, they have a pair of ear-shaped miniature leaves called stipules attached at the base of the leaf stem. To find more typical leaves, one must examine those on slower-growing twigs and twigs not bearing flowers or fruit.

The buds on willows are unusual in being covered with a single caplike scale. Other shrubs and deciduous trees mostly have buds covered with two or more scales or are naked, that is, without a protective cover.

Nearly all residents of the Greater Northwest have admired the whitish gray, feltlike pussy willows that are the first harbingers of spring. These are actually catkins, which are tight, narrow clusters of either male or female flowers, and there is practical importance in differentiating the sexes when collecting them for bouquets. Female flowers develop into tearshaped capsules filled with cotton-enveloped seeds, while the male flowers bear yellow stamens and ultimately shed a profusion of pollen. Avoid collecting willow catkins that are tinged with yellow! Willows bear male and female flowers on separate plants.

A few species of willow have distinct features or habitats that allow them to be recognized rather easily, but many others are difficult even for trained botanists to identify. In some cases, positive identification requires painstaking examination of both female and male flowers, which are found on different plants. To complicate matters, size and shape of the leaves vary substantially within a given species, and willows often hybridize, producing plants with intermediate characteristics. Three species described below commonly grow as small trees.

In addition, the sandbar willows (*S. exigua* and *S. sessilifolia*), which are usually tall shrubs, occasionally reach a height of 25 feet (8 m). Two introduced treelike willows—European willow (*S. alba* x *S. fragilis*) and golden willow (*S. alba vitellina*)—have escaped cultivation and spread along some streams and rivers in the dry interior valleys (Johnson 1995).

Hitchcock and others (1955–69) provide a comprehensive technical classification of Northwestern willows, along with illustrations. Brayshaw (1976), Eliot (1948), and Johnson (1995) provide well-illustrated, less technical guides to individual species. Information on individual species is also available by entering the species' name into a search engine site on the Internet.

Peachleaf willow. *S. amygdaloides* is restricted to the region east of the Cascades, where it typically forms a small tree up to 50 feet (15 m) or more in height lining rivers that thread through the arid sagebrush-grass country. It is especially common along the Snake and Yakima rivers. It is a picturesque tree with two to four leaning trunks and long, slender, weeping branchlets. The distinctive shiny leaves average 2 to 4 inches (5 to 10 cm) long, are about a third as wide, and have long pointed tips. Johnson (1995) observes that the leaves

actually resemble those of almond trees rather than peach, as suggested by the species' scientific name, which means "almondlike."

Whiplash willow. *S. lasiandra*—also called Pacific willow—can be found along streams, rivers, and in wetlands at lower elevations throughout the Greater Northwest. It grows as a large shrub or small tree, up to 50 feet (15 m) tall, and is especially abundant in and west of the Cascades. Here it characteristically inhabits waterways in a mixture with black cottonwood and red alder. British Columbia's largest willow, it is very common in Oregon's Willamette Valley, where the larger trees become ragged, black-barked specimens. Its leaves have a long, tapered tip that is often curved, simulating a whiplash, an important identifying feature of this species. The leaves are long and narrow and have two or more wartlike glands at the base of each leaf blade.

Scouler willow. *S. scouleriana* is the tall

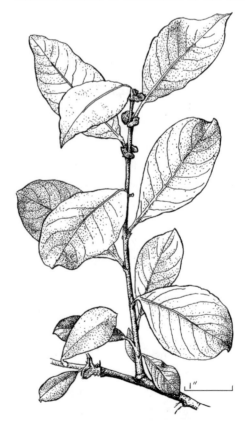

Scouler willow: flowers and fruits; foliage

shrub or multistemmed tree that commonly occupies both uplands and streamsides associated with conifer forests throughout the Greater Northwest. It abounds from sea level to an elevation of 7000 feet (2100 m) in the Rocky Mountains. It contrasts from other willows in being able to flourish on slopes away from water, even in the semi-arid ponderosa pine–Douglas-fir forest. West of the Cascades, it often reaches 40 feet (12 m) in height, whereas on dry inland sites, it is usually no more than 15 feet (4.5 m) tall. Each Scouler willow plant consists of a large root system supporting a clump of one to three dozen slender stems. Scouler willow leaves are oblong, with a rounded or at least not a narrowly pointed tip, and are widest toward the tip.

Ecological Role

Willows are shade intolerant, generally short-lived, and vulnerable to replacement by conifers or larger deciduous trees. Consequently, they depend on disturbances to create open sites that they can colonize. Along rivers and streams, floods accomplish this task. Elsewhere, fire, landslides, volcanic explosions, glaciers, and man-made disturbances fill the bill.

During spring, the minute individual flowers that make up the female catkin mature into capsules containing seeds so tiny that it takes 2 million to 12 million to make a pound (4.5 million to 26 million per kg). The seeds are released in early summer, each having a tuft of cottony down that allows it to float great distances in the wind. Willow seeds are also transported to new growing sites by stream water. The seeds are so tiny that they have little stored food or protective covering. Unlike the heavier seeds of many conifers or oaks, willow seeds do not remain dormant but must germinate within a few days of being shed.

Willow seeds usually do not germinate in dry or shady sites, and the chances for successful regeneration from the frail seeds are poor.

Nature compensates by producing prodigious quantities of them, so that some do happen to land on a suitably moist, open site and, under the right temperatures, regeneration succeeds. Moreover, willow can survive even without seed production since new stems sprout readily from the stumps of willows that are burned, cut, or eaten by animals. Even branches broken in floods can take root where they are deposited. Still, to be successful, the sprouts need an opened habitat.

While the early-blooming willow flowers are enjoyed by humans, they are essential to honeybees, providing their first spring food supply. Bees and other insects gather pollen and nectar from the catkins for rearing their broods.

In fact, willows are immensely important to wildlife in general. They stabilize and shade stream banks, helping keep the water clear and cool, thus maintaining good habitat for trout and other aquatic life. Beavers use willow extensively for food and dam construction. A great variety of songbirds nest and forage in the protective cover of willow thickets. White-tailed deer, grouse, and any number of other creatures find valuable seclusion among the willows.

Deer, elk, and especially moose eagerly chew the young willow twigs and sprouts, especially in winter when other nutritious forage is scarce. Scouler willow is particularly important for big-game forage in the inland mountains. Fires and sometimes logging operations allow it to suddenly become established over large areas of dense upland forest that formerly provided a scant food supply. In some rugged, roadless areas of Idaho's Clearwater drainage, land managers use prescribed fires to restore aging shrub fields where conifers are replacing willows and other important forage plants.

Human History

To say that willows were important and widely used in the everyday lives of Native Americans is understatement. Moerman's (1998) compendium cites nine pages of specific uses of willow by North American tribes. Several references mention chewing willow bark as an analgesic for headache and other pain, apparently presaging the development of aspirin in the late 1800s, which was derived from a substance (salicin) in willow. Some Natives boiled the bitter-tasting bark and used the broth as a remedy for sore throats and tuberculosis.

The Quinault people made a twine from willow bark that was tough enough to serve as the harpoon line for sea-lion hunting. Some Natives used willow wood for starting fires by friction. Willow shoots were perhaps the most widely used basket material in North America. Sometimes willows were deliberately burned to induce the production of vigorous, straight shoots ideal for basketry. Willow shoots are still sought out by basket makers and other artisans.

Several tribes used the tough, slender stems of Scouler willow and other species as frames for sweat lodges and shelters. The springy branches were also fashioned into snowshoes, baby cradleboards, fish traps, and other diverse items. Willow's utility as fish weir poles may have been enhanced by the fact that branches (cuttings) pushed into wet ground will quickly take root. Today willow cuttings are planted to restore damaged wetlands and eroded stream banks.

The Boy Scouts may have borrowed the Natives' technique of making whistles from willow branches. Scouts and other campers also use willow for slingshot forks, toy bows and arrows, and hot-dog roasting sticks. Some country kids are familiar with an unpleasant application of the tough and withy willow shoots, which serve as a switch applied to the naughty child's bare legs.

Willow's greatest value to humans may be its immense contribution to wildlife habitat for both aquatic and terrestrial species. Native Americans often aided willow's productivity by setting fires and by not suppressing lightning fires. This induced existing willows to resprout and allowed establishment of new willow plants from seeds blown into burned areas where the conifer forest was killed or thinned out. With long-term protection from fire and other disturbance, as is the case in many streamside habitats and forests today, willows are outcompeted and displaced by conifers. When small areas are treated with prescribed fire or logging, willows respond with vigorous new growth. Burning is better than cutting the old willows since the tough, fire-killed stems form a cage that protects some of the new shoots from hungry herbivores that otherwise devour all the delectable new growth!

an alpine willow

1"

BLACK COTTONWOOD AND ITS RELATIVES

Populus trichocarpa and *Populus* spp., Willow family—Salicaceae

Black cottonwood is one of the tallest and most massive broad-leaved trees in North America, and it surpasses all others in the Greater Northwest. It is by far the most abundant of the four species of cottonwoods native to our region. To complicate matters, the other three species hybridize with black cottonwood, and some introduced cottonwoods have escaped cultivation and hybridize with the natives! Still, all the Northwest cottonwoods have a lot in common. They are large, spreading, broad-leaved trees that typically border streams and form extensive groves in bottomlands of major valleys. They grow rapidly and provide important habitat for birds, mammals, and aquatic life.

Where They Grow

Black cottonwood has a distribution similar to many other North Pacific coastal trees. It extends from southern Alaska to northernmost California but also spreads inland through the Greater Northwest in a pattern similar to that of western redcedar, but more extensively. It is plentiful along streams and other wet sites at lower elevations but also occupies road cuts, gravel pits, and other disturbed places in all but the driest forest habitats. It barely spills eastward over the Continental Divide into southwestern Alberta and central Montana. It inhabits the mountains of central Idaho and northeastern Oregon but does not reach into the deserts farther south.

Balsam poplar (*P. balsamifera*), a native cottonwood, overlaps the eastern range of black cottonwood and hybridizes with it in southwestern Alberta and the Rocky Mountain Trench of southeastern British Columbia. Plains cottonwood (*P. deltoides* var. *occidentalis*), also a native, extends westward along rivers to the foot of the mountains in southern Alberta and central Montana. Narrowleaf cottonwood (*P. angustifolia*), another native, occupies southern Alberta, southwestern Montana, the greater Yellowstone Park region, and southeastern Idaho. Small, isolated populations of these three cottonwood species are also sprinkled here and there through the inland Northwest but, overall, black cottonwood is most prevalent.

Comparative Appearance

On favorably moist sites such as floodplains, cottonwoods grow tall and develop great, arching branch-trunks that form a light-filtering canopy high overhead. West of the Cascades, black cottonwoods on rich bottomland soils attain heights of 160 to 200 feet (50 to 60 m), and the largest trees have trunks 4 to 6 feet (120 to 180 cm) in diameter. Broad-canopied black cottonwoods up to 100 feet (30 m) tall also dominate floodplains along rivers flowing west from the Rocky Mountains. Exceptionally large black cottonwoods up to 7 feet (2.1 m) thick and 155 feet (48 m) tall are found in the southeast corner of British Columbia, in the Morrissey Grove along the Elk River (Rood and Polzin 2003).

All the native cottonwoods have trunks covered with deeply furrowed gray bark. Magnificent cottonwood bottoms extend along rivers out into the sagebrush-grass country from central Washington to central Montana, where they become stunningly beautiful in autumn as they turn golden yellow.

Cottonwoods and aspen are both members of the genus *Populus*, but cottonwoods have stout twigs and large, gummy buds, while aspen has slender twigs and nongummy buds. They also have different flower structure and occupy

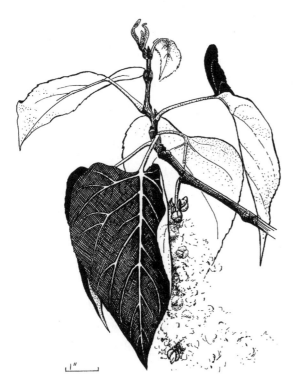

black cottonwood

different habitats. Our native cottonwoods can be distinguished from other Northwestern trees by their large, broad (except narrowleaf cottonwood), almost triangular, pointed leaves. These are deep green above and silvery white or pale green below. A gusty summer wind gives the trees a fluttering two-toned appearance. The large buds—about ¾ inch (2 cm) long—are filled with aromatic, sticky orange gum.

Cottonwoods, like willows, bear male and female flowers on separate trees. The female flowers mature into 4-inch-long (10-cm-long), grapelike bunches of light green capsules. The capsules split open in early summer, releasing minute plume-bearing seeds into the breeze. The cotton-covered seeds float through the air day after day and pile up in drifts a few inches deep—thus the name "cottonwood."

A few simple characteristics allow separation of the native cottonwoods, but hybrids can confound identification.

Left to right: narrowleaf cottonwood, plains cottonwood, balsam poplar (with two-part seed capsules), black cotton-wood (with three-part capsules)

Narrowleaf cottonwood. This species differs from the other natives in having many leaves that are two and a half or more times longer than broad.

Plains cottonwood. This species has broadly triangular leaves, flat across the base, with large, rounded teeth on the margins and often a pair of prominent glands at the junction of the leaf stem.

Balsam poplar. This species and black cottonwood have broadly egg-shaped leaves drawn to a pointed tip, with fine teeth on the edges. The seed capsules of balsam poplar are pointed, and they split lengthwise into two parts, while those of black cottonwood are rounded and split into three sections.

Ecological Role

Cottonwoods are very intolerant of shade and grow best in full sunlight. In most of its extensive range, black cottonwood must compete to some extent with more shade-tolerant conifers. It succeeds by rapidly colonizing burned, bulldozed, or other disturbed sites and growing more rapidly than conifers. On a good site in western Washington, free-growing nine-year-old black cottonwood saplings were nearly 50 feet (15 m) tall. The tiny cottonwood seeds require a moist seedbed for germination, and seedling survival depends on continued moist conditions during the first month.

On floodplains, periodic inundation and deposition of fresh sediment is necessary for cottonwood seed germination. To allow root development, the water table in the soil must not drop by more than about 1½ inches (4 cm) per day. Stream-flow regulation from dams and irrigation withdrawals has reduced both rejuvenating floods and summer stream flow, resulting in declining populations of cottonwoods along many rivers.

Cottonwoods have shallow root systems that snake across a bottomland site just below the surface. Where these roots are scraped or injured, they often sprout new aerial shoots. Most cottonwoods can also sprout from cut or broken stumps, and new trees can be generated by sticking young shoots (cuttings) into moist soil. After logging operations or floods, cottonwood trees occasionally regenerate from fragments of roots or branches that became partially buried in soil. When a load of black cottonwood logs was left through a rainy winter and spring on a railroad car in western Washington, it was soon engulfed in a forest of sprouts.

On upland sites in moist areas, cottonwoods are eventually displaced by conifers that grow up beneath and through them. However, on heavy bottomland soils that experience high water tables or flooding in the spring and drought-stress in late summer, cottonwood's shallow, spreading root systems allow it to dominate with minimal competition from conifers. West of the Cascades, Sitka spruce and western redcedar are the most successful conifer companions in cottonwood bottoms. In drier regions of the interior, perhaps surprisingly, ponderosa pine codominates bottomlands with cottonwood, while Douglas-fir and most other conifers cannot cope with the alternately flooded and dry soil.

Cottonwood's rapid growth does not produce a durable tree. The wood is weak but heavy in live trunks due to the large quantities of water these trees store. Even during a dry spell, water will flow from the surface of a freshly cut cottonwood stump. Large upper limbs split off in strong winds or in snowstorms that happen while the trees are leafed out. Clinging ice often snaps the trees, and the waterlogged trunks may split when they freeze.

Cottonwood communities are very productive wildlife habitats. Unlike in dense conifer forests, filtered sunlight shines through the canopy, and the leaves provide nutrient-rich litter. This allows a profusion of smaller deciduous trees, fruiting shrubs, and herbaceous plants to thrive, which in turn makes good nesting habitat for songbirds that migrate from the tropics.

Cottonwood trunks consist of soft, rot-prone wood encased in durable bark. Wood-peckers hammer these trees, creating an abundance of cavities used for nest sites by animals ranging from small birds to great horned owls, wood ducks, flying squirrels, and raccoons. Big, horizontal upper limbs serve as foundations for the platformlike nests of bald eagles and ospreys. Canada geese sometimes use these nests too and provide quite a sight when they land ponderously in the treetop. Blue herons also build their stick-pile nests atop the cottonwood canopy, sometimes a few dozen nests constituting their noisy colony.

Beavers use cottonwood for food and for building dams, sometimes chiseling through and toppling trees 24 inches (60 cm) thick, though often giving up after having chewed only partway through a big tree.

black cottonwood chewed by beaver

Human History

Native people had a multitude of uses for cottonwood. They relished the sweet inner bark and sap (Hart 1976; Moerman 1998). They fed the inner bark and foliage to horses, the bark especially in winter when other forage was scarce. They cooked up the buds along with animal fat to make salves and other medicines. They also processed the inner bark and leaves for medicinal use. They made dyes of various colors from fruit capsules and buds. They burned the dry wood inside tepees because it produced little smoke.

Today some people burn cottonwood in stoves because if it's dry it seems to drive soot out of the chimney when it's temporarily substituted for hotter-burning Douglas-fir or pine. Cottonwood gives off little heat and yields voluminous ash. Although the wood is soft and easy to cut, the bark of old trees is so hard that sparks fly when a whirring chain saw touches the bark. Large rounds of cottonwood are often mushy enough to absorb two or three steel wedges without splitting, but this resistance can be overcome, east of the Cascades, by waiting for temperatures of 10 degrees F (−12 C) or colder. The same rounds split easily with a clinking sound when frozen.

Our cottonwoods yield cream-colored lumber that is light in weight and not very strong but useful for a number of utility purposes. It excels as pulp for premium-grade book and magazine papers. Introduced hybrid cottonwoods are grown experimentally in agricultural plantations in the Columbia Basin as a highly productive source of pulpwood and biomass for energy generation. Similarly, plantations of black cottonwood in western Washington and southwestern British Columbia can be harvested for pulpwood in ten to fifteen years. For all we know, this book is produced from a cottonwood plantation! (However, producing pulp or industrial fuel from intensively managed plantations may not be as economical as using wood waste from lumber mills.)

QUAKING ASPEN

Populus tremuloides, Willow family—Salicaceae

Quaking aspen, also known as trembling aspen, would surely win the title of Most Colorful Tree in the mountain West. In autumn, Colorado's radiant, aspen-clad slopes draw legions of sightseers. In late spring and summer, aspen's bright green and silvery leaves shimmer and whisper almost incessantly. At the onset of fall, aspens turn a glorious yellow, golden, and occasionally reddish. Even when the trees are bare in winter, photographers and artists are attracted by their creamy-white bark with its distinctive black markings.

Aspen groves are sprinkled here and there across the Greater Northwest, often tucked away in mountain canyons east of the Cascade crest. Along the eastern slope of the Rockies in northern Montana and Alberta, aspen forms sizable woodlands. Aspen plays a special role as wildlife habitat and it has unusual traits, including an ability to propagate for thousands of years through sprouts from a communal root system without regenerating from seeds.

Where It Grows

Quaking aspen is the most widely distributed tree in North America, extending 4000 miles (6500 km) across the northern United States and Canada from the Atlantic coast to western Alaska. It is a major component of both the northern hardwood forest and the boreal conifer forest. In western North America southward from Canada, aspen becomes more and more confined to high-mountain habitats. It ranges southward at increasing elevations in the mountains to northern Mexico. It grows near sea level in some places west of the Cascades and as low as 2000 feet (600 m) in northern Idaho and interior British Columbia, but reaches

7000 feet (2100 m) in the Yellowstone Park area and 11,000 feet (3350 m) in Colorado.

Small, widely scattered aspen groves inhabit lowlands west of the Cascades, including the lower Fraser Valley and the vicinity of Victoria, British Columbia, and a few locations in Washington's Puget Sound region and Oregon's Willamette Valley. Aspen is far more common east of the Cascade crest and especially in the Rocky Mountains. In mountain country east of the Cascades, aspen commonly grows near watercourses, in moist meadows, beneath rugged canyon walls, in boulder piles, in avalanche chutes, near seeps and springs, and elsewhere at the edge of the conifer forest. Although some of these sites may appear to be rather dry, aspen's presence often indicates that water is available a few feet below the surface in spring and early summer.

Appearance

Aspen is notably smaller than most cottonwoods. The larger aspen trunks on a good site often attain 50 to 60 feet (15 to 18 m) in height and 10 inches (25 cm) in diameter during their 80- to 100-year life span. These trees develop a narrow, domelike crown made up of slender, irregularly bent limbs that stand out straight from the trunk.

Quaking aspen is easy to identify based on several features, including its sound. Some Native peoples named it "noisy leaf." Its leaves are almost round, about 1½ to 2½ inches (4 to 6 cm) across, but with an abruptly pointed tip. They are attached to the twig via a long, flattened petiole (leaf stem) that causes them to quiver in the slightest breeze. (To confirm that the petiole is flattened, try to roll it between your fingers.) The leaves are green above and pale silvery on the underside, giving the canopy

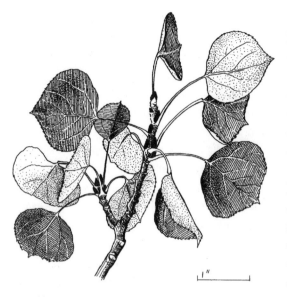

quaking aspen

a shimmering appearance as the leaves flutter. Like cottonwoods, aspen leaves are attached in an alternate arrangement along the twigs. However, unlike cottonwoods, aspen buds are small—about ¼ inch (5 mm) long—and not filled with sticky gum.

Aspen has smooth, whitish bark—not peeling off in layers like paper birch—with black marks and splotches here and there. Juvenile stems have pale green bark, and exceptionally large old aspens develop heavily fissured gray bark on the lower trunk.

Aspen seeds are tiny—3 million per pound (6.5 million per kg)—and are similar to cottonwood in being enveloped in cottony down. Because they lack stored food or a thick protective coating, the seeds remain viable for only a week or two. New aspens occasionally arise in abundance from seeds, when site and weather conditions are exceptionally favorable. As described below, however, aspen's prolific sprouting ability compensates for inconsistencies in establishment of seedlings.

Ecological Role

Aspen is a smaller, more-compact tree than its relatives the cottonwoods, and it ascends much higher in the mountains. Its small size and little leaves are no doubt advantageous when it comes to surviving the wet snowfalls that inundate the mountains in late spring, summer, or early fall when the trees are leafed out. Heavy snows in June break off many of the aspens and even lower-elevation cottonwoods every decade or two in the Rocky Mountains.

Within a few years after an aspen seedling has become established, it can produce a large colony of genetically identical stems arising from its vigorous root system. The group or colony of stems produced vegetatively from a single aspen is termed a clone. When fire, cutting, or other damage kills the original stem, sprouts or suckers arise from the shallow, spreading roots. Anyone who has tried to yank out a very small aspen while clearing land soon learns that it is securely attached to large horizontal roots that snake along a few inches beneath the surface. Thus, nearly all apparent "saplings" are actually root suckers. Moreover, most aspen groves are in reality clones wherein each stem arises from the common root system.

An aspen clone often covers a few acres (1 ha or more). A clone in Utah covers 107 acres (43 ha) and consists of about 47,000 stems. Although an individual aspen stem rarely lives more than 100 years, upon its death it is replaced by new sprouts from the same parent root system. Thus a clone can perpetuate itself for centuries, perhaps even for millennia, if conditions remain favorable.

Evidence that a single grove of aspens is a genetically identical clone can be seen in early autumn. At this time, some aspen patches are uniformly golden in color, others are yellowish, and others are still green. Each clone begins to enter winter dormancy on its own genetically determined schedule, probably keyed to day length. Similar clonal behavior can be seen in the spring as individual clones leaf out at different times. A clone is also distinctive in terms of other genetically controlled characteristics, including sex (each clone bears only male or only female flowers), leaf shape and size, and resistance to diseases.

Aspen bark tastes bitter to humans, but many animals eagerly feed upon it. Snowshoe hares, elk, moose, deer, livestock, and beavers feed on aspen foliage, twigs, and bark and sometimes girdle the stems just above the level of the snowpack. Beavers spend much time logging aspen, cutting it up into chunks, and caching it underwater near their dens to serve as winter food. Biologists estimate that to supply daily needs, an adult beaver consumes the bark from a 2-inch-thick (5-cm-thick) sapling.

Aspen groves provide food and nesting sites for a great variety of animals. Ruffed grouse prefer aspen as habitat year-round. Migratory songbirds nest and feed in aspen. Aspen groves provide far more forage and biodiversity than do conifer forests. They also utilize less water, allowing springs and streams to run fuller (Gifford and others 1984).

Historically, relatively frequent fires helped maintain an abundance of aspen over large areas in the inland mountains where this light-demanding species has to compete with longer-lived, shade-tolerant conifers. However, since the late 1800s, the pattern of burning has been disrupted by livestock grazing (which removed grassy fuel) and fire suppression. This has allowed conifers to largely replace aspen in many areas.

In Yellowstone National Park, aspen largely gave way to conifers. Then the extensive fires of 1988 set the stage for a prodigious crop of aspen seedlings in burned areas (Kay 1993). However, the large population of elk and other grazing wildlife zeroed in on the succulent seedlings and suppressed their development. In many places, wildlife populations have been displaced by agriculture and suburban development and now concentrate in the aspen-conifer forest. Where aspen groves are particularly imperiled, land managers sometimes cut or burn them and their immediate surroundings and then fence the area. This stimulates vigorous sprouting and provides protection from browsing animals long enough for stems to grow above grazing height and to build a large root system.

Human History

Native Americans used aspen medicinally, especially its bark (Moerman 1998). Pioneers also employed aspen bark for its quinine and other alkaloids. These substances provided relief from bodily pains, fevers, infections, and colds.

In the early 1800s, trappers and traders who roamed the mountain West knew that where there were aspen, they would find beaver. The trapper would set an aspen stick strategically in a hole in a beaver dam to lure the flat-tail into a trap, so that men in eastern cities could wear beaver hats. By the mid-1800s, beavers were nearly annihilated in many areas, but then fashion changed, and beavers, their pelts no longer in vogue, made a comeback.

Aspen wood is cream colored, lightweight, and soft. It wears without forming splinters and is therefore suitable for outdoor benches and playground structures. Like cottonwood, it yields high-quality wood pulp, a primary use of aspen in central and eastern Canada. Western aspen is less abundant, less accessible, and relatively little used for forest products. It is denser than cottonwood and cleaner and easier to handle, and it makes better firewood.

Aspen's principal values for modern society lie in wildlife habitat and other environmental attributes. Because of low flammability, aspen groves serve as firebreaks and are thus very desirable in the vicinity of woodland home sites. Homeowners should not get too friendly with aspen, however. It is easily propagated but should be used with caution as an ornamental since its root system can spread extensively and clog septic systems!

Ramona Hammerly

ALDERS

Alnus spp., Birch family—Betulaceae

About thirty-five species of alder inhabit moist and wet sites throughout most of the northern hemisphere, some even extending southward through the South American Andes. Four species occupy the Greater Northwest. Alder leaves and especially the roots are important to the ecosystem because they enrich the soil with nitrogen and other nutrients.

Where They Grow

Alders border streams and other wetlands; two species also spread out extensively across moist upland slopes. Northwestern alders can often be distinguished by their contrasting distributions and life-forms as well as by characteristics of their foliage.

Red alder (*Alnus rubra*) and Sitka alder (*A. sinuata*) are most abundant near the Northwest coast, ranging from southern Alaska to northern California. Red alder is a midsized tree that occupies large areas at low elevations west of the British Columbia Coast Range and the Cascades, with small, isolated populations in northern Idaho. It extends from sea level up to about 3000 feet (900 m) in elevation.

Sitka alder is primarily a very large shrub that forms extensive thickets on moist slopes at mid- to high elevations in the coastal and moist inland mountains. It is the major component of junglelike shrub-fields that fill avalanche chutes and other openings in moist high-mountain forests of the Greater Northwest. Vertical swathes of deep-green Sitka alder spill down mountainsides as seen from highways crossing the Cascades, Selkirks, and Rocky Mountains. Sitka alder also grows as a patchy layer among open canopies of subalpine fir and other conifers in moist subalpine basins. It forms luxuriant thickets along the southern Alaskan coast. In Glacier National Park, Montana, its thickets provide dangerous opportunities for grizzly bears and humans to suddenly bump into each other on an overgrown trail!

Thinleaf or mountain alder (*A. incana*, also known as *A. tenuifolia*) and white alder (*A. rhombifolia*) are inland species largely restricted to streams and other wetlands. Thinleaf alder is a very small, bushy tree that is widespread along watercourses among lower-elevation conifer forests and sometimes grows at middle elevations in the mountains east of the Cascade Divide. Unlike red and Sitka alders, thinleaf alder seldom ventures away from water, and its occurrence indicates the presence of springs, seeps, or streams.

White alder is a small to midsized tree that grows in the warmest inland valleys and canyons. Unlike other Northwest alders, it has an affinity for warm, dry climates, where it grows along watercourses—for instance, along the lower Columbia River east of the Cascades and the Snake River, including Hells Canyon. Similarly, white alder occupies the middle of the Willamette and Rogue River valleys of western Oregon, whereas red alder replaces it in nearby foothill and mountain drainages.

Comparative Appearance

Alders have spreading canopies composed of rather large—3 to 6 inches (7.5 to 15 cm) long—egg-shaped leaves with sawtoothed edges. The leaves are attached to twigs in an alternate arrangement and are unusual in being shed in autumn while still essentially green. Like other members of the birch family (but unlike willows and cottonwoods), alders bear both male and female flowers in catkins on the same tree. The male catkins are bright yellow and several

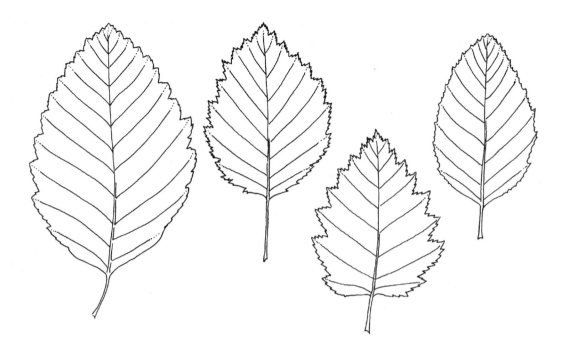

Left to right: red alder, Sitka alder, thinleaf alder, white alder

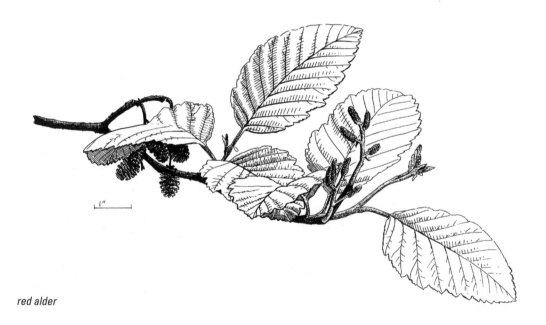

red alder

inches long, and they hang like tassels from the branches in early spring before the leaves are fully developed. Then they disintegrate. The female catkins are woody, persist year-round, and look superficially like tiny conifer cones. They are ½ to ¾ inch (1 to 2 cm) long.

Red alder. Red alder is our largest alder and the most plentiful and commercially important broad-leaved tree in the coastal Northwest. Groves of red alders 10 to 20 inches (25 to 50 cm) in diameter intermingle with young Douglas-fir forests west of the Cascades. Red alders attain their maximum height of 100 to 110 feet (30 to 33 m) in about sixty years and then lose vigor as heart rot sets in. On good sites, red alders can reach 70 to 80 feet (21 to 24 m) in height by age twenty, outgrowing all other trees except black cottonwood, which is nowhere near as abundant as alder on upland sites.

Red alder differs from the other species in having leaves whose margins are rolled under (downward) and in having short, rust-colored hairs on their pale undersides. These alders have smooth, gray bark that is mottled or nearly covered with very light gray lichen, making them superficially resemble paper birch. However, the birch has white bark that peels off in sheets.

Sitka alder. Sitka alder is usually shrubby, and its branches can be distinguished by their stalkless buds, which contrasts with the stalked buds of other alders. Only occasionally, where this species descends to lower elevations in canyons west of the Cascades, does it become a small tree, up to 30 feet (9 m) tall. Any hiker who has traversed tangles of "slide alder" without a trail will remember the intertwined, springy, sprawling stems—3 to 6 inches (7.5 to 15 cm) thick and 10 to 15 feet (3 to 4.5 m) tall—that are as hard to squeeze through as they are to walk upon. Elk seem to negotiate these thickets with ease, however. The resilient, slanted stems are well suited to surviving the snow avalanches that mow down erect trees.

Thinleaf alder. Thinleaf or mountain alder is a tall shrub or small multistemmed tree often 6 inches (15 cm) thick and 25 to 30 feet (8 to 9 m) tall. The leaves have small teeth superimposed on larger teeth and feel thinner than leaves of red alder and white alder.

White alder. White alder is a small tree, often with multiple trunks about 12 inches (30 cm) thick and 50 to 60 feet (15 to 18 m) tall arising from a single clump. It may have been named for the very pale green, almost silvery color of its leaves when they emerge in spring. White alder stands out from the others in having rounded, rather than pointed, leaves and reddish brown bark, rather than gray, on mature trunks. Earlier, in midwinter, the trees put on a colorful display as showy yellow male catkins bloom in the otherwise naked canopies.

Sitka alder

thinleaf alder

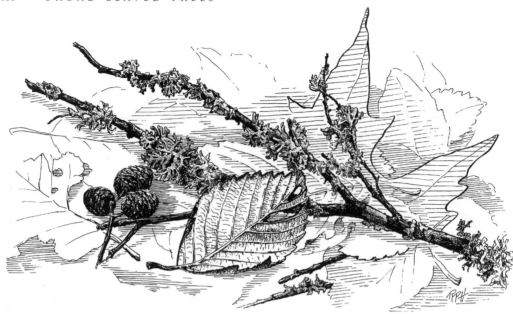

alder twig, leaves, and cones on forest floor

Ecological Role

Alders, like some legumes, have the ability to extract nitrogen from the atmosphere via bacteria in swellings or nodules on their roots. The nitrogen is then added to the soil from the roots and also from the leaves, which fall when still green and abound in nutrients. Unlike conifer needles, alder leaves decompose rapidly to form a rich humus amendment that improves soil tilth.

Because of its abundance, red alder delivers large amounts of nitrogen to enrich forest soils. Red alder stands have been found to supply between 120 and 290 pounds of nitrogen per acre (130 to 320 kg per ha) annually to the soil. From Alaska to Oregon, Sitka alder characteristically pioneers fresh, gravelly sites at the foot of retreating glaciers. Studies show that Sitka alder adds nitrogen to the soil at an average of 55 pounds per acre (60 kg per ha) per year, helping convert the sterile glacial terrain to soil capable of supporting a conifer forest.

Prior to the mid-1900s when fire suppression became very effective west of the Cascades, fires—along with floods, catastrophic windstorms, etc.—were the disturbances that killed conifer forests and initiated their replacement by stands of red alder. Alder groves themselves often served as natural firebreaks since these broad-leaved trees are much less flammable than conifers. Their foliage and leaf litter does not carry a fire well, and their thin bark is sufficiently resistant to protect them from light surface fires. Today, logging, clearing for land development, and epidemics of insects and disease have largely replaced fire in creating opportunities for red alder. Every few years, severe outbreaks of tent caterpillars defoliate most of the red alders over large areas, but despite the disastrous appearance of this damage, the trees recover quickly the next year. Red alder seeds are light—650,000 per pound (1.5 million per kg)—and are showered over virtually the entire landscape west of the Cascades and British Columbia Coast Range by the wind. In initial growth, red alder often exceeds Douglas-fir. Its seedlings often attain 3 feet (0.9 m) the first year.

Red alder is so vigorous and abundant especially on logged, burned, and other disturbed sites west of the Cascades that it could be considered the broadleaf counterpart of the omnipresent coastal Douglas-fir. In fact, red alder colonizes disturbed sites even more readily than Douglas-fir does, because it sprouts from stumps and shallow roots as well as regenerating from copious seed crops. So why doesn't red alder dominate most of the lower-elevation coastal forest? Although it outgrows coastal Douglas-fir for the first 25 years, it is very shade intolerant and seldom lives 100 years. Also, red alder helps create conditions favorable for the giant conifers that replace it.

Human History

Red alder has long been useful to humans. Coastal Natives extracted red, orange, and brownish dyes from its bark. A common application of alder dye was to make fish nets nearly invisible to fish (Moermann 1998). Red alder was second only to western redcedar for utensils and other carvings. Red alder coals were used for smoking salmon, a tradition that enterprising tribal people provide today in the form of festive salmon bakes for conferences and other special occasions.

Blackfeet, Kutenai, Flathead, and Nez Perce peoples boiled the bark of thinleaf alder to obtain reddish and orange dyes, which they used to color their bodies, clothing, and other articles (Hart 1976). Some Flatheads even dyed their hair a flaming red with alder bark, which requires no added mordants to set the color be-cause apparently its tannin serves this purpose.

Early foresters and timbermen often considered red alder a "weed tree" because it took over disturbed sites and outcompeted more-valuable conifers. However, today this species is more highly regarded due to an understanding of its ecological contributions, how it can be managed, and its increasing value for a variety of products.

Red alder is now considered a Cinderella tree in forestry circles. Its moderately dense, even-grained wood has good woodworking and staining qualities that have made it popular for furniture and a number of other specialty products. Its success in colonizing barren ground and its role in boosting soil nutrition has many applications for reclamation of damaged land. It is considered as an alternative tree crop to rehabilitate sites where the soil is infused with root rots that destroy young conifers. Because of its rapid growth and sprouting ability, it has potential for biomass plantations for electric energy production. Alder serves as clean-burning, noncrackling firewood, and it is valuable in horticulture, especially since it often emerges naturally where sorely needed to revegetate road cuts and other bulldozed areas or to provide screening in suburban areas.

alder log on forest floor

Ramona
Hammerly

PAPER BIRCH AND WATER BIRCH

Betula papyrifera and *B. occidentalis*, Birch family—Betulaceae

About fifty species of birch trees and shrubs inhabit mainly moist and cool areas in the northern hemisphere. Like alders, birches bear both sexes of flowers on the same tree; however, the female catkins disintegrate when ripe, unlike the woody alder catkins. The Greater Northwest has two treelike birches and two species of low-growing "bog birch" shrubs, *Betula glandulosa* and *B. pumila*. The trees are paper birch, which extends south from the boreal forest, and water birch, which occupies the interior West.

These distinctly different tree species hybridize in the inland Northwest and produce a spectrum of intermediate forms. Several characteristics distinguish these species and help to identify their intermediate forms:

Paper Birch	Water Birch
bark peels off in sheets	bark does not peel
bark nearly white	bark dark coppery brown
leaf tip with a long sharp point	leaf blunt or only slightly pointed
twigs smooth	twigs covered with warty glands

PAPER BIRCH

Where It Grows
Paper birch is a major forest tree all across the northeastern United States, Canada, and central Alaska. In the Greater Northwest, it is generally confined to lower elevations. It inhabits most of British Columbia except Vancouver Island, where it is reported only from the southern tip. It spreads southward, west of the Cascades as far as Everett, Washington, and reaches south in moist valleys and canyons of the Inland Empire

to northeastern Oregon. It extends southward through the Rockies to northern Montana. Being intolerant of shade, paper birch is often seen growing in open woodlands and moist pastures along river valleys and in logged or other partially cleared areas.

Appearance
Paper birch can be identified at quite a distance by its whitish, papery bark. Two to five trunks commonly arise from a clump. The largest trees on deep valley-bottom soils reach 80 to 100 feet (24 to 30 m) in height and 18 to 24 inches (45 to 60 cm) in diameter during their approximately 100-year life span. Paper birch leaves are 1½ to 3 inches (4 to 7.5 cm) long, generally larger than those of water birch, and are rather coarsely toothed.

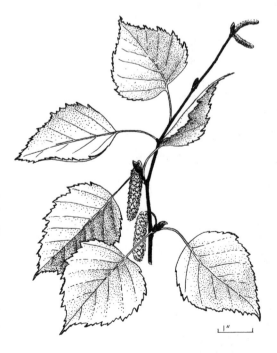

Opposite: paper birch

paper birch

Ecological Role

Paper birch seedlings—1.5 million per pound (3 million per kg)—grow well on mineral soil or a moist rotten stump, but they don't survive in leaf litter. Successful seedlings attain only 3 to 4 inches (7.5 to 10 cm) in height during their first year, whereas sprouts from cut or burned stumps grow as much as 24 inches (60 cm). Moose, white-tailed deer, and other browsing animals feed heavily on sprouts and saplings and can restrict successful regeneration.

If more than a century passes without fire, massive blowdown, logging, or other disturbance, paper birch will be overtopped and crowded out by longer-lived, more shade-tolerant conifers or even by black cottonwood. Through the ages, fire has served as both the killer and the perpetuator of paper birch. Because of their thin, flammable bark, these trees are easily killed by fire, but fire also provides light and growing room for birch stump sprouts and mineral soil for seedlings.

Human History

Paper birch bark was used as a firestarter by Native peoples, but it is renowned for its use in birch-bark canoes, such as the one made by Henry Wadsworth Longfellow's *Hiawatha*. The bark was peeled in sheets and sewn together over a frame, often of cedar, to make a fast, lightweight craft for use on the northern lakes and rivers. The thread was often made from tree roots, and thread holes were filled with pitch from conifers. To his chagrin, however, explorer David Thompson found that many paper birches in the inland Northwest had bark too thin for making canoes (Nisbet 2005). The bark is impermeable to water and was also used for roofing, buckets, utensils, and baskets.

Peeling bark from living paper birch trees is not acceptable in most areas today because it leaves a permanent unsightly scar by exposing the dark underbark and may injure the tree.

However, useful bark strips can be taken from a downed tree since the bark is very durable. In fact, the wood in downed trunks of paper birch often rots away, leaving an intact cylinder of bark lying on the forest floor. John Worrall of the University of British Columbia attributes the bark's durability to its high wax content.

Paper birch wood is moderately heavy, hard, and strong; it is used for furniture and pulpwood in the northeastern United States and eastern Canada. Because of its limited abundance in the Northwest, it has little commercial use here, but people who live near some of the more extensive stands consider it the premier firewood. It splits easily, burns cleanly, and has a high heating value.

The graceful form and attractive white bark of paper birch make it desirable as an ornamental. However, the bark doesn't turn white until trees are ten or twelve years old; consequently, introduced birches that develop white bark earlier are generally chosen.

WATER BIRCH

Where It Grows

Water birch is a distinctively different and very interesting tree. Whereas paper birch is restricted to the northern part of the continent, water birch is a denizen of the West, extending from the Yukon Territory to mountain habitats in northern New Mexico and Arizona and southern Nevada. It is an inland species, widespread in the Greater Northwest but only east of the British Columbia Coast Range and the Cascades. While paper birch is restricted to cool, moist, forested regions, water birch grows along small streams that thread their way into some of the driest deserts.

Water birch often grows squeezed into a slitlike rock gorge where a snow-fed stream gushes over its roots. It lines the lower reaches of mountain streams amid conifer forest and also follows the waterways out into sagebrush-grass deserts. In the high desert of eastern Idaho and

water birch

southwestern Montana, water birch is some-times the only tree growing along streams in 7000-foot-high (2100-m-high) valleys.

Appearance

Water birch is a tall shrub or small tree consisting of several tightly clumped vertical stems. Along waterways in the high desert, its dark, spindly stems commonly grow about 15 feet (5 m) tall, while on streams in the lower-elevation coni-fer forests it can reach 45 feet (14 m) in height and 8 to 10 inches (20 to 25 cm) in diameter. It attains relatively large size where it hybridizes with paper birch; for instance, between Coeur d'Alene and Cascade, Idaho.

It contrasts with paper birch in having bark that is almost black when young and turning reddish-brown to copper colored as it matures. Also, the bark does not loosen and peel in sheets. The bark is speckled with small, light, horizontal patches of lenticels, or breath-ing pores. Water birch leaves are small, only ¾ to 1¾ inches (2 to 4.5 cm) long, and the fine twigs are covered with wartlike glands.

Ecological Role

Water birch's small, frail appearance is deceptive, since it alone is able to survive a climate where summer frost is frequent and snow can fall in any month. Birches bear a very small nutlet with a papery wing on each side. These are often pro-duced in prodigious quantities and spread far and wide in the wind. The tiny seeds grow into

water birch

delicate seedlings that can survive only under a narrow range of moisture, light, and seedbed conditions. Seeds are an important food source for chickadees and other small birds, while male catkins and buds benefit ruffed grouse.

Human History

Although it is an attractive and interesting small tree, water birch has been little noticed or used by people in bygone or recent times.

GOLDEN CHINKAPIN

Chrysolepis chrysophylla, Beech family—Fagaceae

Golden chinkapin, also spelled chinquapin, is one of the Northwest's most unusual trees. This evergreen broad-leaved tree is native to western Oregon and northern California. On favorable semi-open habitats, it becomes a handsome, medium-sized tree, but on harsher sites or in a dense stand of conifers, it grows as a small, spindly tree or bushy shrub. Golden chinkapin's full canopy of leathery leaves and creamy white blossoms resembles tanoak (*Lithocarpus densiflorus*), also found in southwestern Oregon; however, rather than an acorn, chinkapin's fruit is chestnutlike and surrounded by a spiny bur. Golden chinkapin and tanoak are among a group of trees considered to be living links between the chestnuts (*Castanea*) and oaks (*Quercus*), and "chinkapin" is a Native American term for chestnut. Chestnut trees are deciduous, while golden chinkapin and its closest relatives (the two *Chrysolepis* species of North America and the numerous *Castanopsis* species of tropical Asia) are evergreen.

Where It Grows

Golden chinkapin ranges from the coastal lowlands to as high as 6000 feet (1800 m) on the crest of the Oregon Cascades. It typically becomes a good-sized tree only on moderately moist sites in low-elevation valleys of southwestern Oregon and northwestern California. Elsewhere—on dry sites, at higher elevations, among crowded conifer forests, and in northwestern Oregon—it is primarily a small tree or bushy shrub. In the Coast Range, it reaches nearly as far north as Corvallis, Oregon, and it extends through the Cascades to the Columbia River Gorge. An isolated colony of small chinkapins grows north of the Columbia at Big Lava Beds

north of Carson, Washington, and far-flung outlier populations are found near Eldon on Hood Canal about 140 miles (225 km) north of the Columbia (Kruckeberg 1980).

Appearance

Chinkapin trees growing in the open often have luxuriant, pyramidal canopies reaching the ground and standing out as if they were ornamentals. Under crowded conditions, the foliage becomes sparse. The biggest chinkapins in southwestern Oregon attain about 36 inches (90 cm) in diameter and 100 to 120 feet (30 to 35 m) in height. Their straight, branch-free lower trunk is covered with bark that has deep, vertical furrows and resembles a mature conifer. Chinkapin bark is reddish brown on the ridges, with the brilliant red inner bark appearing in the fissures.

Throughout the long flowering season, chinkapin trees are strikingly beautiful, their dense, glossy green foliage covered with elongated clusters (spikes) of creamy-white flowers, similar to those of chestnut. These showy blossoms are the male or pollen-producing flowers, and they give off a musky odor that seems rather rank to humans but does an effective job of attracting bees and other pollinating insects on hot summer days. The only other Northwestern native with similar flowers is tanoak, and these two species are hard to distinguish at a distance, but close up, the chinkapin stands out because its leaves have a golden-yellow undersurface. Chinkapin's stiff, leathery leaves are narrow and 2 to 5 inches (5 to 12 cm) long, with long-pointed tips.

Chinkapins bear edible nuts about ½ inch (1 cm) in diameter and similar in taste to the hazelnut or filbert (*Corylus cornuta*) native to West

golden chinkapin

to maintain itself among the mixed conifer–broadleaf forest with Douglas-fir, incense-cedar, tanoak, California black oak (*Quercus kelloggii*), and other species. Most of its conifer associates grow taller and eventually overtop it; but chinkapin benefits from fire or logging because in open habitats it regenerates readily from stump sprouts as well as seeds. Historically, its abundance in the lower elevations of southwestern Oregon reflects a history of relatively frequent fires.

In contrast, golden chinkapin's shrubby form is tolerant of shade and seems well adapted to survival, regardless of disturbances, on warm, dry sites and soil types characterized by high moisture stress. Shrubby chinkapin and associated chaparral species can outcompete and exclude conifer seedlings and thus form persistent shrub fields on harsh sites in southwestern Oregon. In the Siskiyous, the shrubby form of chinkapin is abundant on dry, rocky sites, while the tree form occurs on north-facing slopes and on sites with deep soils.

Despite its close relationship to chestnut, golden chinkapin is resistant to the devastating blight that has destroyed American chestnut (*Castanea dentata*). Chinkapin is generally little affected by other diseases or insects, although old trees often develop heart rot. Some of the larger trees are estimated to be more than 300 years old.

Human History

Native Americans ate golden chinkapin nuts raw, and also roasted them. They also collected and stored them for winter food (Moerman 1998). However, often the husks do not contain fully developed nuts, and extracting nuts from their spiny casings is a chore now mostly left to squirrels. Golden chinkapin wood is moderately heavy, hard, and strong but is seldom used commercially because good-sized trees are so widely scattered.

Coast lowlands. Chinkapin nuts, like chestnuts, are surrounded in a husk covered with sharp, branched spines. Remains of these armored fruits, locally called "porcupine eggs," litter the ground beneath chinkapin trees and shrubs and challenge anyone clad in flimsy footwear.

In southern Oregon, chinkapin is often part of a community of robust shrubs called chaparral that includes manzanita (*Arctostaphylos* spp.), buck brush (*Ceanothus* spp.), and others. To complicate identification, the chinkapin shrubs could be either golden chinkapin or the closely related "bush chinkapin" (*C. sempervirens*), which is always a shrub and ranges southward through the mountains of California. Or they could be an intermediate form resulting from hybridization of the two chinkapin species.

Ecological Role

Golden chinkapin has a sort of multiple personality. The tree form is relatively intolerant of shade and requires occasional disturbances

TANOAK

Lithocarpus densiflorus, Beech family—Fagaceae

Tanoaks, like chinkapins, are part of the evolutionary linkage between chestnuts (*Castanea*) and oaks (*Quercus*). Because tanoaks are not true oaks, the name is properly written as one word. Tanoaks have flowers similar to chestnuts and chinkapins. They bear acorns like oaks except that the acorn cup is covered with spines, reminiscent of the husks on chestnuts and chinkapins. Tanoaks consist of at least 100 species of evergreen trees inhabiting tropical Southeast Asia and the East Indies and not found elsewhere, except for our single, more cold-hardy species in Oregon and California. Our tanoak resembles golden chinkapin in both appearance and ecology, but there are fundamental differences in the leaves and fruit. Also, tanoak differs in being an aggressive competitor, able to prosper in conifer-dominated forests with or without disturbance. This ability allows it to become abundant within its small native range.

Where It Grows

Tanoak occupies the Coast Ranges from southwestern Oregon to central California and extends inland to Mount Shasta and the northern Sierra Nevada. In Oregon, it grows between sea level and about 4000 feet (1200 m) elevation, and its general northern limit is near Myrtle Point on the Coquille River. It grows best on the humid seaward slopes of the Coast Ranges: Most of the large tanoaks in Oregon are confined to Curry County along the extreme southern coast. Smaller tanoaks are scattered eastward almost to Grants Pass and Oregon Caves in Josephine County.

Appearance

Open-grown tanoaks have great, globe-shaped crowns 70 to 90 feet (20 to 25 m) tall, with evergreen foliage so dense it obscures the stout trunk and long, spreading branches. Their robust canopies are all the more impressive during spring and early summer when festooned with cream-colored blossoms, which are pollen-bearing catkins. These are borne upright, as in golden chinkapin, and they also have a similar musky odor. (Oak catkins are pendant.)

Tanoaks growing among tall coastal Douglas-firs or redwoods raise their limb-free trunks high overhead to support a narrow crown of upswept branches. They reach up 120 feet (35 m) or more but are still over-topped by the conifers. Mature tanoaks are covered with dark gray to brown bark that has heavy ridges separated by deep fissures.

Tanoak leaves are oblong, 3 to 5 inches (7.5 to 13 cm) in length, and thick and leathery. The upper surface is pale shiny green, while the

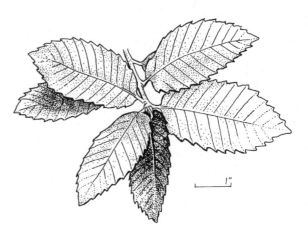

variant leaf form of tanoak

tanoak

underside has a bluish white fuzz that wears away during summer. The leaves have prominent parallel veins often ending in a tooth on the leaf margin, but sometimes the leaf edges are smooth.

Tanoak's fruit distinguishes this species from all other North American trees. Here is an obvious oaklike acorn, but it is nestled in a spine-covered cup. The acorn matures in its second year and is bitter, like those of black oaks. It is about ¾ inch (2 cm) long and projects out from the shallow cup. The acorns are heavy, about 110 per pound (240 per kg), and tanoaks with full canopies often produce large crops of acorns every other year—several hundred pounds of acorns per acre in a tanoak stand on an annual basis. Tanoak acorns are a rich source of food consumed by animals ranging from squirrels to band-tailed pigeons, deer, bears, and raccoons.

Ecological Role

Tanoak and coastal Douglas-fir are the signature species of the mixed evergreen forest that characterizes the coastal mountains of southwestern Oregon and northwestern California. Here a "Mediterranean" climate of mild, wet winters and hot, dry summers nurtures a unique kind of forest where tall conifers co-dominate with shorter evergreen broad-leaved trees. Tanoak and other evergreen broadleaves—golden chinkapin, canyon live oak (*Quercus chrysolepis*), Pacific madrone (*Arbutus menziesii*), and California-laurel (*Umbellularia californica*)—are able to carry on growth processes during the damp winters, while deciduous trees are dormant. Moreover, during hot, dry summers, their tough, waxy leaves reduce water loss. Although the evergreen broadleaves prosper in this narrow coastal region, they do not survive farther inland where colder and drier winters prevail or farther north along the coast where colder wet conditions tip the balance more in favor of conifers and deciduous broadleaf trees.

Tanoak is tolerant of shade and thus competition from larger conifers. Although it can endure shade and domination by conifers, it flourishes when fire, windstorm, or logging kills or opens up the forest. Tanoak responds quickly to disturbance by prolific sprouting and regeneration from seed, sometimes establishing so much vigorous new growth that it prevents establishment of conifers. New sprouts and seedlings of many broad-leaved trees are heavily consumed by deer and other herbivores, but tanoak is not similarly vulnerable. Fresh tanoak leaves and twigs are covered with abundant fine hairs that deer evidently don't like to inhale (U.S. Forest Service 1990).

Historically, frequent, low-intensity fires in some of these forests may have limited the amount of tanoak. Douglas-fir, redwood, and some other conifers are fire resistant and survived undamaged while tanoak trees are often killed. Tanoak sprouts would not succeed so well where conifers remained dominant. Tanoak trees injured by fire or other wounds are susceptible to a variety of rotting fungi, which shortens the tree's life.

Human History

Native peoples along the southern Oregon and northern California coast obtained one of their primary foods from tanoak. They ground and washed the acorns in hot water to remove the bitter taste, then prepared them as mush or bread. Tanoak acorns were favored as food because they are oily and rich and have an agreeable acid taste (U.S. Forest Service 1990).

A century ago, large quantities of tanoaks were felled and their bark stripped for commercial extraction of tannin used in producing leather. This is the origin of the tree's common name. Its tannin was considered superior in making heavy leathers because of its mix of tannic and other acids.

Tanoak wood is heavy, hard, strong, and shock-resistant, similar to commercially available oak lumber. It has potential for manufacture into flooring and furniture, for instance. However, limited accessibility to tanoak trees suitable for lumber has largely prevented commercial use. It makes good firewood.

OREGON WHITE OAK OR GARRY OAK

Quercus garryana, Beech family—Fagaceae

Stout, craggy oak trees with broad, rounded canopies stand scattered across a rolling landscape of sun-bleached grass. This scene is reminiscent of California's golden foothills, but the trees are Oregon white oaks growing in dry valleys west of the Cascades from west-central Oregon to southernmost British Columbia, where they are called Garry oaks. Historically, open oak woodlands and oak-sprinkled prairies were heavily occupied by Native Americans. Later, these habitats were among the first areas settled by Oregon Trail pioneers. Today, Oregon white oak is recognized as a special tree because it is the cornerstone of an increasingly scarce and highly diverse plant and animal community.

Where It Grows

Fifteen species of oak are native to California, and three of them as well as their relative tanoak reach southwestern Oregon. However, Oregon white oak grows 400 miles (650 km) farther north than the others, occupying the warmest, driest sites west of the Cascades. It spreads along the rain-sheltered, southeastern coast of Vancouver Island from Victoria to Courtenay and inhabits two localities on the British Columbia mainland: Sumas Mountain and Yale in the Fraser River Canyon. Southward, patches of Oregon white oak grow in the San Juan Islands and at Sequim in the rain shadow of the Olympic Mountains in Washington. Oregon oak is now rare in most of the Puget Sound area but is still found at the Fort Lewis Prairies south of Tacoma, Washington. It becomes more common south of Chehalis; its dark, rounded form is seen on the south-facing hills east of Interstate 5.

Oregon white oak extends upstream along the Columbia River past the Dalles, occupying dry hills and then spreading north along the parched eastern foothill slopes of the Cascades to the drainages west of Yakima. Otherwise, Oregon oak is mostly restricted to west of the Cascades.

It is plentiful in warm, dry habitats of the Willamette and Umpqua river valleys in Oregon, but from the Rogue River drainage southward, it is increasingly replaced by California black oak and other more southerly species, especially on moderately moist sites. Still, Oregon white oak retains a presence in the mixed oak woodlands throughout much of northern California.

Appearance

Oregon white oak is a tree of modest stature but striking appearance. Its dark green foliage stands out at the end of big, long, crooked limbs that radiate from the top of a stout trunk covered with gray, fissured bark. On fertile valley soils, mature trees 36 inches (90 cm) in diameter and 80 feet (25 m) tall are fairly common. The biggest oaks on Sauvie Island in the Columbia River floodplain northwest of Portland, Oregon, are 5 feet (1.5 m) in diameter and perhaps as much as 500 years old, although ages of venerable oaks are hard to determine because of heart rot. On dry, infertile sites, the oaks are much smaller, and the maximum horizontal spread of their canopy may exceed the tree's height. On extremely rocky, wind-exposed sites, Oregon oaks grow as tall shrubs.

Oregon white oak and California black oak (see the next chapter) are the Northwest's only native deciduous oaks. (Evergreen oaks have thick, leathery leaves.) Oregon white oak has dark green leaves with rounded lobes, whereas the leaves of California black oak are yellow-green and have bristle-tipped lobes. Oregon white oak's leaves average about 5 inches (13 cm) long and 3 inches (7.5 cm) wide and have five to seven lobes. They are lustrous dark green on the upper surface and pale green with fine, rusty hairs below. The waxy upper surface and hairy underside evidently helps them retain moisture during the long, droughty summer.

Oregon oak's acorn develops in one season. It is about 1 inch (2.5 cm) long and is heavy—about 85 per pound (190 per kg). Good nut crops are borne about every other year and can produce 1000 pounds per acre (1100 kg per ha).

Large, bushy clusters of the leafy (Christmas) mistletoe *Phoradendron flavescens*, a parasitic plant, are often seen in the crowns of oak trees. Mistletoe clumps and lichens hanging from the gnarled, leafless limbs impart an eerie appearance to old oak trees on a winter night.

Oregon oaks often have large, round galls attached to their leaves and twigs. These hard-shelled, hollow spheres are calluses in the foliage induced by two species of gall wasps (harmless to people), which use them as egg chambers (Furniss and Carolin 1977). The leaf galls, called poppers, are a favorite of children, who stomp on them to make a popping sound.

Ecological Role

Some species of oak grow almost exclusively on certain kinds of soils, but Oregon white oak is more of an opportunist, growing wherever it will not be readily crowded out by conifers or more aggressive broad-leaved trees. Douglas-fir and bigleaf maple, for example, are not only more tolerant of shade than oaks are, they also grow faster and have replaced oak communities at an alarming rate. Today oak is mostly restricted to the driest areas; shallow, rocky soils; and south-facing slopes—and even in these habitats it may be giving way to other trees and tall shrubs. But how then can we account for the historic abundance of Oregon white oak even as far north as southern British Columbia?

To understand the ecology of Oregon white oak, we need to consider the role that human activities have played, probably for thousands of years. Oregon white oak forms self-perpetuating woodlands only in habitats too arid for other more-competitive trees, and few sites west of the Cascades are actually too dry for Douglas-fir. Yet mid-nineteenth-century government land surveys and other evidence confirm that open oak woodlands and prairies with scattered oaks covered more than a million acres in the Willamette Valley alone (Boyd 1999; U.S. Forest Service 1990).

In 1826, botanical explorer David Douglas became the first of many journalists to witness the fires set annually by Native Americans in the Willamette and other valleys. Native peoples burned these valleys to favor production of camas (*Camassia*) and other food plants and to herd deer and attract them to areas by producing succulent new forage (Davies 1980).

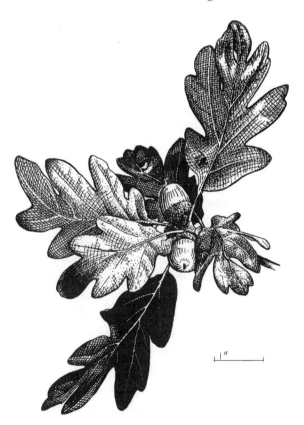

Oregon white oak (Garry oak)

Frequent burning favors the oak since older trees are moderately resistant to fire damage. Fire induces stump sprouts and root suckers in oak. (In contrast, the slow-growing Douglas-fir saplings on dry sites are readily killed by fires.) Also, oak seedlings have a low survival rate in sod or heavy duff and are more successful when this material has been burned.

Evidence from many sources now indicates that the expansive oak woodlands and prairies historically found west of the Cascades were largely a result of deliberate burning by aboriginal people. In these areas, dry lightning storms are uncommon, and even fewer occur when vegetation is parched enough to carry fire; thus it is doubtful that lightning ignitions alone could have perpetuated the oak communities. In the 1840s and 1850s, thousands of Oregon Trail pioneers established homesteads west of the Cascades among the oak woodlands and prairies. The Native peoples and their burning practices were displaced, and within a century the oak communities, especially those in relatively moist sites, were crowded out by Douglas-fir and other woody vegetation, or they were destroyed by land development.

Today, conservation organizations and government agencies recognize the plight of the Oregon white oak and its associated native prairie communities. The Garry Oak Meadow Preservation Society headquartered in Victoria, British Columbia, is concerned about declining oak communities, which are among British Columbia's most diverse terrestrial ecosystems, containing many imperiled species. In western Washington, the Nature Conservancy estimates that only 3 percent of the original oak-prairie communities still exist, and many of those are being colonized by Douglas-fir or invaded by Scotch broom and other noxious plants. Washington's Department of Fish and Wildlife lists measures for restoring oak woodlands, which it considers priority habitat because of its myriad of plants

yellow bells in Oregon white oak habitat

and animals, including species rarely found elsewhere. The acorn crop is a special feature of oak communities that provides abundant food for diverse wildlife.

Fire ecologist Jim Agee (1996) has evaluated different techniques for restoring Oregon white oak communities. He points out that many of these habitats have deteriorated to the point that simply reintroducing fire may not help. Douglas-fir or aggressive weeds might regenerate better than the few remnant oaks. Coordinated restoration treatments may be needed, including removal of conifers, weed control, fuel removal, burning, and planting of oaks and native herbs.

Human History

Native peoples made heavy use of Oregon white oak acorns, eating them raw, roasted, or sun-dried; making them into soup, mush, pancakes, or bread; and also storing them (Moerman 1998). Some anthropologists suspect that these people long ago aided the northward spread of this tree by carrying acorns. Another theory is that these oaks and other warm-climate plants, including Pacific madrone, spread northward in the warmer climatic period that the Northwest experienced a few thousand years ago (Long and others 1998).

Botanist David Douglas discovered Oregon white oak in the 1820s and named it for Nicholas Garry, an official of the Hudson Bay Company who aided his explorations. During the late 1800s and early 1900s, Oregon white oak supplied much of the hardwood lumber needs of the Northwest. Its wood compares with eastern oaks in many qualities, including hardness. It is fine-grained, heavy, hard, and strong and was used for agricultural implements, wedges for felling trees, furniture, flooring, and ship construction.

Today, little Oregon white oak is harvested for lumber, in part because of the modest supply and the fact that much of it grows on countless small properties not managed for producing timber. However, the oak commands high prices for firewood and fence posts, uses aided by the fact that the wood splits readily. The heartwood is so durable that oak fence posts last almost twice as long in the ground as those of western redcedar.

Today the greatest value of craggy old Oregon white oaks probably lies in the way they enhance wildlife habitat and scenery. However, while visiting oak woodlands, particularly in the Willamette Valley, it is a good idea to watch out for its major undergrowth associate, poison oak (*Rhus diversiloba*), which forms both a low shrub and a vine in the trees.

silhouette of Oregon white oak (Garry oak)

CALIFORNIA BLACK OAK

Quercus kelloggii, Beech family—Fagaceae

California black oak commonly borders dry meadows, boulder piles, and other openings in the ponderosa pine forest high up in the Oregon Siskiyous and the mountains of California. This oak also spreads across the low interior valleys of southwestern Oregon, where its luxuriant green foliage stands out amid parched, grassy slopes baking in oppressive summer heat. The sturdy, forked trunk and massive limbs of old trees are covered with blackish bark.

Where It Grows

In Oregon, the California black oak is confined to interior valleys west of the Cascades, ranging north as far as Eugene. In the dry valleys and foothills southward from Roseburg, it becomes more and more abundant, while Oregon white oak becomes less prominent. It inhabits well-drained, stony, and droughty soils but, unlike Oregon white oak, does not tolerate floodplains or other wet sites. In the far south of Oregon and into California, black oak also ascends to middle elevations in the mountains, where it is one of the few large broad-leaved trees that penetrate the ponderosa pine–mixed conifer forest. For example, in the vicinity of Mount Shasta, it attains elevations of 6000 feet (1800 m).

Appearance

California black oaks growing in an open stand have a broad, bright-green canopy like bigleaf maple, but the oak occupies much drier sites than maple will tolerate. Vigorous, open-grown California black oaks have a dense canopy that obscures the large inner branches. In contrast, an old oak has sparse foliage that reveals its picturesque form and crooked, spreading branch-trunks. Mature black oaks on valley sites commonly reach 36 inches (90 cm) in diameter

and 80 feet (25 m) in height, and occasionally one will develop into a massive monarch. Surprisingly, considering that this species is most abundant in California, the largest-known black oak inhabits the Siskiyou National Forest in southwestern Oregon, where it stands 9 feet (2.7 m) thick and 124 feet (38 m) tall (Jensen and Ross 2003). Old black oaks commonly have a haggard appearance due to heart rot and weather damage, as from heavy, wet snowfalls. They have broken branch-trunks and cavities used by wildlife.

Black oak leaves are bright green, 4 to 10 inches (10 to 25 cm) long, and distinguished by pointed, bristle-tipped lobes—usually seven of them. In May, when new leaves emerge from the buds, they are red and velvety. By June they are full-grown, bright yellow-green and translucent in the sun. In autumn, the leaves range from tawny yellow to golden brown.

The tree's acorn measures 1 to 1½ inches (2.5 to 4 cm) long and is cradled in a deep cup. It ripens during the second year and serves as a major food for wildlife, which seem unaffected by its bitter, tannin-rich taste.

Ecological Role

California black oak is even less tolerant of shade and competition than its associate, ponderosa pine. However, black oak also extends into low-elevation sites too dry for ponderosa in the interior valleys of southwestern Oregon. Saplings of ponderosa pine and other conifers can grow up beneath and through a black oak canopy. On the other hand, black oak saplings can ascend through some of the chaparral shrub communities. Black oaks require some direct sunlight, and they die when overtopped by other trees. As young black oaks mature amid an increasingly crowded stand,

California black oak

the nuts into these pockets, pointed end first, for future use. It may store hundreds of acorns in an individual tree, flush with the surface so as to be inaccessible to squirrels. Anyone who has experienced the raucous harangue of an angry squirrel can imagine the scolding that sometimes greets this woodpecker.

In mountain areas, California black oak has lost ground to conifers due to fire suppression. Returning some approximation of historical fire disturbances, using prescribed or natural fires or removal of competing trees, could help restore oak habitats.

Sudden oak death, a disease caused by *Phytophthora ramorum*, is often deadly to California black oak and tanoak and has spread along much of the northern California coast since its discovery in 1995 (Barrett and others 2006). This worrisome disease has been found in nursery stock in many states, and quarantine has been instituted to slow its spread.

Human History

Native Americans of many cultures relied on the oil-rich acorns of California black oak as a staple food (Moerman 1998). These people located summer encampments among black oak groves and toiled laboriously, pounding the nutmeats into meal, often using cup holes (mortars) in boulders or bedrock. They leached out most of the bitter tannin by soaking and washing the meal in stream water. Leached meal or flour was then prepared variously as soup, mush, gruel, porridge, pancakes, biscuits, and bread. Acorn crops were also stored in granaries for future use.

In Oregon, the wood of California black oak is prized as fuel, but little of it is harvested for manufactured products. In California, its greater abundance has brought about commercial use as paneling and furniture, enhanced by the attractive grain and pattern. The wood's hardness and finishing qualities also make it suitable for flooring.

they often extend toward a hole in the overhead canopy, sometimes leaning fifteen or twenty degrees to reach it. In conifer-dominated stands, relict oaks persist in boulder piles or other harsh microsites.

Fire is an important factor in black oak communities. The habitat has long, dry summers and historically burned every decade or two in fires of low or medium intensity. Large black oaks, particular those in rocky places, often survived fire, but each blaze killed some trees and created openings that made room for oak seedlings. Old, partially rotten oaks would burn out but be replaced by vigorous sprouts arising from the stump.

California black oak is important for wildlife because of its acorn crops and nesting cavities. The acorns are an abundant, high-quality food eaten by many birds and mammals and stored for use in winter when other foods are scarce. The acorn woodpecker, a denizen of black oak communities, is a case in point. Called *el carpintero* by Spanish Californians, this red-crowned bird hammers acorn-sized holes into tree trunks, utility poles, or buildings and jams

CANYON LIVE OAK

Quercus chrysolepis, Beech family—Fagaceae

Canyon live oak, abundant in California, extends northward into southwestern Oregon. It is easy to recognize by its small, leathery leaves, some of which resemble holly leaves. Canyon live oak plays multiple roles. It is the rugged little evergreen clinging to cliffs and rock gorges; but in an open valley, it becomes a broad-crowned shade tree. In the mixed evergreen forest, it grows tall and slender, with a sparse canopy, while on hot, dry ridges it takes on shrubby form as a member of mountain chaparral (brush) communities.

Where It Grows

Canyon live oak occupies much of the foothill and mountain country in California, and scattered populations inhabit mountains that rise out of Arizona's deserts. It spreads northward in Oregon as far as the canyons and ridges near Roseburg. It grows in Oregon's Coast Range, a few miles inland from the ocean, and extends inland to the western slopes of the southern Cascades. It is plentiful along Interstate 5 in the Siskiyou and Klamath mountains from Canyonville, Oregon, to Mount Shasta, California, and along US 199 from Grants Pass, Oregon, nearly to Crescent City, California.

Appearance

Canyon live oak is most conspicuous as the small evergreen broad-leaved tree clinging to rock-walled canyons, its crooked trunk leaning out and supporting an irregularly shaped canopy. As an open-grown valley tree, its short,

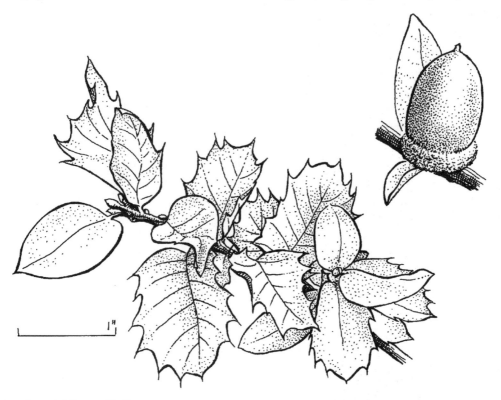

canyon live oak foliage and fruit

sturdy trunk supports a dense, rounded canopy whose horizontal spread often equals or exceeds its height. Mature, open-grown live oaks commonly attain 36 inches (90 cm) or more in diameter, 60 to 80 feet (18 to 24 m) in height, and 80 feet (24 m) or more in maximum canopy spread.

Trees and shrubby forms of this species that have foliage within easy reach are readily identified by their small, shiny, dark-green evergreen leaves. However, the tall, slender canyon live oaks that grow in the mixed-evergreen forest are harder to identify because their foliage is high overhead. Still, the thin, grayish brown, scaly bark distinguishes them from the associated tanoak and Pacific madrone.

Canyon live oak leaves exhibit confusing variety, sometimes even on the same branch. The leaves are oval and have a pointed tip. They range from 1 to 3 inches (2.5 to 8 cm) long and are about half as wide. The most diagnostic leaves have spiny edges, like holly. This is juvenile foliage, most common on young trees and on sprouts at the base of older trees. Canopy leaves on older trees tend to be smaller and have smooth edges.

The acorn is 1 to 2 inches (2.5 to 5 cm) long and held in a thick but shallow cup that has golden-colored hairs on its scaly outer surface. The nuts are heavy—ranging from 50 to 150 per pound (110 to 310 per kg)—and a large, open-grown tree can produce a crop weighing as much as 400 pounds (180 kg).

Ecological Role

Canyon live oak grows as both a tree and a shrub in the mixed evergreen forests of southwestern Oregon. It is less tolerant of shade and competition than the associated Douglas-fir, tanoak, or golden chinkapin but more tolerant than Pacific madrone. On productive sites, it appears after fire or logging, as a result of stump sprouts and regeneration from seeds, but it is eventually outgrown and replaced by the other species. On drier sites, it persists longer, and on rock cliffs and boulder piles it remains the dominant tree by default.

The reasons behind its supremacy in occupying rocky canyons are not clear, but it seems to excel in sending roots deep and widespread through the crevices. Canyon live oak is very drought tolerant and thus able to regenerate and persist in shrubby form on hot, dry ridges—along with manzanita (*Arctostaphylos*) and buck brush (*Ceanothus*). On these sites, the shrubby canyon live oaks may represent a distinct variety (var. *nana*) or a hybrid with the shrubby huckleberry oak (*Q. vaccinifolia*). Here, chaparral develops after fires, and forest trees become established very slowly, if at all.

Canyon live oak's ability to colonize rock lands and other harsh sites benefits watershed stability and wildlife habitat. Its plentiful acorn crop is a major asset for wildlife. Band-tailed pigeons swallow the acorns whole, and their powerful gizzards do the shelling.

Human History

Native Americans used the acorns of canyon live oak as a staple food much like the nuts of California black oak. One California tribe leached them all winter in swampy ground, to remove the bitter tannic acid, before boiling or roasting them for eating in spring (Moerman 1998).

The wood of canyon live oak is extremely heavy, hard, strong, and stiff. Early settlers called this tree maul oak because they were able to use it for sledgehammers and wood-splitting wedges. They also employed it for wagon tongues, wheels, and axles.

The wood makes an attractive multicolored paneling, but it is seldom harvested commercially. However, it is prized as firewood.

NATIVE FRUIT TREES

Prunus, Pyrus, Crataegus, and *Celtis*

Several of the Greater Northwest's native species bear edible fleshy fruits and at least sometimes grow as "trees"—mostly with a single stem attaining at least 20 feet (6 m) in height—although they often occur as tall, multistemmed shrubs. Most of these native "fruit trees" are members of the rose family (Rosaceae), which also includes the domestic cherry, apricot, and peach (all species of *Prunus*) as well as apple, pear, and mountain-ash. Our natives include cherry trees, plum trees, crab apple, and hawthorn. One other native fruit tree, hackberry, is a member of the elm family (Ulmaceae).

***

Note: See also the Fruit Trees section in the Naturalized Trees chapter at the end of Part 2.

BITTER CHERRY (*Prunus emarginata*) AND CHOKECHERRY (*P. virginiana*)

Where They Grow

Bitter cherry is widely distributed in the Greater Northwest west of the Continental Divide, whereas chokecherry is even more prevalent in our region and extends clear across North America. Both species commonly form tall shrubs, but in moist sites and mild climates they sometimes grow as trees.

Comparative Appearance

Both species have oval leaves that can be readily distinguished from those of most other native trees by a pair of knoblike glands that are attached to the base of most leaf blades in bitter cherry and to the leaf stem near the blade in chokecherry. Bitter cherry leaves are 1 to 3 inches (2.5 to 8 cm) long and have a rounded tip; chokecherry leaves are 1½ to 4 inches (4 to 10 cm) long and have a pointed tip.

Bitter cherry has small, round clusters of fragrant white flowers; chokecherry has cylindrical clusters of white flowers, 4 to 6 inches (10 to 15 cm) long. Both species bear cherries about ½ inch (1 cm) long that range in color from red to purple and black.

Ecological Role

Flowering bitter cherry and chokecherry trees attract honeybees and other pollinators, and the trees hum with activity in the spring. The fruit crop is devoured by a variety of birds. The large, stone-hard seeds pass unharmed through birds' digestive systems and are deposited at some other site. Seeds that land in a burned, cutover, or otherwise disturbed area have the best chance of becoming established. However, the seeds can also survive in the upper soil layers for decades and then germinate after the area experiences a fire. The closely related pin cherry (*P. pensylvanica*), which becomes treelike east of our region, is also called fire cherry because it suddenly appears in quantity after forest fire as a result of seeds that lay dormant in the soil.

One variety of bitter cherry (*P. emarginata* var. *mollis*) grows primarily as a tree, up to 10 inches (25 cm) in diameter and 50 feet tall (15 m), in moist low-elevation forests west of the Cascades and in northern Idaho. Its distinctive bark is reddish brown with light-colored horizontal bands similar to the bark of water birch. This variety typically gets established after fire or logging and grows rapidly for perhaps thirty years, but after that it is overtopped and crowded out by red alder, Douglas-fir, or other forest trees. In these situations, bitter cherry seldom lives fifty years, but it produces seeds that are ready to spring from the ashes or bare ground next time the forest is disturbed.

bitter cherry

In moist low-elevation pasturelands and streamside habitats, particularly in northern Idaho, chokecherry becomes a tree up to 12 inches (30 cm) thick and 60 feet (18 m) tall (Johnson 1995). However, throughout the Greater Northwest, chokecherry plants are most often multistemmed, bushy shrubs 12 to 20 feet (3.5 to 6 m) tall. In spring, chokecherries stand out from the other trees and shrubs, clothed in clusters of creamy-white blossoms. Robust clumps of chokecherries are even scattered along ephemeral stream courses that thread their way into semi-arid grasslands. Chokecherry twigs are a favorite food of deer and elk, and in some areas the plants are so heavily browsed that they are unable to grow above knee height.

Human History

Northwest Natives peeled the bark of bitter cherry trees, polished it to a rich red color, and wove strips of it into their decorative baskets (Moerman 1998). They used both bitter cherry and chokecherry as medicines; the latter was commonly applied for relief of stomach complaints (Hart 1976). When Captain Meriwether Lewis became violently ill with abdominal cramps and fever while exploring the upper Missouri River on June 10, 1805, he drank an astringent tea from chokecherry twigs and soon "was entirely relieved from pain and in fact every symptom of the disorder forsook me" (Ambrose 1996, 235).

Chokecherries are the most frequently recorded plant foods cited in North American ethnobotanical studies (Moerman 1998). Native people harvested chokecherries after the first freeze, which made them sweeter (Hart 1976). Most of this crop was sun-dried and stored for later use. Women pulverized the berries, seed included, making a finely ground material they formed into cakes, which they dried in the sun. The berry meal was a major ingredient in pemmican and an amendment used with other foods.

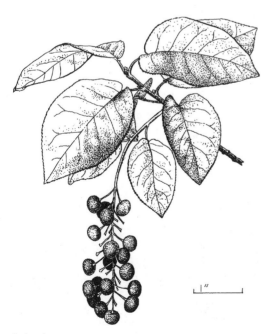

choke cherry

Birds love both species, but today humans find bitter cherry true to its name, while chokecherry is sweet but quite tart when fully ripe. No amount of sugar is adequate to make bitter cherries palatable, whereas chokecherries are often sweetened and made into jelly, syrup, or wine (Johnson 1995).

KLAMATH PLUM (*Prunus subcordata*) AND AMERICAN OR WILD PLUM (*Prunus americana*)

Where They Grow

Klamath plum is generally a thick-stemmed shrub when growing on poor soils, but on moist valley sites it can become a small tree about 6 inches (15 cm) in diameter and 20 feet (6 m) tall. Its main distribution is in foothill country of northern California, but it extends north into Oregon, especially east of the Cascades from Klamath Lake and Summer Lake to Bend, where it can be seen along pasture fence lines. It is widely scattered in the Rogue River drainage and other interior valleys west of the Cascades as far north as Salem.

American or wild plum is a rare resident of valleys in western and central Montana that becomes more common farther east. A few of these small trees are reported in western Montana, near Hamilton and in Sanders County.

Klamath plum flower and fruit

Comparative Appearance

Klamath plum's treelike form has a short, stout trunk and broad, dome-shaped crown, like a dwarf domestic fruit tree. However, it also has scraggly branches with thornlike spur shoots. It bears small, rounded leaves with blades less than 2 inches (5 cm) long, usually with a few glands at the leaf base. The leaves of American or wild plum are more oval and pointed than those of Klamath plum (which is not found in Montana).

The apple-blossom-like flowers of Klamath plum are about ¾ inch (2 cm) across, much larger than those of bitter cherry and chokecherry. The fruit is nearly 1 inch (2.5 cm) long, purplish red or yellowish, and tart but juicy. East of the Cascades, plums ripen after the leaves turn multicolored—red, orange, and yellow—and drop off. The orange-to-red fruit of American or wild plum is similar to that of Klamath plum.

Ecological Role

These little plum trees are scarce, but their fruit is highly sought out by a variety of wildlife species, which in turn inadvertently help distribute the undigested seeds and thereby aid regeneration.

Human History

It may be that the American or wild plum trees in western Montana arose from seeds brought back by Native Americans who customarily traveled east to hunt bison on the Great Plains (Lackschewitz 1991). A diarist who marched with General Crook of the U.S. Cavalry in the 1876 Indian campaigns just east of the Montana border wrote that the starving soldiers "including the General stampeded into a [American] plum patch, going down on our hands and knees to pick up the ripe fruit that the wind had shaken off" (Schuyler 2006). The soldiers captured a large Indian cache of dried fruit and credited the wild plum and wild cherries with saving them from scurvy.

PACIFIC OR OREGON CRAB APPLE
(*Pyrus fusca*)

Where It Grows

The Pacific or Oregon crab apple inhabits the cold, foggy coastal forest zone from Alaska to northern California, an unusual environment for a fruit tree. It often borders beach meadows or swamps along the oceanfront but also grows in moist pastures and streamside thickets at low elevations west of the Cascades in association with red alder, bigleaf maple, willows, and cascara.

Pacific crab apple

Appearance

Pacific crab apple often forms scrubby thickets along the coast but develops a trunk 8 to 10 inches (20 to 25 cm) thick and 20 to 30 feet (6 to 9 m) tall under less-exposed conditions. Like Klamath plum, it has thornlike spurs on its twigs.

Crab apple leaves are egg-shaped and 2 to 3 inches (5 to 8 cm) long, and they often have shallow lobes or notches like those of domestic apple trees. Another name proposed for this species, *P. diversifolia*, recognizes its diverse leaf shapes. The leaves are dull, dark green on the upper surface, paler and generally with whitish hairs underneath. They turn scarlet and bright orange in the fall.

This little tree bears typical apple blossoms, waxy and white or rose colored and delightfully fragrant. The apples are about ¾ inch (2 cm) long and yellow with pink cheeks, and they hang in small clusters from rather long stalks. Their flesh is thin, rather dry, and extremely sour.

Ecological Role

Crab apple is appreciated by grouse, bears, and no doubt other animals.

Human History

Native peoples of the Pacific coast also used the crab apple as food, eating it freshly picked or storing it in baskets until it ripened more fully (Moerman 1998). Pacific crab apple has been known to science since it was described in 1792 by naturalist Archibald Menzies, who found it near present-day Port Angeles, Washington. Its fruit makes good home-canned preserves.

The tree grows slowly, attaining 100 or more years of age and producing wood that is fine-grained, heavy, and hard. Northwest Natives used this wood for prongs of their seal spears and for wedges to split western redcedar. Early grist mills in Ontario, Canada, used a similar crab apple wood for their gears.

BLACK HAWTHORN (*Crataegus douglasii*)
Where It Grows

One of our native fruit trees has true thorns and "false" apples: the hawthorn or thorn-apple. Hawthorns hybridize freely and so are a very complex, taxonomically unstable genus containing at least a few hundred species and varieties in North America. However, tree enthusiasts in the Greater Northwest need not cope with this confusing plethora, since we have only two broadly recognized species of hawthorn. One of these, Columbia hawthorn (*C. columbiana*), is primarily shrubby, grows in scattered locations east of the Cascades, and can be distinguished by its impressive 2-inch (5-cm) thorns.

In contrast, black hawthorn is very widespread in the Greater Northwest, and it attains tree size—up to 10 inches (25 cm) thick and 25 or 30 feet (8 or 9 m) tall on rich valley-bottom soils. More commonly, however, it forms multi-stemmed clusters dotting pastureland, each consisting of tough, spindly, crooked trunks supporting a broad, brambly canopy about 15 feet (4.5 m) tall. It is locally abundant in moist fields and along streams at lower elevations.

Appearance

Black hawthorn is distinguished by branches armed with a multitude of tough, slender thorns ½ to 1 inch (1 to 2.5 cm) long. The twigs grow in a zigzag manner, which enhances the density of the canopy and makes the spiny armor even more effective. Black hawthorn leaves are 1 to 2 inches (2.5 to 5 cm) long and often rather fan-shaped, with small, shallow lobes or deep notches, but quite variable. The flowers are white and like small apple blossoms. The fruit is black, about ½ inch (1 cm) long, and contains three to five bone-hard seeds.

Ecological Role

These small, dry fruits are eagerly eaten by birds, bears, and some other animals. In open, semi-arid country where magpies and hawthorns are abundant, nearly every large hawthorn hosts at least one magpie nest. Often there are two or three of the intricately woven stick-pile dwellings, one of which is the birds' current residence. Magpies negotiate their way through the dense, thorny foliage with amazing ease and agility. The Magpie Forest is a conservation reserve featuring black hawthorn and native prairie near the campus of Washington State University in Pullman.

Human History

The black hawthorn fruits are of little interest to humans. That hawthorns can be used to make an effective barrier was recognized by medieval Anglo-Saxons, whose word *haw* meant "hedge."

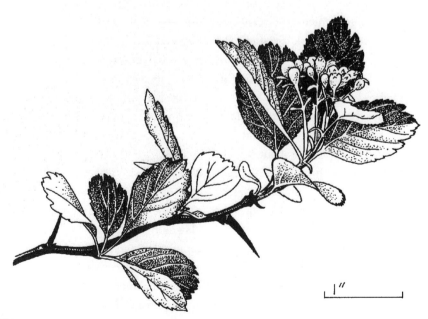

1"

black hawthorn

NETLEAF HACKBERRY (*Celtis reticulata*)

Where It Grows

Keen observers puzzle about the identity of the craggy, hunched-over broad-leaved tree that inhabits some of the driest, most forbidding desert canyons in the Northwest. Netleaf hackberry is strikingly unusual. Out of 150 or so members of the elm family worldwide and a few dozen in North America, netleaf hackberry is the only one native to the Greater Northwest. Moreover, its northwestern occurrence is restricted to austere and largely treeless habitats, unconnected to its main distribution hundreds of miles away along the Colorado River and farther south. The Northwest's hackberry trees may be a relict of the warmer climate period (Hypsithermal period) when this species was probably more widespread in the interior West.

Netleaf hackberry is the only common tree in the bottom of furnacelike Hells Canyon of the Snake River forming the boundary between northeastern Oregon and Idaho. It is also seen on the south side of the Columbia River east of the Dalles and along the lower reaches of the Deschutes, John Day, Salmon, and Clearwater rivers. However, rather than lining the watercourses as cottonwood and willows do, hackberry often grows mostly in rocky sites well above the water.

Appearance

Considering its growing conditions, it is not surprising that netleaf hackberry becomes a squatty dwarf with a crooked trunk. Large old trees in Hells Canyon are commonly 12 to 15 inches (30 to 40 cm) thick and 20 to 30 feet (6 to 9 m) tall, but in some areas hackberry grows as a gnarled shrub. When it grows in the productive alluvial soils along the rivers, or when it is cultivated, it grows relatively straight and tall, with a trunk 24 inches (60 cm) or more in diameter.

Hackberry produces an extensive network of crooked limbs that supports a thick canopy. The leaves are 2 to 3 inches (5 to 8 cm) long and egg-shaped. Like elm leaves, they are lopsided at the base—one side being larger than the other. They are thick and dull green, and

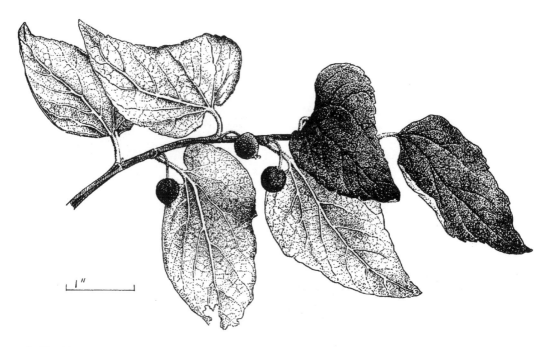

netleaf hackberry

they feel rough or coarse. The tree's common and scientific names denote the prominent network of veins visible on the underside of the leaves. Another unusual feature is its smooth, gray bark that has projecting corky ridges. Thick foliage hides most of the cherrylike fruits, which are ¼ inch (6 to 7 mm) thick and are attached singly at the base of leaves near the branch tip. The fruits are reddish-brown to purple and have a sweet but thin pulp.

Ecological Role

Hackberry is exceptionally tolerant of drought, inhabiting places that receive as little as 7 inches (180 mm) of precipitation in an average year. Summer temperatures reach 110 degrees F (43 C), accompanied by relative humidity of 5 to 10 percent. It seldom occupies the productive alluvial soils along rivers. The fruits are harvested by birds. In the Idaho river canyons, hackberry is a favorite food of beavers, while mule deer and bighorn sheep browse the young twigs (Johnson 1995).

Human History

Little is known about early human use of hackberry in the Northwest. If any fruits are left by birds, they can be picked as late as midwinter, a season of short duration in hackberry country. In the desert Southwest where it is more abundant, the Navahos and other Native peoples used the fruits extensively as food (Moerman 1998).

BIGLEAF MAPLE

Acer macrophyllum, Maple family—Aceraceae

The Midwest, East, and South have several species of large, spreading maples, whereas the West has only one: bigleaf maple, which nevertheless is an admirable representative. Bigleaf maple is in a class by itself, being North America's largest maple and having by far the biggest leaves. Unlike Eastern maples that are quite cold hardy, bigleaf maple is adapted to the mild climate west of the Cascades. Also, it is a trademark species of the coastal rain forest because it hosts long, heavy drapes of hanging moss and lichens, reminiscent of scenes from a Southern swamp. Bigleaf maple is familiar to people living west of the Cascades as the most common and eminently suitable shade tree in residential areas and parks—and many of these highly valued maples sprang up on their own.

Where It Grows

Bigleaf maple is widespread west of the Cascades and British Columbia Coast Ranges, from the north end of Vancouver Island and nearby Sullivan Bay on the mainland, southward to California. In much of the coastal Northwest, it grows from sea level to about 1500 feet (450 m) in elevation, but it ascends as high as 4000 feet (1200 m) in southwestern Oregon and sometimes higher in the mountains of California, where it becomes less common. Small populations are reported in a few moist canyons on the east slope of the Cascades; otherwise, it is absent from the inland Northwest. The species' northern limit and its scarcity east of the Cascade crest probably reflect sensitivity to cold temperatures. Its relatively low upper-elevational limits suggest an inability to complete its annual growth in a short, cool summer that is bracketed by occa-

sional dumps of heavy, wet snow, disastrous to trees with large leaves and spreading crowns.

Appearance

In productive valley sites where it is not crowded by conifers, bigleaf maple develops a broad, outstretched crown. The stout bole is commonly 36 to 48 inches (90 to 120 cm) in diameter and separates into great branch-trunks 10 to 15 feet (3 to 4.5 m) above ground. The canopy of an open-grown bigleaf maple is nearly as wide as the tree is tall. Exceptionally large bigleaf maples attain 6 feet (1.8 m) in diameter, and the tallest ones attain 125 feet (38 m) or so. According to the American Forestry Association, the country's largest maple is one of this species in Clatsop County, Oregon: 11 feet (3.4 m) in diameter and 101 feet (30 m) tall. In contrast, when bigleaf maples grow in dense stands, they develop a narrow crown situated high up on a relatively slender trunk. The bark on young trees is light gray-brown and smooth but becomes darker and with interlacing ridges on old trunks.

This species is easily distinguished from other native and introduced maples by its exceptionally large leaves. The leaf blades are 8 to 12 inches (20 to 30 cm) across, and their stalks are 6 to 12 inches (15 to 30 cm) long. The leaves have five lobes deeply cut into them, in a palmate pattern like fingers and thumb on a hand. The leaf stems also differ from most other maples in exuding milky sap when cut. All maples bear their leaves, twigs, and buds opposite each other in pairs, which aids identification year-round.

In late April and early May, the translucent, yellow-green new leaves are unfolding and only half-grown while copious clusters of fragrant yellow blossoms 4 to 6 inches

bigleaf maple twig with seeds

(10 to 15 cm) long fill the canopy. These hanging blossoms teem with honeybees and other
insects gathering nectar and pollen on warm
spring days.

   Bigleaf maple depends on insects to fer-
tilize its flowers, and evidently this works well
since it is a prolific seed producer. Its fruit, like
that of all maples, is a double samara, meaning
it consists of two large, hair-covered seeds fused
together. In bigleaf maple, the joined seeds each
have a 1½-inch (4-cm) wing attached so that

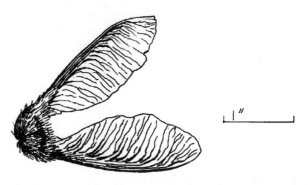

bigleaf maple fruit

bigleaf maple blossoms

squirrel extracting bigleaf maple seed

the fruit resembles a broad V. When launched from the tree into a stiff breeze, the fruit spins like a helicopter. Bigleaf maples begin to produce fruit when only ten years old, and some of the crop hangs on the trees through fall and winter, providing nutritious food for Douglas squirrels, finches, and evening grosbeaks when other seeds are scarce.

Ecological Role

Bigleaf maple is not a pioneer species comparable to red alder, which readily colonizes disturbed areas. Instead, it is considered relatively tolerant of shade and competition. However, it is not as tolerant as vine maple, which is able to survive beneath a dense conifer canopy. Bigleaf maple gradually increases in areas that are recovering from fire or logging, and later it is gradually shaded out as conifers overtop it. It sprouts vigorously from cut stumps and produces seedlings readily in open areas as well as beneath established conifer stands, but successful establishment is unlikely beneath conifers. Each spring, countless seeds from the previous season's crop germinate on the forest floor and in suburban flower beds, in vacant lots, and even from cracks in sidewalks. In the forest, perhaps only one in a million of these new seedlings is able to root into mineral soil in a spot where there is adequate growing space for it to grow up and become a tree.

Bigleaf maple is a major constituent of river bottom and streamside hardwood communities along with red alder, black cottonwood, and willows, but it cannot tolerate long-term flooding as cottonwood can. It inhabits meadows, pastures, old fields, and many young forests that arise after logging or fire. It occupies a broad range of habitats, from the hot, dry valleys of southwestern Oregon to the rain forests of the Olympic Peninsula and

Opposite: bigleaf maple in rain forest

the west side of Vancouver Island. In these ultrahumid habitats, old, spreading maples survive in small openings among conifers three times as tall. The maples are draped with hanging club moss (*Selaginella oregana*) and other mosses and lichens that can weigh up to four times as much as the tree's foliage—and more yet when saturated with rain or clinging wet snow (Nadkarni 1984). Bright green licorice ferns (*Polypodium glycyrrhiza*) grow out of the moss litter high up in these 200- to 300-year-old rain-forest maples.

Bigleaf maple can grow on nutrient-poor soils (albeit as a smaller bushy tree), including rock slides, but wherever it grows, its abundant leaf litter enriches the soil. The fallen leaves, blossoms, and seeds contain high concentrations of potassium, calcium, and other important nutrients.

Human History

Northwest Native peoples used bigleaf maple in many ways. They sprouted seeds for food (comparable to alfalfa sprouts today), wove inner bark into baskets, covered food in cooking pits with the leaves, and carved the wood into dishes, spoons, and canoe paddles (Moerman 1998).

Bigleaf maple's wood is valued for specialty lumber and fuel, although the oldest trees often have heart rot. The heartwood is light reddish brown, fine-grained, moderately heavy, and moderately hard and strong. The wood is not suitable for flooring but is used in furniture and decorative veneer. It is a preferred wood for piano frames. It takes a high polish and often has interesting grain, such as in curly or bird's-eye maple. Some mature trees have large burls on their lower trunk, which are prized by skilled wood crafters for their beautiful grain patterns.

Bigleaf maple has sweet sap that can be collected in winter and made into syrup, although this is not done commercially because the produce is of lower quality than syrup made from the eastern sugar maple (Ruth and others 1972). John Worrall, of the University of British Columbia, also points out that the Northwest coast doesn't have the crisp February weather that induces sap flow in eastern maples.

Today, bigleaf maple is probably the most common native shade tree west of the Cascades. Its stout, spreading limbs are a favorite site for children's tree houses. The tree turns a beautiful bright orange-yellow in fall, and for better or worse, its prodigious leaf-fall can be turned into compost. It is sometimes planted as a shade tree in England but is not successful in climates having cold winters.

SMALLER MAPLES

Acer spp., Maple family—Aceraceae

Small, often shrubby maples inhabit all but the driest and coldest forests in the Greater Northwest. Normally not very noticeable, these maples stand out in early autumn when they light up mountainsides with splotches of red and orange. One rather variable species, Rocky Mountain maple, is widely distributed across our region. Another, vine maple, is confined to the Cascades and the coast. Native populations of two other maples—bigtooth maple and boxelder—reach the eastern edge of the Greater Northwest.

ROCKY MOUNTAIN MAPLE AND DOUGLAS MAPLE (*Acer glabrum*)

Where They Grow

This species consists of two intergrading subspecies, and others have also been proposed. Such variability is understandable considering that it has adapted to diverse habitats ranging from low to moderately high elevations along the coast from Alaska to California and from northern interior British Columbia southward in the Rockies and desert mountains to southern Arizona.

Comparative Appearance

Where not suppressed by conifers, Rocky Mountain maple commonly forms a tight cluster of relatively straight, slender, vertical stems reaching 20 to 30 feet (6 to 9 m) high, occasionally 40 feet (12 m) or more in moist, productive valleys. The larger stems are often about 5 inches (13 cm) thick, but sometimes they grow to 10 inches (25 cm) or more thick.

The leaves typically have three main lobes

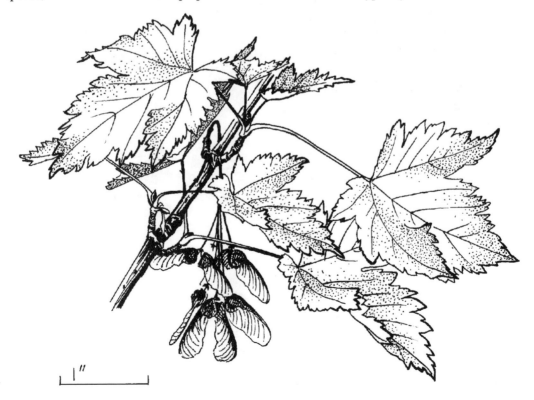

1"

Douglas maple with fruits

vine maple

and are 2 to 5 inches (5 to 13 cm) wide. The fruit is a double samara of two fused seeds each with an attached large wing. The wings spread out to form a ninety-degree angle. The variety most common west of the Continental Divide (*A. glabrum* var. *douglasii*), called Douglas maple, has reddish twigs.

Ecological Role

Rocky Mountain maple is very abundant in the inland mountains, where it is a major component of brush fields that arise after severe fires and serve as prime winter forage for deer and elk. Often the maple clumps appear to have been pruned of all low-hanging twigs as a result of browsing by wild herbivores. Hungry elk sometimes break slender maple stems to get at the new growth that is above their reach. Rocky Mountain maple resprouts vigorously when killed by fire, logging, or similar disturbance. When crowded and overtopped by conifer forest, it loses vigor and barely produces new twig growth. This species is less common west of the Cascades but can be found on dry, open, rocky sites including cliffs and rock slides.

Human History

Native peoples used the straight, strong, slender stems of Rocky Mountain maple for snowshoe frames, bows, and other utility purposes (Moerman 1998).

VINE MAPLE (*Acer circinatum*)

Where It Grows

Vine maple grows as a large, multistemmed shrub and a small, single-stemmed tree in openings and also beneath dark forest canopies. It is common on moist sites along the Northwest coast, from Bute Inlet about 135 miles (220 km) northwest of Vancouver, British Columbia, to the Klamath Mountains of northern California. It occupies humid sites on the east slope of the Cascades, up to about 3000 feet (900 m) in elevation, and westward to the ocean but, surprisingly, is rare on Vancouver Island. It is not found inland beyond the Cascades.

Appearance

Hikers west of the Cascades recognize vine maple as being an "octopus" tree whose slender, crooked trunks and long limbs sprawl across the understory of a conifer forest, sometimes forming a formidable barrier. In openings, vine maple grows more erect but still is short, with long, irregular branches and a trunk seldom as much as 10 inches (25 cm) thick.

Vine maple's leaves average 3 to 4 inches (8 to 10 cm) across and have seven or nine lobes with triangular points, making them somewhat star-shaped. In spring the delicate emerging leaves are bright yellow-green when the clusters of small flowers with red and green parts appear. Vigorous young shoots are reddish. The flowers are soon replaced by red-winged fruits. These double samaras differ from those of other native maples in having wings that spread in

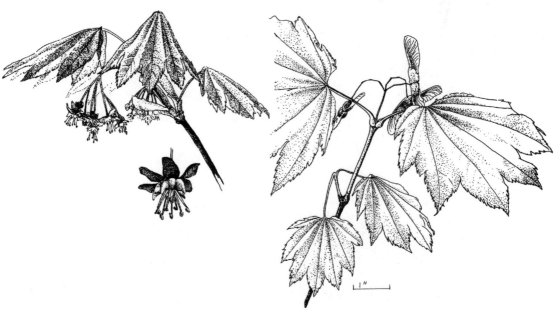

vine maple: in flower (with close-up); in fruit

opposite directions, at 180 degrees, as opposed to making a V. At summer's end, the leaves turn multicolored. Trees in partial sun have leaves that vary from scarlet to pink and orange while some are yellow or still bright green.

Ecological Role

This little tree contributes considerable coloration to a somber, conifer-dominated landscape. On open canyon walls, vine maples stand out from far away as splotches of brilliant red. When it grows in clearings and avalanche chutes, vine maple becomes a bushy, multistemmed tree. Prostrate limbs and stems flattened to the ground by heavy, wet snowfalls can take root in the damp organic soil.

Human History

The Quinault people of the Olympic Peninsula referred to vine maple as "basket tree" because they wove its long, straight shoots into open baskets used for carrying clams and fish. When it is cultivated as an ornamental, in moist cool climates, vine maple becomes a bushy, multistemmed tree as attractive as many of the exotic maples.

BIGTOOTH MAPLE (*Acer grandidentatum*)
Where It Grows

This small tree's form and habitat are similar to Rocky Mountain maple. It is found immediately south of our region in the cen-

tral Rocky Mountains of southeastern Idaho (as far north as Rexburg) and ranging south through Utah.

Appearance

It is distinguished by the few large, rounded teeth on its leaves, in contrast to the many small, sharp teeth on leaves of Rocky Mountain maple. Bigtooth maple's leaves turn brilliant red in autumn.

Ecological Role

Bigtooth maple is a conspicuous member of a tall shrub–broadleaf tree community that envelops lower slopes of the central Rockies, along with boxelder, aspen, mountain-mahogany (*Cercocarpus*), and scattered conifers. This contrasts with the conifer-dominated lower slopes associated with most of the Northwest's mountains.

Human History

There is little record of human use of this species, but its varied, bright fall coloration has attracted increased interest in it for landscaping applications.

BOXELDER (*Acer negundo*)
Where It Grows

Known as Manitoba maple in Canada, boxelder is widely distributed in central and eastern North America and common south of our area in the western United States.

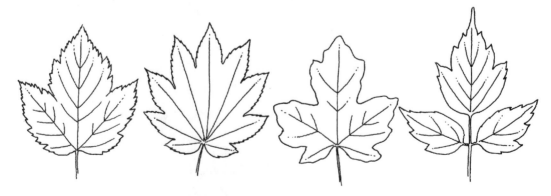

Left to right: Douglas maple, vine maple, bigtooth maple, boxelder

Appearance

Boxelder is a small to medium-sized tree distinguished by leaves that often have a maple-like shape, except that they are divided into three to seven leaflets. The fruit is a V-shaped double samara typical of maples.

Ecological Role

Most boxelders in the Greater Northwest were planted or became naturalized and spread along streams and other moist habitats. However, native boxelders are scattered along the Missouri River and its tributaries westward to the vicinity of Great Falls, Montana. Also, native populations are found immediately south of our region along the Snake River in southeastern Idaho (Johnson 1995).

Human History

Up until the midtwentieth century, midwestern boxelders were widely planted in western communities and on farmsteads because they are hardy and grow quickly, providing shelter and shade. These trees proved to be easily damaged and short-lived, and they also serve as habitat for boxelder bugs (*Boisea trivittata*), which become an annoying household pest.

CASCARA

Rhamnus purshiana, Buckthorn family—Rhamnaceae

Cascara is a little tree that has no value for lumber but is renowned as a medicinal, well known to woods-wise residents of the Northwest Coast. It is a small, often multistemmed tree that grows scattered among much larger conifers, alder, maple, and cottonwood. It is easily identified by its distinctive leaves, buds, and fruit. Cascara bark was used as a laxative by indigenous peoples and adopted in formal medical practice in the nineteenth century.

cascara buckthorn in spring with flowers and developing fruit

Where It Grows

Cascara grows in moist and wet sites at low elevations west of the Coast Range in southern British Columbia and west of the Cascades southward to northern California. Small populations inhabit streamsides on the east slope of the Cascades. Cascara is also widespread at low elevations in the wet inland forest region centered in northern Idaho and the Selkirk region of southeastern British Columbia.

Appearance

Cascara is a tall, multistemmed shrub or small tree. Open-grown trees often have a single stem and rather broad, bushy crown. West of the Cascades, cascara trees sometimes produce a trunk up to 12 inches (30 cm) or more in diameter and 30 to 40 feet (9 to 12 m) tall, if they escape the bark strippers. The bark is very thin and it ranges in color from dark brown to ashy gray, often with chalky white patches; its surface is broken into small scales.

The leaves are elliptical with blades 2½ to 6 inches (6 to 15 cm) long. They have ten to twelve pairs of prominent, parallel veins extending in a chevron from the midvein to the leaf margin, standing out like ribs. Although the leaves are alternatively arranged along the twigs, leaves on new growth are often attached nearly opposite each other. The foliage turns brilliant yellow in autumn.

Cascara is readily identified in winter by its buds, which are unique among northwestern trees in being "naked." That is, the tiny, folded embryonic leaves and shoots they contain are not encased in bud scales. Only a layer of brownish woolly hairs provides some protection to the delicate buds.

The small, greenish flowers are borne in clusters among the leaves. They mature into a dark purple, cherrylike fruit about ⅓ inch (8 mm) long that contains the same bitter chemical as the bark and is considered inedible to humans.

Ecological Role

Cascara fruit is, however, relished by birds as well as raccoons and other mammals. Animals do not digest the hard seed inside the fruit, but they inadvertently propagate cascara across the landscape, when the seed passes through their

cascara buckthorn in fall with ripe fruit

digestive tract. Thus, cascara is often found growing along pasture fences where birds have perched. Cascara also sprouts vigorously from the stump when killed by fire or cut down; for example, by bark strippers. Cascara requires a moist site and a mild climate, and although it is often common amid young forests west of the Cascades, it is seldom abundant. It is tolerant of shade and can survive beneath a moderately dense stand of tall trees.

Human History

Cascara bark was used as a laxative, tonic, and a cure-all by many of the Greater Northwest's Native peoples (Moerman 1998). They introduced it to Spanish missionaries in northern California, who called it *cáscara sagrada*, meaning "sacred bark." This is also the name of the extract from this species that is used pharmaceutically as a laxative throughout the world. Cascara was

introduced into formal medical practice in the United States in 1877, and it soon replaced the berries of its European relative, *Rhamnus catharticus*, as the medically endorsed laxative.

Cascara bark is harvested from wild trees in spring, when the sap is running and the bark strips readily. By the early 1900s, as much as 5 million pounds (2 million kg) of the thin bark was collected and shipped to pharmaceutical companies annually. Cascara bark was in heavy demand during World War II, when it was used in the "CC" pills often prescribed for ailing servicemen and -women. By that time, the coastal states and the province of British Columbia had established regulations aimed at sustaining a continuous supply of this species. The foremost concern was that bark strippers should leave a cut stump still covered with bark. This allows the tree to sprout vigorously. Some enterprising rural Northwesterners started small plantations of cascara.

The bark from a 6-inch-thick (15-cm-thick) tree is said to produce about 2000 doses of the laxative. Many college students and rural residents supplemented their income for a few weeks in spring by gathering the bark, known to locals as "chittam bark." Buyers questioning whether a batch of bark comes from cascara or a similar-appearing alder, for example, can verify by tasting it—cautiously. When chewed, fresh "chittam bark" is intensely bitter and can temporarily numb the taste buds. Cascara bark must be dried and aged for a year to be usable, because fresh bark produces strong, often violent effects. By the 1960s, demand for cascara bark had eased somewhat due to the introduction of synthetic laxatives, but a moderate demand continues for this mild natural laxative used in many drugs.

OTHER MEMBERS OF THE BUCKTHORN FAMILY

Alderleaf buckthorn. *Rhamnus alnifolia* is a closely related species that forms a shrub, generally less than 5 feet (1.5 m) tall, growing in moist forests east of the Cascades. It can be distinguished by its five to seven pairs of parallel leaf veins, as opposed to the ten to twelve pairs in cascara. This species was also used as a laxative by Native peoples.

California buckthorn. *R. californica* is an evergreen shrub that spreads north into the Siskiyous of extreme southwestern Oregon. This species too was used as a laxative by Native peoples.

Sticky-laurel. The genus *Ceanothus* makes up an interesting group of shrubs in the buckthorn family. Some of these normally shrubby species occasionally become as a small tree. One of these is *C. velutinus* var. *laevigatus*, called sticky-laurel, which sometimes forms a spreading tree about 20 feet (6 m) tall in lowlands west of the Cascades. It has gummy, glossy, oval evergreen leaves averaging about 3 inches (8 cm) long.

Blueblossom or wild-lilac. Another is *C. thyrsiflorus*, a shrub with clusters of pale blue flowers. In a few instances along the coast in southwestern Oregon, it develops into a small tree. It also has shiny evergreen leaves, averaging about 1½ inches (4 cm) long.

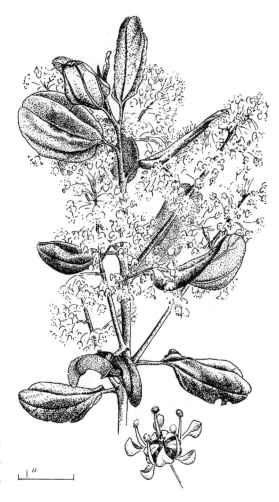

sticky-laurel (Ceonothus), with close-up of flower

PACIFIC DOGWOOD

Cornus nuttallii, Dogwood family—Cornaceae

Pacific dogwood is the most beautiful flowering tree in Northwest forests, and it is British Columbia's Provincial Flower. Dogwood produces its floral display in the somber shade beneath all the largest West Coast trees, including the mammoth Douglas-fir, Sitka spruce, western redcedar, redwood, and giant sequoia. Pacific dogwood is also highly prized as an ornamental and is widely cultivated west of the Cascades. Some lucky homeowners even have one or more dogwoods growing wild in their suburban woodlot. Given a modicum of sun and growing room, dogwoods put on an even more impressive blossoming spectacle. A threat to these lovely trees arose suddenly in the 1980s when many wild and cultivated dogwoods were attacked by an introduced disease. This plague has now has been studied and evaluated in terms of long-term effects and strategies for control.

Where It Grows

Pacific dogwood is associated with the cool but mild and moist climate found at low elevations near the Northwest coast. It grows west of the Coast Range in southern British Columbia and within and west of the Cascades southward to California. Like bigleaf maple, vine maple, Oregon white oak, and Pacific madrone, among others, it does not extend northward past Vancouver Island into the increasingly cold maritime climate. Like these other species, dogwood occurs only sporadically in small populations on the eastern slope of the Cascades. Its only occurrence east of the Cascades is in northern Idaho's Clearwater River canyon, an inland area where red alder and other Pacific coast plants are also found in what may have been a refuge during the (Pleistocene) Ice Age (Daubenmire

1975). Southward in northern California, it retreats to higher elevations and spreads through the relatively humid midelevation forest on the west slope of the Sierra Nevada.

Appearance

When growing under tall conifers, mature Pacific dogwoods commonly develop a slender trunk 6 to 12 inches (15 to 30 cm) in diameter and a sparse but spreading canopy 30 to 50 feet (9 to 15 m) high. Open-grown trees are generally shorter but have a broad, full canopy. The trunk is covered with smooth, reddish brown bark, which becomes scaly at the base of older trees. Dogwoods live as long as 150 years.

The leaves, twigs, and buds are borne opposite each other, and the leaves themselves have opposite pairs of prominent veins that curve parallel to the leaf margin. The leaves are oval and 3½ to 5 inches (9 to 13 cm) long. They are bright green on top and lighter on the underside, and they turn bright orange, red, or purplish in the fall.

Pacific dogwood in spring with blossom

The dogwood's big, showy "flower" is actually a dense cluster of small inconspicuous flowers—a flower "head" like the center of a daisy—set amid four to six creamy white floral leaves, or bracts. This creates a radiant blossom 4 to 6 inches (10 to 15 cm) across. They appear primarily in spring but sometimes also in fall when the buttonlike flower head, more than 1 inch (2.5 cm) across, is bright red. The red parts are elongated fruits, which although bitter are eaten by many birds and animals, including bears.

Pacific dogwood is closely related to the beloved flowering dogwood (*C. florida*) of the eastern United States. Meriwether Lewis, on April 5, 1806, correctly concluded that Pacific dogwood differed from the eastern species,

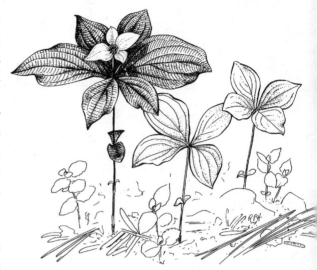

bunchberry dogwood

based on its smooth bark and larger size, but nearly twenty years later, botanist David Douglas mistook it as being the same species. Then in the 1830s, naturalist Thomas Nuttall visited the Pacific dogwoods and found, among other differences, that our dogwood (which is named after him) has four or six floral bracts, compared to four in flowering dogwood. Pacific dogwood also has larger blossoms, and its floral bracts are smooth and not notched at the tip like those of flowering dogwood.

The only other dogwood in our region that has similar blossoms is a low-growing sub-shrub on the forest floor. This little plant, known as bunchberry dogwood (*C. canadensis*), is widely distributed beneath moist, cool forests of the Greater Northwest and has leaves and blossoms that appear to be a miniature version of the Pacific dogwood.

Ecological Role

Pacific dogwood is tolerant of shade and therefore able to survive beneath a conifer canopy. Studies of the closely related eastern dogwood (*C. florida*) reveal that it carries out maximum photosynthesis under less than one-third of full

1"

Pacific dogwood in fall with fruit

sunlight. This related species has a shallow root system and is easily stressed by drought, which also seems applicable to Pacific dogwood. Nevertheless, Pacific dogwood does well in fuller sunlight, provided moisture is adequate, and it sprouts from the stump if cut—for instance, incidental to a logging operation.

Pacific dogwood is present in many forest types west of the Cascades but is seldom a major constituent. Studies of the eastern dogwood, likely applicable to Pacific dogwood as well, have found that the foliage and fruits are especially rich in nutrients. The shed foliage breaks down rapidly and provides calcium, phosphorus, magnesium, sulfur, and several minor elements to the soil. The high calcium and fat content of dogwood fruit suggest why it seems to be an important food for wildlife.

An introduced plague, anthracnose disease, has damaged or killed many wild and cultivated Pacific and eastern dogwoods. The fungus *Discula destructiva* is the culprit, and it was evidently introduced into the United States in New England and Washington State in the 1970s (see *www.plantclinic.cornell.edu*). The fungus first appears as tan spots and blotches on the leaves of infected trees. When the entire leaf is affected, the infection proceeds into the twigs and ultimately the trunk, where cankers produce split or buckled bark. Spores that spread the fungus develop underneath leaf spots and on stem cankers.

Plant scientist Douglas Justice of the University of British Columbia has observed that most native dogwoods have successfully survived attacks of this disease (see *www.ubc botanicalgarden.org*). Healthy dogwoods are much more able to cope with the disease than are trees stressed by drought or other injuries. The small native population in Idaho's Clearwater River canyon (near Lowell on US 12) is particularly hard hit, perhaps because this habitat is exposed to a harsher climate than what is experienced west of the Cascades (Johnson 1995).

Human History

Native peoples apparently made only limited use of Pacific dogwood as a medicinal (Moerman 1998), which may seem surprising in view of Dr. John K. Townsend's successful treatment of two feverish children from the Cowlitz tribe in the 1830s (Townsend 1839, 241): "My stock of quinine being exhausted ... I determined to substitute an extract of the bark of the Dogwood (Cornus Nuttallii). . . . I soon chipped off a plentiful supply, returned, boiled it down . . . with most of the Indians standing by . . . to comprehend the process. . . . I administered to each of the children about a scruple of the extract per day. The second day they escaped the paroxysm, and on the third were entirely well."

In medieval times in northern Europe, nails for construction and skewers—called "dags"—were made from the very hard wood of the tree *Cornus sanguinea*. From "dagwood" the name evolved to "dogwood" (Johnson 1995). *Cornus* means "horn," in reference to the hard, hornlike wood.

Most of the Pacific dogwood and eastern dogwood that was once harvested was made into shuttles for textile mills because of its toughness and ability to stay smooth under continuous wear. Plastics now fill this need.

Today, the major human use of Pacific dogwood is for its aesthetic value in the wild and for cultivation as an ornamental. Dogwoods in suburban settings can be aided in resisting fungal disease by applying mulch around the base (but not against the trunk), watering around the base during dry periods, and removing fallen leaves and diseased branches. A white-flowering Asian dogwood (*C. kousa*) shows good resistance to the disease and is easier to cultivate.

PACIFIC MADRONE

Arbutus menziesii, Heath family—Ericaceae

Pacific madrone—also called madroña and known in Canada as arbutus—could hardly be mistaken for any other northwestern tree. It is the only good-sized evergreen broad-leaved tree found in any appreciable quantity north of Eugene, Oregon. Madrone is a picturesque West Coast tree recognizable from far away. It is commonly seen arching out over the salt water in Puget Sound or other inlets. It is a fixture in cities and towns, especially common on steep, undeveloped lots and in seminatural parks. Even where it forms a large tree, set amid suburban landscaping, the tree was generally there first or grew up as a volunteer.

Where It Grows

Madrone inhabits the lowlands along the Strait of Georgia in southwestern British Columbia as far north as Kelsey Bay (about 50 degrees N latitude). It occupies most of the lowlands west of the Cascades in Washington and Oregon. It also inhabits the coastal mountains of northern California and the northern Sierra Nevada, but south of Monterey it becomes increasingly scarce and confined to the immediate coast. Although its entire distribution in the Northwest lies within about 100 miles (160 km) of the ocean and saltwater inlets, madrone is most abundant in relatively dry microclimates, such as along British Columbia's Sunshine Coast, around Puget Sound, and in the interior valleys of western Oregon. Even there, it tends to be most plentiful on dry, rocky sites and south-facing hills. The few other species of madrone trees (*Arbutus*) in the western hemisphere dwell in warm climates, including the mountains of southern Arizona, Mexico, and Central America.

Appearance

In favorable situations, madrone grows 50 to 80 feet (15 to 25 m) tall. The trunk, commonly about 24 inches (60 cm) thick, curves upward and often divides as it forms a broad, spreading crown. Even squeezed in among conifers, madrone's main trunk usually curves upward and forms a somewhat spreading canopy. The trees can survive three centuries or longer, and when growing on a fertile, open site, they occasionally attain great size. The largest madrone in Oregon, near Portland, is reported (Jensen and Ross 2003) to be 7.5 feet (2.3 m) thick and 84 feet (26 m) tall, with a maximum spread of 88 feet (27 m).

Madrone produces a virtual kaleidoscope of colors accentuated by its extraordinary bark, which is orange-brown or terra-cotta and shreds off all summer in ragged, papery strips to reveal the smooth, chartreuse inner bark. Near the base of old trunks, the bark becomes brown with flaky, gray scales.

Madrone leaves are elliptical, 3 to 5 inches (8 to 13 cm) long, and thick and leathery. They are shiny dark green above and pale silvery green below, resembling leaves of rhododendron (*R. macrophyllum*), which is also in the heath family. In June, shortly after the new crop of leaves has become fully grown, the second-year leaves turn orange to red and begin to fall.

In May, the tree bears grapelike clusters of small, white to pinkish, urn-shaped flowers, often in profusion. They have a strong, sweet odor that attracts honeybees. Clusters of orange-red berrylike fruits ripen in autumn and persist into December. They have a rough granular surface and a mealy pulp surrounding a knot of small, bony seeds.

Pacific madrone, with close-up of flower cluster

Ecological Role

Madrone is relatively intolerant of shade and thus is replaced by Douglas-fir and other conifers except on exceptionally dry, rocky sites where harsh growing conditions prevent conifers from forming a closed stand. It inhabits the driest sites in the San Juan Islands—a thin layer of soil atop bedrock—where annual precipitation averages only 15 inches (380 mm). Here, and on some stony, south-facing hills in southwestern Oregon, madrone is reduced to a small, scraggly tree. Madrone is exceptionally tolerant of salt water, often occupying ground barely above the highest tide and with foliage hanging down nearly into the briny liquid.

Madrone's thin bark makes it highly vulnerable to fire, but it is ultimately favored by fire or logging that kills other trees, since its seedlings require open conditions and it also sprouts vigorously from the base of burned or cut stems. As a result of historic fires, logging, and other disturbances, madrone is able to occupy a broad range of sites, since it is not particular in regards to soil type, geology, or topography, and its seeds are apparently well dispersed by birds and other animals. Madrone rarely grows in pure stands and is associated mainly with Douglas-fir. In the Willamette Valley, it also accompanies Oregon white oak, and in southwestern Oregon it is part of the mixed evergreen forest, a rich assortment dominated by Douglas-fir and tanoak.

Madrone fruits are a favorite food for several species of birds, including band-tailed pigeons and quail. Stomach analysis of one pigeon revealed 111 madrone berries, so many that the bird could not fly. Birds are believed to be a major factor in disseminating and inadvertently planting madrone seeds.

Human History

Some Native peoples dried, soaked, and otherwise prepared madrone berries for food, sometimes storing them for future use (Moerman 1998). A few tribes chewed the leaves or cooked them to make a cold remedy. The Karok people residing along the Klamath River used madrone berries as bait for steelhead fishing.

Early Spanish California first called this tree *madroño*, meaning "strawberry tree," because it resembled the strawberry madrone (*A. unedo*), which has large, bright-red berries with a bumpy surface and grows in the Mediterranean region. Early Californians reportedly preferred madrone for making the charcoal used to manufacture gunpowder.

Pacific madrone leaf and fruit

Madrone wood is reddish brown, heavy, and extremely hard but tends to warp and check as it dries, and so it is relatively little used commercially. It yields handsome veneer for paneling that has a rich color, luster, and grain pattern similar to the highly prized (and scarce) eastern black cherry (*Prunus serotina*). Madrone makes excellent firewood. It cuts like a softwood when green but becomes very hard when dry and is very challenging to split with a maul.

Increasingly, madrone is valued as a colorful ornamental and shade tree. It can be propagated from cuttings. It seems to prefer dry summer conditions, however, and often declines in yards that are heavily irrigated. Residents with madrones in their yard are well aware that it is continually shedding something—bark, leaves, flowers, fruit. A mature madrone will give the homeowner plenty of exercise in the form of raking.

Widespread decline has been observed in madrone trees, especially in the Puget Sound area. Despite its tolerance of drought and poor soils, madrone is sensitive to environmental changes caused by humans. Historically, madrone benefited from relatively frequent fires that allowed it to regenerate and thinned out Douglas-fir and other vigorous competitors. In addition to fire suppression, other detrimental changes are associated with construction and land development that damages stems and roots and alters natural drainage, artificial irrigation, fertilization, and use of herbicides. Decline is characterized by foliage dieback and black stem cankers, which is a natural process that can be accelerated by human activities. Several internet websites (accessible by listing "madrone decline" in a search engine) provide information about ongoing investigations of causes of decline and measures for its mitigation.

CALIFORNIA-LAUREL

Umbellularia californica, Laurel family—Lauraceae

California-laurel, also known in the Northwest as Oregon-myrtle, is one of several trees restricted to the "Mediterranean" climatic region of California and southwestern Oregon. This evergreen broad-leaved tree is in the same family as the classical laurel (*Laurus nobilis*) of the Old World that was fashioned into a wreath to crown distinguished men. Like other members of the laurel family, California-laurel has spicy-scented leaves and wood. When growing in uncrowded situations, this tree is commonly rather short but has a broad, rounded canopy so dense that it hides the trunk. The "myrtle-wood" harvested from this species is famous for its beauty and is made into bowls and other decorative products that are marketed to visitors along the southern Oregon coast.

Where It Grows

California-laurel inhabits the Oregon coast southward from the vicinity of Reedsport at the mouth of the Umpqua River, extending up river valleys and lower slopes in the coastal mountains and spreading about 60 miles (100 km) inland. Southward, it occupies California's coastal lowlands and mountains and the lower west slope of the Sierra Nevada, but it becomes less abundant in southern California. Within this coastal and mountain distribution, California-laurel attains tree size on a wide variety of soils and topography, provided there is a moderate supply of moisture. On especially hot, dry, or windy sites, it is reduced to a dense, shrubby form.

Appearance

Along the southern Oregon coast, California-laurel is most often a multistemmed tree, with a wide, spherical canopy extending almost to the ground. Such trees are seen at Humbug Mountain State Park, south of Port Orford; but here on storm-lashed headlands, California-laurel forms huge, wind-pruned shrubs. In productive valley bottomlands, mature trees 150 or more years old range from 60 to 100 feet (18 to 30 m) tall and 24 to 36 inches (60 to 90 cm) thick, but most trees of this size were long ago harvested or cleared for agriculture. Remnant stands of well-formed trees are found at Loeb State Park near Brookings and Coquille Myrtle Grove State Park south of Myrtle Point. Open-grown trees on fertile sites sometimes attain colossal size—Oregon's record tree, in Curry County, is 13 feet (4 m) in diameter and 88 feet (27 m) tall (Jensen and Ross 2003).

The leaves are evergreen, arranged alternately on the twigs, 3 to 6 inches (8 to 15 cm) long and about one-third as wide. They have smooth edges and a pointed tip and are dark green above and paler below. The bark is thin, smooth, and gray-brown on young stems and becomes dark reddish brown and scaly with age. Both leaves and bark are readily identified by the pungent, camphorlike scent they give off when bruised. The odor can pain the sinuses and cause headaches in some people if they breathe in too much of it—hence its local names, "pepperwood" and "headache tree."

The small, yellowish green flowers are borne in clusters. They bloom at an unusual season, from January to March, before the crop of new leaves develops. The fruit is the size and shape of a large, plump olive, about 1 inch (2.5 cm) long. It appears in groups of two or three, attached at the base of leaves. As the fruit matures, its thin pulp changes from green to yellow or purple. It contains a single large seed, bigger than an olive pit.

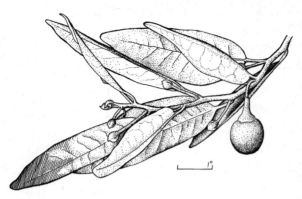

California-laurel

Ecological Role

Although confined to the West Coast's "Mediterranean" climatic region, California-laurel inhabits diverse microclimates ranging from the fog-shrouded coast to scorching hills of the interior valleys. It occupies nearly all types of rock and soil, as well as habitats ranging from steep mountain slopes, exposed ridges, coastal bluffs, and bedrock to fertile valleys, alluvial flats, and deep canyons. It adapts to variable conditions by assuming different growth forms, from slender and tall on moist, fertile soils to stout and spherical, and finally to shrubby as sites become increasingly dry and windy. It is part of the mixed evergreen forest, dominated by Douglas-fir and tanoak, as well as the western hemlock forest and even the mountain brush (chaparral) communities. Pure stands once occurred in coastal and inland valleys but are now very scarce.

California-laurel is able to regenerate and grow under heavy shade and is thus considered shade tolerant. There is more bare ground under its canopy than beneath other trees, apparently because its leaf litter releases chemicals that inhibit most vegetation. However, it grows more slowly than associated conifers, which can overtop it. Because of their thin bark, California-laurel trees are readily killed by fire, but they resprout vigorously. Young sprouts are a choice food for deer in spring and summer when the strong chemicals in the leaves are at their lowest concentrations.

Human History

Native Americans used the leaves crushed or cooked as a pain reliever and cold remedy (Moerman 1998). They roasted and ate the large nuts or made them into a meal or bread. Some tribes used the boughs or smoke from burning them to rid their beds of fleas.

Today, the leaves are harvested locally, and sometimes sold, as a spice for cooking, but they have a stronger flavor than the traditional bay leaves from European laurel. One botanist notes that a few of the leaves added to flour will ward off mealworms.

The wood of mature trees is moderately hard and heavy, rich yellowish brown to grayish brown, and often mottled with darker streaks, and it has a spicy odor. It works well with tools and polishes nicely. It commands the highest prices among western hardwoods and is used in custom paneling, cabinets, and gun stocks. Wood from large burls on coastal trees is highly prized for its beautiful grain patterns and is used for decorative clocks and wood carvings marketed as Oregon-myrtle.

Botanical explorer David Douglas extolled the elegance of this tree, was impressed by the foliage's strong scent, and foresaw its use as an ornamental. It is commonly planted for hedges, for windbreaks, and as an indoor or outdoor ornamental, but it is not hardy in the colder coastal or inland climates.

OREGON ASH

Fraxinus latifolia, Olive family—Oleaceae

Oregon ash might be viewed as a typical eastern hardwood that got misplaced to the west side of the continent. About sixteen species of ash attain tree size in the United States and southern Canada, roughly half of them residing in the East and Midwest and the remainder in canyons and washes of the desert Southwest. Except, that is, for Oregon ash, which inhabits low-elevation valleys west of the Cascades. It is a medium-sized tree that grows mostly in wet habitats. Its light-green foliage made up of pinnately compound leaves, as well as its distinctive fruits, render it easy to identify. Oregon ash's wood compares favorably to the valuable lumber associated with eastern ashes, but it is seldom used for hardwood products because of its limited availability and distribution.

Where It Grows

Oregon ash inhabits most of the lowland valleys west of the Cascades from the Seattle and Aberdeen areas of Washington south to northern California. Farther south, along streams in the Sierra Nevada, it becomes scarce and very small. In the valleys of western Oregon and southwestern Washington, it commonly occupies wet ground, including swales, sloughs, wet meadows, swamps, stream courses, and bottomlands.

Appearance

When growing in the open, Oregon ash develops a broad crown, almost as wide as that of bigleaf maple, but when part of a denser stand, it produces a taller, narrower form more like that of red alder. On good sites, the ash attains diameters of 16 to 30 inches (40 to 75 cm) and heights of 60 to 80 feet (18 to 24 m) in 100 to 150 years. Occasionally on rich bottomland soils, an ash will grow considerably larger in its 200-plus-year life span. On dry or other poor sites, such as in the Columbia Gorge west of the Dalles, Oregon, Oregon ash is stunted and quite small.

The leaves and branchlets are attached in pairs, opposite each other. Leaves are pinnately compound, composed of five to seven oval leaflets attached in pairs to a linear stalk with an additional leaflet at the tip. The leaves are conspicuously lighter green than those of associated broadleaf species, and they turn bright yellow and fall off earlier in autumn. In winter, Oregon ash is distinguished by its stout twigs, with opposite branching arrangement and opposite buds. Unlike those of bigleaf maple, ash twigs are covered with woolly hairs.

Oregon ash flowers are small and rather inconspicuous. Male and female flowers are borne on separate trees; thus, only female trees produce the clusters of ash fruits. These are winged samaras like those of maples except that ash samaras are single, while those of maples are fused together in pairs. Oregon ash samaras are 1 to 2 inches (2.5 to 5 cm) long and shaped like a canoe, with the small seed located near one end.

Even the bark of Oregon ash is distinctive. It is dark gray-brown and has a pattern of deep fissures and ridges that creates a woven appearance.

Ecological Role

Oregon ash is intolerant of shade and can eventually be replaced by more competitive trees such as bigleaf maple or conifers. Damaging floods, blowdowns, or other disturbances that create open habitat provide an opportunity for

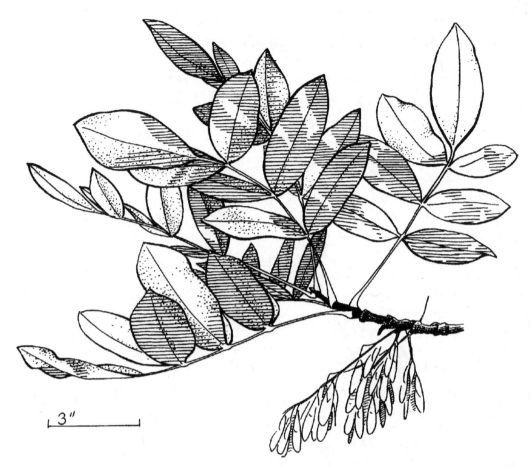

Oregon ash twig

ash to regenerate. In addition to reproducing from the wind-disseminated seeds, Oregon ash sprouts vigorously from cut stumps or fire-killed trees. In open sites, young ash trees grow vigorously for sixty years or so, as they attain most of their ultimate height. Thereafter, growth slows considerably.

Oregon ash is well adapted to soggy ground. Its root system is moderately shallow but extensive and wide-spreading, rendering the tree exceptionally wind-firm. Ash is also able to tolerate flooding better than many of its associates, especially Douglas-fir and grand fir.

Deer and elk browse foliage and sprouts of Oregon ash. Use of this species' seeds is not well known, but seeds of the comparable eastern ash (*F. americana*) are eaten by many animals, including wood ducks, quail, songbirds, and squirrels.

Human History

Oregon ash is plentiful in the bottomlands of the Cowlitz River Valley south of Mount Rainier, and the Cowlitz Tribe used its wood for canoe paddles and digging sticks (Moerman 1998). Similar species of ash have long been preferred by Europeans and, later, by European Americans for comparable purposes—notably, tool handles and sports equipment.

The wood of Oregon ash, like that of eastern white ash (*F. americana*), is light in color, somewhat lustrous, hard, strong, stiff, high in shock resistance, flexible, and workable with machines, and it wears smooth with use. Because eastern ash is much more abundant, Oregon ash has had limited commercial application. Wide-ringed young growth is more elastic and thus is favored for handles and baseball bats. The fine-grained growth of older trees is more brittle. Because it splits readily and has a high heating value, it is prized for firewood.

Because of its rapid growth rate, symmetrical shape, and hardiness, Oregon ash is commonly planted as an ornamental or shade tree within and beyond its native range—for example, in the eastern United States and Europe.

Green ash. *F. pennsylvanica* is native to eastern and midwestern North America, with native populations reaching central Montana along the Yellowstone and Missouri rivers. Widely planted for windbreaks and shade trees, green ash has also escaped cultivation and established naturalized populations in some Idaho valleys (Johnson 1995). Leaflets of green ash are mostly long-pointed, whereas those of Oregon ash are rounded or bluntly pointed.

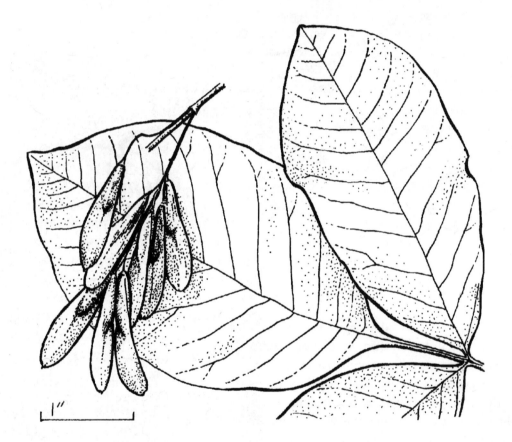

1"

Oregon ash close-up of leaves and fruits

NATURALIZED TREES

The Northwest's native trees have evolved into their present forms—the species we recognize—through millions of years. Their modern distributions have been established within the last 12,000 years or so, since the retreat of the most recent glacial period or Ice Age. Each species' distribution continues to adjust to changes in climate and disturbance patterns linked to fire suppression, livestock grazing, logging, and land development.

Although the native trees described in preceding chapters dominate our undeveloped lands, several species that were introduced by humans have established naturally regenerating populations in the wild. These "naturalized" trees might sometimes be mistaken for natives. This chapter describes naturalized trees that have been recognized by botanists. No doubt, additional species are becoming naturalized. For instance, Siberian elm (*Ulmus pumila*) is an escapee from cultivation that may soon join the ranks of those listed below. Also, tamarisk or "salt-cedars" (*Tamarix* spp.) are tall, flowering shrubs with scalelike leaves that have invaded desert stream banks in central Oregon and southwestern Idaho, and some will likely attain tree size (Johnson 1995).

Many other introduced tree species occasionally regenerate in the wild as a result of seed dispersal but have not established self-perpetuating populations—for example, the European mountain-ash (*Sorbus aucuparia*) in lowlands west of the Cascades. Some cultivated trees around abandoned homesteads might be considered historical relics, and some, such as fruit trees, might represent varieties that are now rare and valuable as a horticultural resource.

Thus far, no treelike conifers have become naturalized to any appreciable extent in the Greater Northwest. Several species of nonnative broad-leaved trees and some tall multistemmed shrubs have established self-perpetuating populations in some localities. Green ash (see the Oregon ash chapter) and boxelder (see the smaller maples chapter) have native populations at the eastern edge of our region but are also introduced and naturalized elsewhere in the Northwest.

FRUIT TREES

Several fruit trees have become naturalized in low-elevation river valleys, particularly in central and southern Idaho (Johnson 1995), as well as in Washington and Oregon. These are listed below, along with distinguishing characteristics.

Mazzard or sweet cherry. *Prunus avium* is the parent of sweet cherry trees grown in warmer parts of the Greater Northwest. Introduced from Europe, where it has been cultivated for centuries, and disseminated by birds, it grows wild in the Willamette Valley and in some other low-elevation valleys of the inland Northwest. Mazzard cherry forms dense, shrubby thickets beneath second-growth oak communities in the

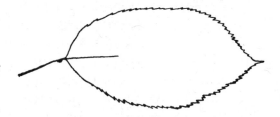

Mazzard cherry leaf silhouette

Mahaleb cherry leaf silhouette

Willamette Valley, but it becomes a good-sized tree when growing in the open. It can be distinguished by its larger, sweet fruit (like that of domestic cherries but smaller); big leaves—3 to 6 inches (8 to 15 cm) long—and dark bark that peels like that of paper birch.

Mahaleb cherry. *Prunus mahaleb* is a small, spreading tree that was introduced to serve as the rootstock for grafted domestic cherry trees. It is colonizing disturbed areas in the Spokane Valley and other low-elevation sites in northern and central Idaho. The leaves are 1 to 2 inches (2.5 to 5 cm) long, nearly as wide, and shiny on their upper surface. Fruits are borne in small clusters like that of bitter cherry and are black when mature, about ¼ inch (6 mm) across, and very bitter.

Apricot. *Prunus armeniaca*, the domestic fruit tree, is colonizing several sites in the Snake, Salmon, and lower Clearwater river canyons of Idaho and no doubt adjacent areas in Washington and Oregon. The leaves are 2 to 3 inches (5 to 8 cm) long and nearly round but with a pointed tip. The fruit is the same as a domestic apricot but smaller.

Cherry plum. *Prunus cerasifera* is a small domestic tree cultivated as a rootstock for other plums that can be found growing wild, especially in the lower Clearwater, Salmon, and Snake river canyons of Idaho. It has white flowers about ¾ inch (2 cm) across that appear very early in spring. It bears sweet, spherical plums 1 inch (2.5 cm) in diameter. When ripe, these are yellow or dark red on different trees. Thorns are present on some trees.

White mulberry. *Morus alba* was probably brought to the Northwest for its raspberrylike fruit, although its foliage is used to feed silkworms and it provides timber in China, where it is native. Its seeds are dispersed by animals, and it spreads through root sprouts. It colonizes lower canyons of the Snake, Clearwater, and Payette rivers in Idaho. The sweet, ripe fruit varies from white to pale purple, red, or black

white mulberry leaves, flowers, and fruit

white mulberry lobed leaf silhouette

and is about ½ inch (1 cm) long. Leaves are quite variable, but some have lopsided bases and others have deep lobes.

English or Persian walnut. *Juglans regia* is the common walnut used in baking, and the trees were planted in warm inland valleys for their nut crops. Animals disperse the nuts, and well-established populations of these trees inhabit side streams in Hells Canyon and along

English walnut leaf silhouette

the lower Salmon River in Idaho. Leaves are pinnately compound with five to seven leaflets, and the leaves are attached in an alternate arrangement on the branches, unlike the similar but opposite leaves of ash. The fleshy husk peels off when the familiar, thin-shelled nut inside is mature.

SHADE TREES

Frémont cottonwood. *Populus fremontii* is native to the Southwest and was evidently planted as a shade tree around farms in southwestern Idaho, where it is now colonizing riverside habitats (Johnson 1995). It grows with both eastern and black cottonwoods, and probably with hybrids as well. It can generally be distinguished by its broadly triangular leaves that have large, curved teeth.

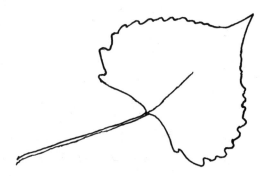

Frémont cottonwood leaf silhouette

Silver maple. *Acer saccharinum* is a fast-growing shade tree native to the East and Midwest. Its seeds mature in early spring and float down streams during peak flows (Johnson 1995).

silver maple leaf silhouette

They can then germinate and become established near the high-water line. The leaves are more deeply lobed (or "cut") than those of native maples, and they have bright silvery undersides.

Tree-of-heaven. *Ailanthus altissima* is a fast-growing tree that can spread problematically in urban settings; it was featured in the novel and movie about tenement life, *A Tree Grows in Brooklyn*. This species colonizes disturbed sites along highways near rivers, notably along the Columbia River west of the Dalles. This tree has very large, pinnately compound leaves 12 to 48 inches (30 to 120 cm) long, with twelve to forty-one leaflets. The leaves are attached in an alternate pattern on the branches. Flowers of male trees have a strong, unpleasant odor. The fruit is a single samara, like that of ash, except that the seed is in the center of the papery wing. These samaras are borne in large clusters, and many remain on the tree during winter.

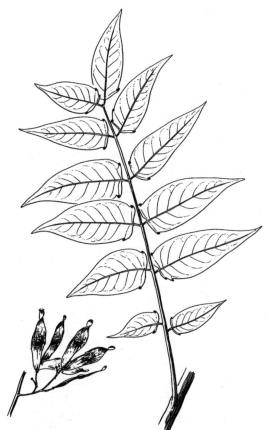

tree-of-heaven

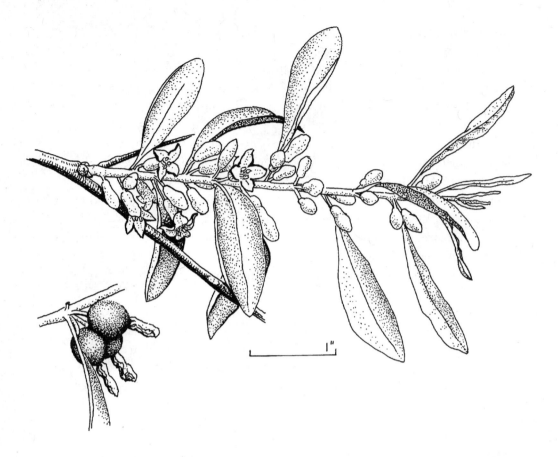

Russian olive fruit and flowers

TROUBLESOME TREES

Two other naturalized trees are widespread and in some areas pose a threat to native vegetation.

Russian-olive. *Elaeagnus angustifolia* is an extremely hardy tree from the steppes of central Asia that was widely cultivated in the dry interior Northwest for windbreaks and wildlife habitat. However, it has now colonized large areas along streams, irrigation ditches, seasonal marshes, abandoned fields, and forest edges in eastern Washington, eastern Oregon, southern British Columbia, and southern Idaho. Its roots can "fix" nitrogen—absorbing it from the atmosphere—which allows this species to grow vigorously on bare, gravelly surfaces and displace the native cottonwoods and willows that would otherwise dominate. The heavy, dense shade of Russian-olive also blocks sunlight needed for native trees and undergrowth plants.

Colonizing Russian-olive is very difficult to control because it produces basal sprouts and root suckers when cut, cleared, or burned.

Russian-olive is a short, spreading tree or tall shrub. The leaves are silvery on both surfaces. Those on mature branches are willowlike, about 3 inches (8 cm) long and only ½ to ¾ inch (1 to 2 cm) wide. Juvenile leaves are egg-shaped. Young trees often have sharp thorns. Flowers are small, yellow, and very fragrant, and by late summer these mature into reddish, dry, but edible berries about ½ inch (1 cm) across that stay on the tree through the winter.

Black locust. *Robinia pseudoacacia* is a small to medium-sized tree native to the Appalachian Mountains and the Ozark-Ouachita region of Missouri and Arkansas. It was widely planted in semi-arid regions of the West as a windbreak and shade tree, sometimes to supply durable fence posts. From extensive plantings, it has now colonized canyons and benches or terraces near streams in southern British Columbia, eastern Washington, eastern Oregon, and central and southern Idaho. Black locust spreads very aggressively from root suckers and stump sprouts, especially into habitats where native vegetation has been degraded. Its extensive root system fixes nitrogen and is able to outcompete other plants.

Black locust is unlikely to be mistaken for any other naturalized or native tree because it is the only one belonging to the pea and bean family, Leguminosae. It has long, hanging clusters of showy white flowers that give rise to legume fruits, like pea pods, 2½ to 4 inches (6 to 10 cm) long. It also has distinctive, pinnately compound leaves 8 to 14 inches (20 to 35 cm) long made up of eleven to twenty-one smooth-edged leaflets. The leaves are arranged alternately on the twigs, and on vigorous shoots the base of each leaf is armed with a pair of spines ½ to 1 inch (1 to 2.5 cm) long.

Black locust can be identified by its bark and its bite. The bark is dark-colored and made up of coarse, interlacing fibrous ridges; the "bite" has been felt by many a tree-climbing youngster who got snagged on its spiny branches.

black locust in flower, with close-up of seed pods

REFERENCES

Most of the information appearing in this book is of a general nature and comes from personal observations or the general reference books below marked by an asterisk (*). Occasionally these general references are cited in the text, when it seems important to identify the source. The other references listed here are more specific and are cited at various places in the text.

Achuff, P. L. 1989. Old-growth forests of the Canadian Rocky Mountain national parks. *Natural Areas Journal* 9 (1):12–26.

Agee, J. K. 1996. Fire in restoration of Oregon white oak woodlands. In General Technical Report INT-GTR-341, U.S. Forest Service, 72–73. Ogden, UT.

Ambrose, S. E. 1996. *Undaunted courage: Meriwether Lewis, Thomas Jefferson, and the opening of the American West.* New York: Simon & Schuster.

Antos, J. A., and D. B. Zobel. 1986. Habitat relationships of *Chamaecyparis nootkatensis* in southern Washington, Oregon, and California. *Canadian Journal of Botany* 64:1898–1909.

Arno, S. F. 1970. Ecology of alpine larch (*Larix lyallii* Parl.) in the Pacific Northwest. PhD diss., Univ. of Montana, Missoula.

———. 2000. Fire regimes in western forest ecosystems. In Effects of fire on flora, ed. J. K. Brown, 97–120. General Technical Report RMRS-23, U.S. Forest Service. Ogden, UT.

Arno, S. F., and S. Allison-Bunnell. 2002. *Flames in our forest: Disaster or renewal?* Washington, DC: Island Press.

Arno, S. F., and C. Fiedler. 2005. *Mimicking nature's fire: Restoring fire-prone forests in the West.* Washington, DC: Island Press.

Arno, S. F., and J. Habeck. 1972. Ecology of alpine larch (*Larix lyallii* Parl.) in the Pacific Northwest. *Ecological Monographs* 42:417–450.

*Arno, S. F., and R. P. Hammerly. 1984. *Timberline: Mountain and arctic forest frontiers.* Seattle: The Mountaineers Books.

Arno, S. F., H. Smith, and M. Krebs. 1997. Old growth ponderosa pine and western larch stand structures: Influences of pre-1900 fires and fire exclusion. Research Paper INT-495, U.S. Forest Service. Ogden, UT.

Barrett, S. W., S. Arno, and C. Key. 1991. Fire regimes of western larch-lodgepole pine forests in Glacier National Park, Montana. *Canadian Journal of Forestry Research* 21:1711–1720.

Barrett, T. M., D. Gatziolis, J. Fried, and K. Waddell. 2006. Sudden oak death in California: What is the potential? *Journal of Forestry* 104 (2):61–64.

Bates, C. G. 1924. Physiological requirements for Rocky Mountain trees. *Journal of Agricultural Research* 24:97–164.

Beal, M. D. 1963. *"I will fight no more forever" Chief Joseph and the Nez Perce War.* Seattle: Univ. of Washington Press.

Blankinship, J. W. 1905. Native economic plants of Montana. Bulletin 56, Montana Agricultural College Experiment Station. Bozeman, MT.

Boyd, R. 1999. Strategies of Indian burning in the Willamette Valley. In *Indians, Fire, and the Land in the Pacific Northwest,* ed. R. Boyd, 94–138. Corvallis: Oregon State Univ. Press.

*Brayshaw, T. C. 1976. Catkin bearing plants of British Columbia. Occasional Paper no. 18, British Columbia Provincial Museum, Victoria.

*———. 1996. *Trees and shrubs of British Columbia.* Vancouver: Univ. of British Columbia Press.

*Brough, S. 1990. *Wild trees of British Columbia.* Vancouver, BC: Pacific Educational Press.

Carlson, C. E., S. Arno, and J. Menakis. 1990. Hybrid larch of the Carlton Ridge Research Natural Area in western Montana. *Natural Areas Journal* 10:134–139.

Cheff, B. Sr. 1993. *Indian trails and grizzly tales.* Stevensville, MT: Stoneydale Press

Cochran, P. H., and C. Berntsen. 1973. Tolerance of lodgepole and ponderosa pine seedlings to low night temperatures. *Forest Science* 19:272–280.

Cooper, S. V., K. Neiman, and D. Roberts. 1991. Forest habitat types of northern Idaho: a second approximation. General Technical Report INT-236, U.S. Forest Service. Ogden, UT.

Daubenmire, R. 1974. Taxonomic and ecologic relationships between *Picea glauca* and *Picea engelmannii. Canadian Journal of Botany* 52:1545–1560.

———. 1975. Floristic plant geography of eastern Washington and northern Idaho. *Journal of Biogeography* 2:1–18.

Davies, J. 1980. *Douglas of the forests.* Seattle: Univ. of Washington Press.

Dickman, A., and S. Cook. 1989. Fire and fungus in a mountain hemlock forest. *Canadian Journal of Botany* 67:2005–2016.

*Earle, C. J. 2006. The gymnosperm database (up-to-date information about all conifers). *www.conifers.org.*

*Eliot, W. A. 1948. *Forest trees of the Pacific Coast.* New York: Putnam's Sons.

Evans, J. W. 1990. *Powerful rockey: The Blue Mountains and the Oregon Trail, 1811–1883.* Enterprise, OR: Pika Press and Eastern Oregon State College.

*Franklin, J. F., and C. T. Dyrness. 1973. Natural vegetation of Oregon and Washington. General Technical Report PNW-8, U.S. Forest Service. Portland, OR.

Frenkel, R. E. 1974. An isolated occurrence of Alaska-cedar (*Chamaecyparis nootkatensis* [D. Don] Spach) in the Aldrich Mountains, central Oregon. *Northwest Science* 48:29–37.

Furniss, R. L., and V. Carolin. 1977. Western forest insects. Miscellaneous Publication 1339, U.S. Forest Service. Washington, DC.

Gende, S. M., R. Edwards, M. Willson, and M. Wipfli. 2002. Pacific salmon in aquatic and terrestrial ecosystems. *BioScience* 52:917–928.

Gifford, G. F., W. Humphries, and R. Jaynes. 1984. A preliminary quantification of the impacts of aspen to conifer succession on water yield—II. Modeling results. *Water Resources Bulletin* 20:181–186.

Gruell, G. E. 1983. Fire and vegetative trends in the Northern Rockies: Interpretations from 1871–1982 photographs. General Technical Report INT-158, U.S. Forest Service. Ogden, UT.

Gruell, G. E., J. Brown, and C. Bushey. 1986. Prescribed fire opportunities in grasslands invaded by Douglas-fir: State-of-the-art guidelines. General Technical Report INT-198, U.S. Forest Service. Ogden, UT.

Gruell, G. E., W. Schmidt, S. Arno, and W. Reich. 1982. Seventy years of vegetative change in a managed ponderosa pine forest in western Montana. General Technical Report INT-130, U.S. Forest Service. Ogden, UT.

Habeck, J. R. 1978. A study of climax western redcedar (*Thuja plicata* Donn.) forest communities in the Selway-Bitterroot Wilderness, Idaho. *Northwest Science* 52 (1):67–76.

Habeck, J. R., and T. Weaver. 1969. A chemosystematic analysis of some hybrid spruce (*Picea*) populations in Montana. *Canadian Journal of Botany* 47:1565–1570.

*Harlow, W. M. 1991. *Textbook of dendrology: Covering the important forest trees of the United States and Canada.* New York: McGraw-Hill.

Hart, J. 1976. *Montana native plants and early peoples*. Helena, MT: Montana Historical Society.

Hartzell, H. Jr. 1991. *The yew tree—a thousand whispers: Biography of a species*. Eugene, OR: Hulogosi.

*Hitchcock, C. L., A. Cronquist, M. Ownbey, and J. W. Thompson. 1955–69. *Vascular plants of the Pacific Northwest*. 5 vols. Seattle: Univ. of Washington Press. Also available in single condensed volume, *Flora of the Pacific Northwest*.

*Hosie, R. C. 1969. *Native trees of Canada*. Ottawa: Canadian Forestry Service.

*Jensen, E. C., and C. R. Ross. 2003. *Trees to know in Oregon*. Corvallis, OR: Oregon State Univ. Extension Service.

Johnson, C. G. Jr. 2004. Alpine and subalpine vegetation of the Wallowa, Seven Devils and Blue Mountains. Pacific Northwest Region, R6-NR-ECOL-TP-03-04, U.S. Forest Service. Portland, OR.

*Johnson, F. D. 1995. *Wild trees of Idaho*. Moscow, ID: Univ. of Idaho Press.

Kay, C. E. 1993. Aspen seedlings in recently burned areas of Grand Teton and Yellowstone National Parks. *Northwest Science* 67:94–104.

Kay, C. E., C. White, I. Pengelly, and B. Patton. 1999. Long-term ecosystem states and processes in Banff National Park and the central Canadian Rockies. Occasional Report no. 9, National Parks Branch, Parks Canada, Ottawa.

Kirk, R. 1966. *The Olympic rain forest*. Seattle: Univ. of Washington Press.

Kruckeberg, A. R. 1980. Golden chinquapin (*Chrysolepis chrysophylla*) in Washington State: A species at the northern limit of its range. *Northwest Science* 54: 9–16.

Lackschewitz, K. 1991. Vascular plants of west-central Montana—Identification guidebook. General Technical Report INT-277, U.S. Forest Service. Ogden, UT.

Lanner, R. M. 1996. *Made for each other: A symbiosis of birds and pines*. New York: Oxford Univ. Press.

Leiberg, J. B. 1900. The Bitterroot Forest Reserve. 20th Annual Report, Part V, 317–428, U.S. Geological Survey. Washington, DC.

*Little, E. J. Jr. 1971 and 1976. Atlas of United States trees. Vols. 1 and 3 (maps of each species' distribution). Miscellaneous Publications 1146 and 1314, U.S. Forest Service. Washington, DC.

*———. 1979. Checklist of United States Trees. Agriculture Handbook 541, U.S. Forest Service. Washington, DC.

Long, C. J., C. Whitlock, P. Bartlein, and S. Millspaugh. 1998. A 9000-year fire history from the Oregon Coast Range, based on a high-resolution charcoal study. *Canadian Journal of Forestry Research* 28:774–787.

Mattson, D. J., K. Kendall, and D. Reinhart. 2001. Whitebark pine, grizzly bears, and red squirrels. In *Whitebark pine communities: Ecology and restoration*, eds. D. F. Tomback and others, 121–136. Washington, DC: Island Press.

McDonald, G. I., and R. J. Hoff. 2001. Blister rust: An introduced plague. In *Whitebark pine communities: Ecology and restoration*, eds. D. F. Tomback and others, 193–220. Washington, DC: Island Press.

Moerman, D. E. 1998. *Native American ethnobotany*. Portland, OR: Timber Press.

Moulton, G. E., ed. 1993. *The journals of the Lewis & Clark Expedition*. Vol. 8. Lincoln: Univ. of Nebraska Press.

Muir, J. 1894. *The mountains of California*. Repr., New York: Doubleday and Co., 1961.

Nadkarni, N. M. 1984. Biomass and mineral capital of epiphytes in an *Acer macrophyllum* community of a temperate moist coniferous forest, Olympic Peninsula, Washington State. *Canadian Journal of Botany* 62:2223–2228.

Nisbet, J. 1994. *Sources of the river.* Seattle: Sasquatch Books.

———. 2005. *The mapmaker's eye: David Thompson on the Columbia Plateau.* Pullman: Washington State Univ. Press

Östlund, L., B. Keane, S. Arno, and R. Andersson. 2005. Culturally scarred trees in the Bob Marshall Wilderness, Montana, USA—Interpreting Native American historical forest use in a wilderness area. *Natural Areas Journal* 25:315–325.

Parker, E. L. 1963. The geographic overlap of noble fir and red fir. *Forest Science* 9:207–216.

Parker, E. L. 1998. The true firs of Crater Lake National Park: A closer look. *Nature Notes from Crater Lake National Park* 29:17–23. Also available online at *www.nps.gov/crla/notes.*

*Peattie, D. C. 1950. *A natural history of western trees.* Boston: Houghton Mifflin Co.

Pfister, R. D., B. Kovalchik, S. Arno, and R. Presby. 1977. Forest habitat types of Montana. General Technical Report INT-34, U.S. Forest Service. Ogden, UT.

Rajora, O. P., and B. P. Dancik. 2000. Population genetic variation, structure, and evolution in Engelmann spruce, white spruce, and their natural hybrid complex in Alberta. *Canadian Journal of Botany* 78:768–780.

Richards, J. H. 1981. Ecophysiology of a deciduous timberline tree, *Larix lyallii* Parl. PhD diss., Univ. of Alberta, Edmonton.

Rood, S. B., and M. Polzin. 2003. Big old cottonwoods. *Canadian Journal of Botany* 81:764–767.

Ruth, R. H., J. Underwood, C. Smith, and H. Yang. 1972. Maple syrup production from bigleaf maple. Research Note PNW-181, U.S. Forest Service. Portland, OR.

Schuyler, W. S. 2006. A letter by Walter Scribner Schuyler [1876]. *Montana: The magazine of western history* 56 (1): 42–49.

Smith, W. K. 1985. Western montane forests. In *Physiological ecology of North American plant communities,* eds. B. Chabot and H. Mooney, 95–126. New York: Chapman and Hall.

Stewart, H. 1984. *Cedar.* Seattle: Univ. of Washington Press.

Stewart, O. C. 2002. *Forgotten fires: Native Americans and the transient wilderness.* Norman: Univ. of Oklahoma Press.

Stoltmann, R. 1987. *Hiking guide to the big trees of southwestern British Columbia.* Vancouver, BC: Western Canada Wilderness Committee.

Strong, C. C. 1970. *White pine: King of many waters.* Missoula, MT: Mountain Press.

*Sudworth, G. B. 1908. *Forest trees of the Pacific Slope.* Washington, D.C.: U.S. Forest Service. Repr., New York: Dover Publishing Co., 1967.

Taylor, A. H., and C. Halpern. 1991. The structure and dynamics of *Abies magnifica* forests in the southern Cascade Range, USA. *Journal of Vegetation Science* 2:189–200.

Tomback, D. F. 2001. Clark's nutcracker: Agent of regeneration. In *Whitebark pine communities: Ecology and restoration,* eds. D. F. Tomback and others, 89–104. Washington, DC: Island Press.

Tomback, D. F., S. Arno, and R. Keane, eds. 2001. *Whitebark pine communities: Ecology and restoration.* Washington, DC: Island Press.

Townsend, J. K. 1839. *Narrative of a journey across the Rocky Mountains to the Columbia River.* Boston: Perkins and Marvin.

Turner, N. J. 1979. *Plants in British Columbia Indian Technology.* Handbook no. 38, Royal British Columbia Museum, Victoria.

*U.S. Forest Service. 1974. Seeds of woody plants in the United States. Agriculture Handbook 450. Washington, DC.

*U.S. Forest Service. 1990. Silvics of North America. Agriculture Handbook 654. Vol. 1, conifers; vol. 2, hardwoods. Washington, DC. Also available online by entering the title into an Internet search engine.

*Van Pelt, R. 2001. *Forest giants of the Pacific Coast*. Seattle: Univ. of Washington Press.

Waring, R. H., and J. Franklin. 1979. Evergreen coniferous forests of the Pacific *Northwest*. *Science* 204:1380–1385.

White, C. A., E. Langemann, C. Gates, C. Kay, T. Shury, and T. Hurd. 2001. Plains bison restoration in the Canadian Rocky Mountains? Ecological and management considerations. In *Crossing boundaries in park management*, ed. D. Harmon, 152–160. Hancock, MI: The George Wright Society.

Zobel, D. B., L. F. Roth, and G. M. Hawk. 1985. Ecology, pathology, and management of Port-Orford-cedar *(Chamaecyparis lawsoniana)*. General Technical Report PNW-184, U.S. Forest Service. Portland, OR.

INDEX

ABOUT THE AUTHOR

Stephen F. Arno first came to know the Northwest's trees as a youngster growing up on the shores of Puget Sound. His forestry education began at Olympic College in Bremerton in 1961 and continued at Washington State University and the University of Montana, where he received a doctorate in forestry and plant science. During summers, he worked as a ranger and naturalist in Olympic and Sequoia and Kings Canyon national parks. In 1970 he began a career as a forest ecologist with the U.S. Forest Service, retiring in 1999 to resume writing about forests for general audiences. His recent books are *Flames in Our Forest: Disaster or Renewal* (Island Press, 2002) and *Mimicking Nature's Fire: Restoring Fire-Prone Forests in the West* (Island Press, 2005). He has practiced restoration forestry on his family's ponderosa pine forest for more than thirty years.

ABOUT THE ARTIST

Ramona Hammerly is a native of the Puget Sound area and a graduate of the University of Washington. She has climbed and roamed through the mountains of the Northwest and continues to hike in the mountains and other natural spaces. She illustrated *Northwest Trees* (The Mountaineers Books, 1977) and *Timberline* (The Mountaineers Books, 1984), both written by Stephen Arno, and has worked primarily in watercolor, pen and ink, etching, and oils.

OTHER TITLES YOU MIGHT ENJOY FROM THE MOUNTAINEERS BOOKS

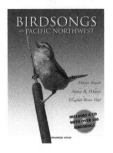

BIRDSONGS OF THE PACIFIC NORTHWEST
A Field Guide and Audio CD
Martyn Stewart, recordist; Stephen R. Whitney and Elizabeth Briars, illustrators
Identify Northwest birds by song and sight in this convenient CD/booklet package.

FIELD GUIDE TO THE CASCADES & OLYMPICS, 2nd Edition
Stephen R. Whitney
You'll find more than 600 species of flora and fauna in this rugged guide meant to be taken into the woods.

NORTHWEST FORAGING

Doug Benoliel
The classic guide to Northwest wild foods, covering 65 edible plants

BEST WILDFLOWER HIKES
Washington
Art Kruckeberg
Take a guided tour of the state's wild flora with Washington's most respected botanist.

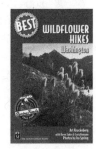

THE OWL AND THE WOODPECKER
Encounters with North America's Most Iconic Birds
Paul Bannick; foreword by Tony Angell
An intimate blend of personal field notes, rich natural history, and stunning photographs in the wild.

THE MOUNTAINEERS, founded in 1906, is a nonprofit outdoor activity and conservation organization whose mission is "to explore, study, preserve, and enjoy the natural beauty of the outdoors. . . ." Based in Seattle, Washington, it is now one of the largest such organizations in the United States, with seven branches throughout Washington State.

The Mountaineers sponsors both classes and year-round outdoor activities in the Pacific Northwest, which include hiking, mountain climbing, ski-touring, snowshoeing, bicycling, camping, kayaking, nature study, sailing, and adventure travel. The organization's conservation division supports environmental causes through educational activities, sponsoring legislation, and presenting informational programs.

All its activities are led by skilled, experienced instructors who are dedicated to promoting safe and responsible enjoyment and preservation of the outdoors.

If you would like to participate in these organized outdoor activities or the organization's programs, consider a membership in the Mountaineers. For information and an application, write or call The Mountaineers, Program Center, 7700 Sand Point Way NE, Seattle, WA 98115; 206-521-6001. You can also visit www.mountaineers.org or email info@mountaineers.org.

The Mountaineers Books, an active, nonprofit publishing program of the organization, produces guidebooks, instructional texts, historical works, natural history guides, and works on environmental conservation. All books produced by the Mountaineers Books fulfill the organization's mission.

Send or call for our catalog of more than 800 outdoor titles:

The Mountaineers Books
1001 SW Klickitat Way, Suite 201
Seattle, WA 98134
800-553-4453
mbooks@mountaineersbooks.org
www.mountaineersbooks.org

The Mountaineers Books is proud to be a corporate sponsor of The Leave No Trace Center for Outdoor Ethics, whose mission is to promote and inspire responsible outdoor recreation through education, research, and partnerships. The Leave No Trace program is focused specifically on human-powered (nonmotorized) recreation.

Leave No Trace strives to educate visitors about the nature of their recreational impacts, as well as offer techniques to prevent and minimize such impacts. Leave No Trace is best understood as an educational and ethical program, not as a set of rules and regulations.

For more information, visit *www.LNT.org*, or call (800) 332-4100.